RE-IMAGINING BLACK WO

Re-Imagining Black Women

A Critique of Post-Feminist and Post-Racial
Melodrama in Culture and Politics

Nikol G. Alexander-Floyd

NEW YORK UNIVERSITY PRESS
New York

NEW YORK UNIVERSITY PRESS
New York
www.nyupress.org

© 2021 by New York University
All rights reserved

References to Internet websites (URLs) were accurate at the time of writing. Neither the author nor New York University Press is responsible for URLs that may have expired or changed since the manuscript was prepared.

Library of Congress Cataloging-in-Publication Data
Names: Alexander-Floyd, Nikol G. (Nikol Gertrude), author.
Title: Re-imagining Black women : a critique of post-feminist and post-racial melodrama / Nikol G. Alexander-Floyd.
Description: New York : New York University Press, [2021] | Includes bibliographical references and index.
Identifiers: LCCN 2020038690 (print) | LCCN 2020038691 (ebook) | ISBN 9781479855858 (hardback) | ISBN 9781479850891 (paperback) | ISBN 9781479820139 (ebook other) | ISBN 9781479824380 (ebook)
Subjects: LCSH: Women, Black—Social conditions. | Women, Black—Political activity. | African American women—Social conditions. | African American women—Political activity. |
Classification: LCC HQ1163 .A44 2021 (print) | LCC HQ1163 (ebook) | DDC 305.48/896—dc23
LC record available at https://lccn.loc.gov/2020038690

LC ebook record available at https://lccn.loc.gov/2020038691 New York University Press books are printed on acid-free paper, and their binding materials are chosen for strength and durability. We strive to use environmentally responsible suppliers and materials to the greatest extent possible in publishing our books.

Manufactured in the United States of America

10 9 8 7 6 5 4 3 2 1

Also available as an ebook

Dedication

I dedicate this work to

a builder, my sister-in-law, Yvette Alexander (1964–2015);

a visionary and artist, my uncle and godfather,

Donald Lee "Aldox" Alexander (1951–2016);

and

a healer, my sister, Kathy Alexander Holmes (1961–2019).

CONTENTS

FIGURES AND TABLE

Introduction

Melodrama, Liminality, and Post-Politics: Neoliberal Racial and Gender Formation in the New Millennium

I have taught a course for some years, "Sex, Race, and Videotape: The Politics of Gender, Race, and Television in Law and Society," that has demonstrated to me time and again popular culture's ever increasing importance in shaping the political views of young people in particular, and the broader public more generally. In one especially memorable moment, a student pressed me to allow her to assess a then new television program, *Grey's Anatomy*, as part of an assignment. The students were tasked with applying some of the key concepts they learned about racism, sexism, and class inequality in analyzing one of several movies or TV programs. This student, a young, conscientious, white female, enthusiastically endorsed the show, highlighting the show's gender and racial diversity. When I viewed the first season in preparation for assessing her assignment, I had a different response.

Although the plots were certainly engaging, the gender and racial politics seemed driven by liberal definitions of formal equality where a premium was placed on multicultural displays of diversity without any serious grappling with the dicey issues—such as microaggression, super-surveillance, and double standards—that white women and racial minorities confront in real workplaces (Puwar 2007). This student's perspective on the show represented a common mindset that caused me to recalibrate how I taught about racism, sexism, and class inequality. Thereafter, I incorporated different approaches geared toward this new generation and I gained an even greater sensitivity to emerging trends in popular culture. They signaled, as well, larger developments taking shape in US society.

More specifically, since the tumultuous social movements of the 1960s and 1970s have profoundly changed the political and social landscape in many ways, members of the general public, particularly those with no direct memory of that time period or its immediate aftermath, have become increasingly hard-pressed to conceptualize the subtler, yet profound ways in which inequality structures society and politics. Indeed, for many confronted with ubiquitous signs of formal equality or multiculturalism, sustained, broad-scale social activism regarding racism and sexism, for instance, appears to be a vestige of a former era that was once necessary, but is now obsolete (McRobbie 2007). This perspective has gained greater currency not only in popular culture, as found in TV ads, sitcoms, music, and movies, for instance, but throughout political discourse, evidenced by discussions amid the 2008 presidential campaign and the historic election of the first African American president, Barack Obama, about "the end of race," shattering the glass ceiling, and the arrival of a "post-racial, postgender" future.

For more than two decades feminists, along with other scholars and activists, have worked concertedly to identify the impact of these messages that suggest that we are beyond the radical politics of the mid–twentieth century. For feminist scholars, these messages constitute a post-feminist politics (what I prefer to call post–Civil Rights, post-feminist ideology, or "post-politics") where resistance to feminism is not only carried out through direct means or what one might call "backlash," but also through the appropriation and redeployment of feminist history, concepts, and the very term "feminist." Although scholars have assessed the work of academic and political figures, such as Katie Roiphe and Naomi Wolf, associated with certain forms of post-feminism (see, e.g., Génz and Brabon 2009), most analysis of post-feminism has centered on popular culture, particularly in terms of how post-feminism operates via television and film (see, e.g., Modleski 1991; Projansky 2001; McRobbie 2007; Tasker and Negra 2007; Negra 2009). Most of this important body of scholarship, however, pays insufficient attention both to questions of race (Modleski 1991; Springer 2007; Tasker and Negra 2007; Kennedy 2017) and the insinuation of post-feminist, post–Civil Rights ideology into the realm of formal politics, such as elections.[1] This work, *Re-Imagining Black Women*, addresses these two neglected dimensions of post-feminist, post–Civil Rights ideology by presenting a black feminist analysis that takes into account the gender, race, and class dynamics of post–Civil Rights, post-feminist ideology, particularly as they impact black women and black gender politics. Integrating insights from political science, women's and gender studies, black studies, cultural studies, media studies, and psychoanalysis, I explore the range and scope of post-feminist, post–Civil Rights thinking across the ideological spectrum, as well as indicating their location within various narrative sites in popular culture and formal politics and how these sites intersect.

My aim is not to conflate the realms of mass-mediated culture and formal politics, but rather to uncover the invisible parameters of these hegemonic ideologies that distort our understandings to the extent that we can no longer claim that inequality exists. Accordingly, I see television and movies as political in that they constitute a "system of [classed and gendered] racialization" (Littlefield 2008, 675–85) through which hegemonic ideologies are refracted and produced and that influence the same "public" that is subject to and participates in formal politics (Condit 1989).

Scholars have examined the connection between popular culture and politics broadly speaking. One noted and early analyst of post-feminism, Tania Modleski (1991), for instance, examined the regressive effects of representations of masculinity in popular movies, such as *Three Men and a Baby*, and the racial mimesis at the center of the hit Eddie Murphy film *Coming to America*. In *Watching Rape*, Sarah Projansky (2001) examines television and movie representations of rape, arguing that the growing inclusion of such representations do not necessarily signal a straightforward triumph of feminist ideals in popular culture. She demonstrates, on the contrary, how representations of rape continue to marginalize rape as an issue of discussion in certain contexts and can serve to voyeuristically display women's trauma, without any change in how rape is dealt with in society. Yvonne Tasker and Diane Negra, in their important collection *Interrogating Postfeminism* (2007), showcase a range of scholars who investigate representations of women in popular culture that, on the one hand, trumpet the success of today's modern woman, while, on the other hand, promote reconstituted, repackaged notions of femininity in relation to middle-class, patriarchal ideals and family formations.

Others have produced focused studies of particular cultural forms, such as Chick Lit (Herzewski 2011), or types of figures, such as single women (Taylor 2012), and, in some cases, argued for embracing varied, conflicting notions of post-feminism and its impact (see, e.g., Génz and Brabon 2009). In *Historicizing Post-Discourses: Postfeminism and Postracialism in United States Culture* (a book I reference throughout this work), Tanya Ann Kennedy (2017, 12) thinks through the connections between post-racial and post-feminist thinking within a historical frame, pointing to the ways in which they "emerge" in cultural discourse. Kennedy highlights post-racial and post-feminist discourses as responses that work to assuage white male anxieties (12). They are affectively connected to systems of meaning that situate oppression within what she describes as "triumphalist" (12–13) narratives of US culture, that is, as oppression that has been overcome. Those who are not convinced are "affect aliens," she claims, borrowing a concept from Sarah Ahmed's work. As it relates to post-racial, post-feminist discourses, affect aliens are deemed out of step and resentful, unable to accept the progressive advance of US culture and politics. Kennedy's analysis is a welcome exception to the general trend of ignoring or sidelining race in relation to post-feminism.

Re-Imagining Black Women extends such scholarship by examining not only popular culture or political rhetoric (although it certainly does this) but also formal politics. By formal politics I mean the production and circulation of power as it impacts, directs, and shapes the operation of the state and its institutions at various levels of scale—from the local to the global. Indeed, given the increasingly intersecting terrains of popular culture and formal politics, this will prove to be an especially important methodology in the future.

This focus enables several critical interventions in my analysis of post-feminist, post–Civil Rights ideology. First, in terms of the absence of a critique of race, one can argue that the dominant conception of post-feminism—that is, that post-feminism operates through appropriating but ultimately undermining the very logics of feminism—have been implicitly based on white, middle-class female experiences (Kennedy 2017). In *Re-Imagining Black Women*, I would like to suggest that by bringing the "margin to center" (hooks [1984] 2015), that is, by situating post-feminism within the context of post–Civil Rights ideology, we can locate the development of these post-feminist ideologies to an earlier point of origin; in this way, we can complicate and clarify our understanding of them as mutually constitutive phenomena. I highlight, moreover, the broader neoliberal shifts of which post-politics are a central part and the production of blacks as liminal subjects before the state and in society. Second, the merging of these two discourses becomes evident, as I argue throughout, in their common use of melodrama as a privileged representational vehicle for reproducing racist and sexist ideologies. Finally, the juxtaposition of popular cultural forms and political discourse, and examination of post-politics across the political spectrum, helps to bridge the gap between the perceived theory/practice divide in feminism. More pointedly, a common complaint among some feminists is that academic theorizing is irrelevant to activism and political happenings outside of academe. My work addresses such concerns by demonstrating how feminist theorizing illuminates our understanding of formal politics and social movements.

In what follows, I lay the groundwork for the rest of the book by first providing an alternative, black feminist reading of the origins of post-politics; its raced, classed, and gendered dimensions; and its connection to neoliberalism. In doing so I explain the importance of melodrama and its attendant concept of liminality, to the expression of post-feminist, post–Civil Rights politics. I explain the nature of this work as an interdisciplinary enterprise, drawing on a variety of fields, including psychoanalysis, and end by providing a chapter-by-chapter outline of the book.

On Neoliberal Social Formation for the New Millennium: "Post"-ing Social Movements in Culture and Politics

For most scholars, such as Negra, McRobbie, and Tasker, post-feminist ideology extends beyond a simple notion of "backlash" in which feminist principles are directly attacked (McRobbie 2007, 27–28; Tasker and Negra 2007, 1–2) to actually trumpet the success of feminism. As feminist cultural studies critic Angela McRobbie (2007, 28), a singularly influential theorist of post-feminism deftly observes, "Postfeminism positively draws on and invokes feminism as that which can be taken into account, to suggest that equality is achieved, in order to . . . emphasize that it is no longer needed, that it is a spent force." Post-feminism, according to McRobbie, evinces several dominant narrative tropes. First, post-feminist ideology operates through subtle messages that situate a clash between generations, where feminist ideology is figured as belonging in the past, something necessary for an older generation of white women. The goals of social justice having been achieved, social equality is something that is now presumed to be the taken-for-granted operating logic for a younger generation. In this context, youth culture is valorized and associated with a liberated individualization whereby young people, personally empowered through educational and economic uplift, can succeed. This focus on individualization feeds a range of self-regulating practices, drawing attention away from social structure and group politics, and toward an "atomized" (Hsu 2006, 146) understanding of individual expression. Second, McRobbie highlights the use of ironic visual imagery, such as ads, that, in lieu of undermining sexist stereotypes, invoke them, either to play upon the notion that they (and feminist criticism of them) are passé, or to image women embracing them forthrightly (McRobbie 2007). In one ad that McRobbie examined, for instance, a noted model executes a strip tease, simultaneously suggesting, but dismissing, a feminist critique of sexual objectification, implying that such a critique is the stuff of an older, now discredited generation (33).

Against this backdrop of the dominant understanding of post-feminism, how does post-feminism—including a specifically subaltern post-feminism—express itself within the context of black politics? Kimberly Springer insightfully explains, "As part of a racialized discourse, one must grapple with post-feminism's place in the post-civil-rights era" (Springer 2007, 253). Importantly, the term "post–Civil Rights," I maintain, admits of several related meanings, including (1) a demarcation of historical time, that is, an "era," that begins with the passage of the 1964 Civil Rights Act, signaling the end of de jure segregation; (2) a politics of opposition to civil rights initiatives, such as voting rights enforcement, during this same swath of historical time; and (3) more increasingly, a school of thought that suggests that we are living in or at least drifting toward a "post-racial" (read: colorblind) society. For our purposes here, it is necessary to clarify that post–Civil Rights politics encompasses not only direct opposition or "backlash," but also an opposition that, like post-feminist opposition, often trades on and affirms certain liberal notions of formal equality. Moreover, also as with post-feminism, post–Civil Rights politics, as a concomitant strategy, appropriates the language of Civil Rights social movements, such as an emphasis on "equality" or "equal opportunity," read through a frame that suggests that equality has been achieved or is now threatened not by racism but by forms of antiracist politics gone amuck. In one noted example, conservative commentator Glenn Beck called for a March on Washington to "Restore America" (Gardner, Thompson, and Rucker 2010). Laden with nationalistic tones that called for a return to US grandeur and honor, something seen as being diminished by President Obama, the march drew fire from Civil Rights advocates because it was done on the anniversary of Martin Luther King Jr.'s famous "I Have a Dream" speech. Occurring close to the site of the historic speech by perhaps the most iconic figure from that period of activism, the conservative march self-consciously invoked language and symbolism of the Civil Rights movement in support of its cause. In a related vein, George W. Bush used the idea of equal opportunity to support his faith-based initiative, which argued for greater funding for churches in the provision of social services (Alexander-Floyd 2007, esp. Chapter 3). This appropriation of feminist and civil rights rhetoric and images has become a mainstay of political framing of conservative and mainstream political and cultural forces. Although such appropriation goes back to at least the 1970s, the nomenclature surrounding it has shifted over time, from "colorblindness" to "post-racial," and reached a different level of maturation with the presidency of Barack Obama (Kennedy 2017, 2–4).

Notably missing from dominant readings of post-feminism and post–Civil Rights politics is an understanding of how sexist and racist forces following the social movements of the mid–twentieth century most impacted black women. As Springer correctly notes, "The social counterpart to institutional post-civil-rights racism [such as assaults on affirmative action] was the welfare queen" (2007, 253). Likewise, the black matriarch/welfare queen has also been a significant element of post-feminist politics for black women, one that, in recent decades, played a major role in transforming US public policy—particularly the sweeping 1996 welfare reform, and subsequent fatherhood and faith-based initiatives—and in generally bolstering neoliberal and conservative dominance.

The image of the black matriarch was made notorious, of course, by the 1965 Moynihan Report. For Moynihan ([1965] 1967), the key problem was that black families were matriarchal, that is, dominated by black women who headed single-parent households, in a society that valued patriarchal families. Because of black matriarchy, he averred, black families suffered socially, economically, and politically. This report had several critical outcomes in terms of, among other things, attitudes about social activism, the resistance to feminism, and the promotion of middle-class respectability and traditional gender roles. First, as others have detailed extensively (see, e.g., Collins 1990; Lubiano 1992; Jewell 1993; Hancock 2004; Jordan-Zachery 2009), for the broader culture, this report facilitated and legitimated political retrenchment that fingered the micro-institution of the family, not the macro-institutional structures controlled by the state, as the source of black people's plight. The notion of black cultural pathology promoted by the report would serve as the narrative framework that would be used to define "the sign of blackness" (Gray 1995) within the current era and that would pose the largest challenge to the Civil Rights and Black Power movements' emphasis on structural change. Second, in line with this thinking, black women have been problematically caricatured as "strong," regardless of their socioeconomic standing: poor women are in control of families, and middle-class, upwardly mobile women are able to succeed, despite the realities of racism. From this vantage point, feminism is not embraced and then discarded. It is said, rather, to have never been necessary. Finally, a middle-class "ideology of respectability" (Higginbotham 1994; White 2001; Harris 2012; Cooper 2017) centered on restoring two-parent, patriarchal homes in black communities has been promoted as the solution to black social and political ills. Consequently, community organizing has been geared toward "saving" the black male and promoting acceptable forms of black masculinity (Alexander-Floyd 2007).

As the above suggests, in the case of black politics, post-feminism can manifest itself as both an explicit "antifeminism," as well as an advocacy of a "new traditionalism" that champions a prefeminist politics (Projansky 2001, esp. Chapter 2).[2] This antifeminism and push for traditionalism is evident in the broader culture as well, as we can see in the Trump administration. Sarah Projansky's extensive discussion of the different manifestations of post-feminism reminds us that the variety of post-feminist themes can be contradictory and appeal to a range of people (Projansky 2001, 86–87). In all their variety, however, post-feminist frames communicate a wish that feminism would go away (Projansky 2001, 87). Moreover, as I discuss a bit more in Chapter 2, specifically in my examination of *Crash* and the 2008 Obama campaign, the stereotypes grounded in black cultural pathology à la Moynihan are used to solidify notions of black liminality, a concept I discuss more below, and juxtapose two black Americas—that is, the underclass, ridden with moral failings that drive their poverty and other social ills, and the middle and upper class, whose members, the most noted being Barack and Michelle Obama, are held out as moral exemplars for their less successful counterparts.

A black feminist analysis exposes the ways in which what we view as post–Civil Rights and post-feminist timeframes and ideologies are not only deeply enmeshed but, indeed, co-constitutive. Post–Civil Rights ideology, for whatever else it represents, has also been elaborated through and constituted a post-feminist politics: it is formulated through the politics of not only race, but gender and class, where black families would come to be situated for political participation and social uplift by attaining middle-class respectability via two-parent families, patterned after an idealized white middle-class family. Likewise, this focus on the family and male uplift, and its attendant focus on self-regulation, personal empowerment, and responsibility, predated the current emphasis on these elements in mainstream white society that have been the subject of so much scholarship on post-feminism. Political scientist Fred Harris also notes that the "politics of respectability predates neoliberalism" (Harris 2012, 105). Although this politics of respectability has a longer historical trail, it nevertheless serves a particular role in the mid–twentieth century in authorizing neoliberalism. More pointedly, once we take the history and social position of black women into account, it is the 1965 Moynihan Report with its raced-gendered individualist frame for upward mobility and assault on black women, not the failure to pass the Equal Rights Amendment or other sociopolitical trends of the 1980s (Projansky 2001, 14–15), that marks the onset of not only a post–Civil Rights but also a post-feminist assault on the social movements of the mid–twentieth century.[3] Thus, as Figure 1.1 illustrates, neoliberal post-politics counters social movement claims to a need for broad-scale change by focusing attention away from macro-structural change. The answer to "what" causes social inequality is found

Figure I.1. The Driving Forces of Neoliberal Post-Politics

in behavior and self-management. The "why," or function of neoliberal post-politics, is the maintenance of elite control and the expansion of global capitalism. Narratives—specifically, melodramas that focus on individuals, relationships, and families—are the vehicle for, or the "how" of, neoliberal post-politics.

This re-periodization is important because it helps us to situate the turn to post-politics as a constituent feature of neoliberalism and to understand the raced, gendered, and classed cultural work that made the ascendance of neoliberalism possible. Neoliberalism is generally identified as an ideological disposition favoring limited government and free and open markets globally. As David Theo Goldberg (2009) argues, however, in *The Threat of Race: Reflections on Racial Neoliberalism*, as a practical matter, neoliberalism does not try to curtail or eradicate the state, as much as lay claim to its authority in support of corporations and the wealthy. In the United States, for instance, calls for lower taxes and an end to big government amounted to deregulation of key financial markets and deficits being settled by drastic changes in social services, most notably the aforementioned 1996 welfare reform. Unsurprisingly, a priority on reducing social services and government regulation and influence toward the public good carried a concomitant focus on devolution of social services to state and local governments and on individual self-help. With a state apparatus focused on restabilizing a government challenged by social movements for racial and gender equality, a post-politics that allows reformist, liberal forms of equality, while thwarting large-scale social transformation, is well-suited to racial and gender management. Elites, moreover, turn to racial management as they confront increasingly diverse democracies, such as in the United States (Goldberg 2009).[4]

Post-Politics, Melodrama, and Liminality

Significantly, a neoliberal, Moynihanesque focus on family rehabilitation and wounded masculinity, with its emphasis on pathos and the resolution of moral crisis, finds its perfect expression in the melodramatic mode. As opposed to a genre with fixed, defining elements, melodrama can be seen as a "mode," that is, a "certain fictional system for making sense of experience" (Brooks [1976] 1995, xvii). It is grounded in "pathos" and embodied in characters that are "victims" or "villains," embodying "virtue" and "virtuelessness," good and evil, respectively (Williams 2001).[5] Melodramas are also often marked by a desire to reclaim an ostensibly beneficial past or state (Williams 2001, 36). As such, melodrama is an optimal medium for quelling or resolving social anxiety. Melodrama, as others have demonstrated, is the prevailing form of narrative expression in film and other forms of cultural production, and arguably in politics as well (Williams 2001; Kelleter, Krah, and Mayer 2007). Importantly, in this current cultural and political milieu, melodrama works by extricating questions of social inequality from the realm of the public, scripted as a masculine domain, and translating it into the realm of the private and individualized world of melodrama, scripted as the special preserve of the feminine (Grindstaff 1994). Indeed, as L. A. Grindstaff (1994) remarks, "Melodrama . . . represents social anxieties or conflicts as sexual and familial ones" and depends "on questions of visibility, representability, pretense, and masquerade" (54). As she further explains, "In film melodrama, crises of representation and identity function to break families apart, then bring them together again at the story's end employing one of a number of formulas: the hero defeats the villain, the 'villain within' is reformed, or the villain turns out to have been the hero all along" (55). Although much analysis of melodrama pertains to literature and culture more broadly, this work takes seriously the impact of melodrama as a political force.

Like political theorist Elisabeth R. Anker, I examine the political dimensions of melodrama, including the way it operates within political discourse. In *Orgies of Feeling: Melodrama and the Politics of Freedom*, Anker maps the ways in which political melodramas became important in the justification for the wars following the attacks of September 11,

2001. Indeed, as she argues, melodrama can be seen as one of several genres, such as jeremiads, within political discourse (2014, 6). Although she deftly examines melodrama as it influences international politics and US national engagement therein, melodrama, as I demonstrate, is also central to domestic concerns and the post-politics that have taken hold of culture and politics within the new millennium. In this sense, with many modern melodramas, the feminist claim that the personal is political is perverted to mean that *only* the personal is political, side-lining or resisting public claims to redress sexism, racism, and class inequality.

Melodrama becomes a privileged mode of post–Civil Rights, post-feminist ideology that functions to redirect attention away from structural inequality and toward individual attitudes and actions through its focus on

(a) *stability of the family*, that is, the micro-institution of the family and reassertion of romanticized forms of white middle-class patriarchy.
(b) *self-regulation* (variously labeled self-development, self-help, or personal responsibility), that assumes social problems are amenable to individual redress.
(c) *social (interpersonal) relationships*, as opposed to institutions or the state, as the site for conflict resolution—relationships that stand in for our understanding of ourselves as a national family or community.
(d) *splitting*, that is, the construction of blacks as *liminal subjects*, who are variously depicted as "good, deserving" citizens or "bad" or abject objects (Tyler 2013).

The construction of blacks as liminal subjects undergirds the other elements—included here—and, therefore, bears particular emphasis. Given its Manichaean focus on good and bad types or villains and victims, melodrama in post-politics renders blacks and, to varying degrees, other racial minorities as liminal subjects in society and before the state. Figure 1.2 illustrates political melodrama's production of liminal subjects, and this splitting of people and groups into good, worthy subjects and bad, abject others.

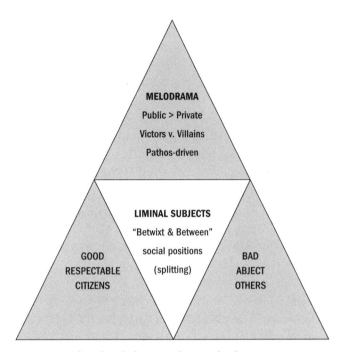

Figure I.2. Political Melodrama and Liminal Subjects

Notably, incarcerated black men and women, highlighted on prison reality shows such as those on MSNBC, are mythologized as to be representative of baseness or "bad" or abject objects, for instance. Imogen Tyler, writing in *Revolting Subjects* (2013), draws on Kristeva's notion of the abject to explore what "being made abject" (see, e.g., 41–46) means. She asserts that those populations, such as migrants or social welfare recipients, who are made abject are denigrated as "human waste" (47), and therefore disposable and outside (although ironically defining) of the state or body politic (46–47). Indeed, as Robert Entman and Andrew Rojecki explain, "As cultural signifiers, blacks now traverse an ill-defined border state, symbolically comprising an uneasy, contradictory mixture of danger/pollution and acceptability. . . . In other words, blacks in American culture are now *liminal* beings" (2001, 50–51 [emphasis in original]).

This liminality operates on macro and micro levels. At the macro level, this liminality is seen in the projection of two "black Americas," noted above. As Figure 1.3 relates, African Americans are seen in dueling polarities—that is, worthy, virtuous ("good") citizens, on the one hand, and unworthy, abject ("bad") figures, on the other. Middle- and upper-class blacks are juxtaposed to urban, poor blacks, who are seen as a drain on the public purse. In a related way, at the micro level—at the level of the individual—blacks are seen as prototypical "super minorities" (a concept I explore in Chapter 2, particularly with regard to President Obama) who are idealized citizen-subjects, or, conversely, as embodiments of abject blackness. This melodramatic duality plays out often in legal dramas. Murder victims, such as Trayvon Martin, are framed as threatening or morally questionable abject figures (see, generally, Johnson, Warren, and Farrell 2015). Botham Jean, shot in his own home by Dallas police officer Amber Guyger, conversely, was avenged in court in no small part because he was framed as an idealized super minority.

Liminality, to be sure, can be seen in dueling representations of black America, as well as in other competing representations of black political figures, such as Condoleezza Rice and Michelle Obama, that demonstrate the social and political ambivalence with which they are confronted, that is, being projected as both idealized and abject subjects. As I discuss in Chapter 1, Rice, for instance, is interpolated variously within storylines of closeness that either frame her as a symbol of the success of integrationism and the arrival of racial and ethnic equality or, conversely, as hypersexualized and treasonous. I suggest that the production of these dueling representations or binary oppositions is, in part, a function of splitting. As I elaborate on in Chapter 1 psychoanalysts suggest splitting is a process, rooted in our early experiences, that map notions of good and evil onto individuals and groups. These conflicting images do not, of course, flatten black female experiences into a monolithic "Sister Citizen" (Harris-Perry 2011) experience; whatever representations are developed of black women, material questions and ideological commitments matter. Rather, assessing this production of blacks as liminal subjects underscores how moral fitness is used as a basis for full participation in society and as citizen–civil society subjects.

Liminality, of course, is best associated with anthropologist Victor Turner, and I draw on his work, as well as that of cultural studies scholar Leah R. Vande Berg (1996). For Turner, liminality conveys the "state of

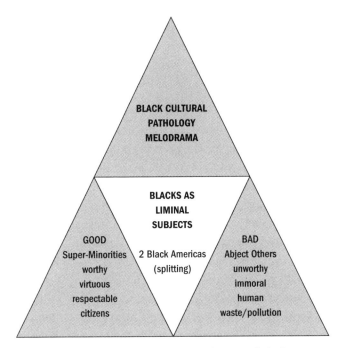

Figure I.3. Black Cultural Pathology Melodrama and Blacks as Liminal Subjects

being 'betwixt and between' social status positions" (Turner, quoted in Vande Berg 1996, 51). It captures the indeterminacy of individuals in this in-between space, as they journey to a new status or position by traversing a "limen" or "threshold." Vande Berg focuses on liminality as a "colonialist process of enculturation" in which dominant societies are seen as having ideal cultural values, which racialized "others" must strive to attain (1996, 52). In my analysis, the crossing of thresholds and/or transitions are, at times, certainly at play, as when, as I discuss in Chapter 1, Condoleezza Rice crosses into membership in the Bush family. Liminality does not necessarily depend on a linear notion of evolution, however. A key difference in my use of the term from Vande Berg and others is that, while internal struggle may be present in individuals, this is not my focus. I am not principally concerned with interiority per se, but rather the ways in which individuals and groups are imagined, that is, represented, perceived, or symbolized.

Narrative Analysis, Critical Race Black Feminism, and Interdisciplinarity

Re-Imagining Black Women utilizes interpretive methodology, focusing specifically on narrative analysis as a method of choice. As I have argued elsewhere (see, e.g., Alexander-Floyd 2003; 2004; 2007), narratives are the central means by which we elaborate political discourse and foment action. Given its relevance to politics, policy, and culture, we can usefully trace its operation in order to map the changing forces that affect not only the operations of state power but also our day-to-day lives. Narratives serve to frame our understandings of culture and politics in ways that both construct and influence interpretations of reality (Schram and Neisser 1997; Fischer 2003). Framing is an important concept across disciplines that helps to explain the ways in which narratives can serve to produce commonsense understandings and influence everything from public policy and social movements to public opinion and media stories; my own work has examined how a focus on black cultural pathology with its emphasis on restoring patriarchy has been a meta-frame for black politics in general and policies, surrounding faith-based and fatherhood initiatives, in particular (Alexander-Floyd 2007). I continue my exploration of narratives and framing by looking at a range of framing devices that one can identify in melodramatic post-racial/post-feminist narratives, including but not limited to storylines, fantasy, and irony. Although narrative analysis is broadly relevant to the study of race, gender, and inequality, in this work I am particularly concerned with the impact of post-politics on the lives of black women and black gender politics.

Indeed, my use of interpretive methodology affirms my commitment to a Critical Race Black Feminism (Alexander-Floyd 2010) or (what I elsewhere refer to as) a black feminist frame of reference (Alexander-Floyd 2007, Chapter 1)—that is, a progressive approach to research and politics that centers on black women as subjects and the black gender politics in which they are embedded. Scholars operating from what I describe as a Critical Race Black Feminist, or Critical Black Feminist, approach (Alexander-Floyd 2010) generally ascribe to several assumptions: (1) that class, gender, and race are mutually constitutive, socially constructed categories (i.e., a constitutive model of identity) (see, e.g.,

McClintock 1995; Fernandes 1997; Harris 1999; Gillman 2010); (2) that while these forces are socially constructed, they are fictions that are very real in their material effects; (3) that scholarship and politics should be aimed at alleviating the disadvantage and domination black women confront; and (4) that radical feminist scholarship must challenge the normative epistemological assumptions of existing disciplines, particularly in their pursuit of Western ideals of rationality and "scientificity" in research.

This project is consistent with the ideographic project of intersectionality (Alexander-Floyd 2012a), that is, the decades-long effort of black feminists to investigate the operation of race, class, gender, sexuality, and other factors in the lives of black women. It includes, of course, Kimberlé Crenshaw's (1989; 1991) articulation of intersectionality, which includes political, materialist, and representational registers, and centers on the co-articulation of racism and sexism and other dimensions of oppression as they impact women of color in general and black women in particular. The term "intersectionality," unfortunately, has been problematically appropriated to account for a range of factors that, in their increasingly more abstract use, may or may not have anything to do with race, not to mention black women (see, e.g., Berger and Guidroz 2009; Dill and Zambrana 2009; May 2015; Collins and Bilge 2016 for a discussion of debates on intersectionality). In this context, I prefer the terms "Critical Race Black Feminism" or "black feminist frame of reference" because they affirm the centrality of black women's experiences as the subject of research and commitment to forging black feminist epistemologies. Through my scholarship I build on and am in dialogue with scholars in a number of discourse communities, but my work is especially and broadly consonant with that of other black feminists in political science, many of whom I cite herein, who explore the inattention or misdirection of emphasis on black political women and black gender politics (see, e.g., Brown 2013; Smooth 2013; Brown 2014; Jordan-Zachery 2017; Harris 2018).

Finally, my use of interpretive methodology within a Critical Black Feminist tradition represents my contribution to interdisciplinarity, particularly within political science and women's and gender studies. As the foregoing suggests, my approach to melodrama necessarily integrates concepts and questions from a variety of disciplines. In addition to research drawn from political science, media studies, cultural studies, and women's and gender studies, this work interweaves psychoanalytic concepts and modes of reading in hopes of advancing a black feminist "psychoanalytic political theory" (Burack 2004). Contrary to conventional scholarly wisdom, which suggests that major African American thinkers and writers have shunned psychoanalysis as irrelevant to black cultural and political thought, black intellectuals have for some time engaged psychoanalytic theory to inform their views and political practice. As Arlene Keizer (2010, 410) observes, "New archival research and new attention to materials long available to critics reveal an extended history of African American involvement with psychoanalytic theory and practice that has rarely been acknowledged or studied." From the 1920s on, thinkers such as Richard Wright, Ralph Ellison, and Zora Neale Hurston (Ahad 2010), as well as more contemporary scholars, such as Daniel José Gaztambide (2019), Paul Gilroy (2006), Hortense Spillers (2003), Michelle Stephens (2014), and the late Claudia Tate (1998), have grappled with psychoanalysis's relevance to US race/gender formations. They have offered important critiques of and correctives to traditional psychoanalysis's implicit Eurocentric, patriarchal frameworks (Keizer 2010). Although I draw on the work of a number of theorists of race and psychoanalysis, the work of Hortense Spillers and Claudia Tate are particularly relevant for the issues I discuss. As I detail in succeeding chapters, Spillers's work on Barack Obama and on black matriarchy play a critical role in my discussion of Barack Obama in Chapter 2 and the figure of Madea in Chapter 3, respectively, and Claudia Tate's meditations on the protocols of race and desire are helpful in my treatment of Condoleezza Rice and in explaining contemporary fixations on black matriarchal figures in popular culture, as I discuss in Chapter 2 and Chapter 3, respectively.

Recent work on race and psychoanalysis has, of course, been marked by what one might call a melancholic turn,[6] that is, an investigation of Freud's notion of melancholia versus mourning in terms of grappling with loss. Scholars such as David Eng and David Kazanjian (2003) and Paul Gilroy (2006) have explored the extent to which postcolonial subjects and/or Others, deprived of genuine, recuperative mourning, which acknowledges and moves beyond loss, are bound instead by the cords of unproductive melancholia, where individuals and groups deny or repress the losses they have endured. The work of Jane Flax (2010) on racial melancholia is particularly resonant with the goals of my project, as she frames her discussion of the subject with the aim of raising some concerns about the rhetoric of "post-racial" politics in the United States. For Flax, US race/gender politics is hamstrung by a refusal to deal with the determinative loss represented in the chasm between the rhetoric of US equality and the reality of a nation founded on human bondage. Moreover, Flax correctly emphasizes that the effects of slavery are visible in the nation's economic development and disparate distribution of resources, as well as in its "psychic register" (Flax 2010, 16). Although I find some of the work on melancholia insightful and, in Chapter 4, advocate speaking the truth about repressed or disavowed political experience as a means of mourning, my work focuses instead on melodrama, as it more directly centers attention on the mechanisms or framing narratives through which post-politics takes shape.

I include psychoanalytic theory and concepts such as defenses, projective identification, and splitting as a complement to the other reading strategies I invoke here, because they are necessary to untangle the full range of forces that constitute racial and gender politics in the United States. Like Jane Flax, I find that many articulations of antiracist politics and theory fall short in explaining the unconscious dimensions of racial domination (Flax 2010). The "political unconscious," that is, "collective psychological dispositions," is fundamental to the operation of what people would describe as individual attitudes or prejudice, and also constitutes a central source of the formation and persistence of the material realities of inequality (Flax 2010, 16). "Such dispositions are themselves material. They inflict material harm and influence the distribution of material goods such as social esteem, status, and prestige" (Flax 2010, 16). As Flax observes, fantasy emerges as a key means of examining the "psychic register" and the political unconscious that animates race and gender politics in the United States, and I investigate some of the dominant fantasies that have emerged as a part of the post-politics of our time, both in formal politics and popular culture, such as movies and music.[7]

Two final points are important to make at this juncture, regarding neoliberalism, post-politics, and fantasy. First, for some, it might seem odd to consider melodrama and neoliberalism, given the former's focus on pathos and the latter's association with rationality. Although neo-liberalism certainly does function in terms of a push for greater rationality and the insinuation of surveillance, regulation, and economic profitability into every aspect of living (see Brown 2017), this, too, is driven by fantasy. The academy provides a perfect case in point. The encroachment of neoliberal paradigms that push for greater efficiency, responsibility, and documentation yields just the opposite, that is, management bloat, a weakening of faculty governance, and administrative confusion. Sarah Ahmed's work on diversity is relevant here. She argues that diversity language is a "non-performative," that is, it does not necessarily do what it states, we have to "follow it around" and examine exactly if and how it manifests and to what ends (Ahmed 2012). Similarly, neoliberal calls for rationality and order are non-performatives. They are fantasies that effect neoliberal agendas, to be sure, but only one set of such fantasies. Melodrama provides a context for others. Second, some might see the recent uptick in protests in the years leading up to and after Trump's election as evidence that post-racial, post-feminist politics are irrelevant, that is, that we are well past a moment when people think activism is unnecessary. On the contrary, however, post-feminist, post-racial politics are, unfortunately, alive and well. In fact, as I discuss in the Conclusion, the fact that some were caught off guard by the political forces that made Trump's presidency a possibility is a testament to the broad reach and impact of post-feminist, post-racial politics. Protests also continue to generally sideline black women, as evidenced, for instance, by ongoing calls to "Say Her Name," that is, to acknowledge the harm visited on black women by police. This persistent deferral of attention to black women enacts a post-feminist impulse in black politics and a post-racial one in feminist activism. Moreover, as I also punctuate in the Conclusion, the melodramatic urtexts and narratives discussed in *Re-Imagining Black Women* still hold sway in popular culture and politics. Post-politics, as previously noted, is best thought of as a repertoire of fantasies, frames, and narratives that ideologically undermine and resist movements for social change. They include what we would see as direct forms of resistance, as well as advocacy for traditionalism and liberal forms of equality, in lieu of social justice. Now, more than ever, there is a need to understand their reach, elaboration, and development.

Outline of Book

In *Re-Imagining Black Women* I focus on areas of black culture and politics that are neglected and repressed, because, as I discuss below, it allows us to better assess the tensions and driving forces of culture and politics. Chapter 1 begins with an examination of a figure who, for some, is an unlikely candidate for analysis of black gender politics: former national security advisor and secretary of state Condoleezza Rice. Since much analysis of black politics, like analysis of black literature (Tate 1998), adheres to a protest model of defining what is authentically black and, therefore, definitive of black politics, black conservatives such as Rice get relatively less treatment, given their ongoing and growing importance on the national scene. Contrary to the protocols of race, which demand attention to black protest in novels, in *Psychoanalysis and Black Novels: Desire and the Protocols of Race* Claudia Tate (1998) examines the lesser-known or uncelebrated works of canonical authors that often foreground other elements of desire. In doing so, she investigates how "the anomalous work not only inscribes but exaggerates a primary narrative, an 'urtext,' that is repeated but masked in the canonical texts" (Tate 1998, 8). Rice as an anomalous subject for scholarly inquiry can yield similar insights. Specifically, we are able to examine the primary narrative or urtext Rice represents—namely, the fantasy of colorblind national community formation.

Although she presents herself and is lauded by others as an example of the United States' progress in terms of race and gender equality, the fantasy of difference-blind inclusion is persistently challenged when it comes to Rice. Indeed, I demonstrate how Rice is constructed as a liminal subject, that is, a melodramatic figure who is represented as both victor and villain. More specifically, I show how this duality is a form of splitting and takes shape via variations on a dominant storyline of closeness that paradoxically work both to create and undermine the US national narrative of color(difference)-blind integration. My central argument is that Rice signifies the liminality of blacks in general and black women in particular and that this liminality is contrary to the triumph of integration she is said to represent.

Chapter 2 expands my treatment of melodrama and the production of blacks as liminal subjects by examining the political beliefs and representations of President Barack Obama. In lieu of viewing President Obama's use of deracialization as a political strategy, I offer an intersectional approach that focuses on President Obama as a post-racial, post-feminist politician. I examine the Moynihan Report as an urtext for black cultural pathology melodrama, a neoliberal frame that anticipated much of what we associate with post-feminism, particularly in terms of self-regulation. I explore black cultural pathology melodrama as it relates to Obama both in terms of his historic 2008 election and his governance. More specifically, I focus on the historic 2008 presidential campaign and the cultural milieu in which it occurred. In order to get at this cultural milieu or "nested context" (Rein and Schön 1993), along with Obama's campaign rhetoric and strategies, I examine *Crash* and *Grey's Anatomy*, popular cultural sites in the general time period of the historic 2008 campaign, in order to capture the resonance of post-feminist, post-racial themes within society during this campaign and to highlight the mutually constitutive nature of culture and formal politics as theaters of engagement and influence.

Drilling down, I identify and trace the various racial and gendered meanings of three melodramatic storylines: individualistic interpretations of inequality, rehabilitation of the family and wounded masculinity, and racial and gender redemption centered in "fantasies of miscegenation" (Courtney 2005). I expose how Obama's personal history, campaign rhetoric, and policies fit within melodramatic frames that focus on pathos; channel public problems into personal spaces, particularly the family; and redirect efforts toward social uplift (T. F. Reed 2008) and personal responsibility. In this vein, I assess how Obama is variously figured as a "magical Negro," or prototypical inversion of black stereotypes, as an example of a new generation of leadership that nevertheless affirms patriarchal modes of black leadership, and a symbolic father who serves as an exemplar of middle-class respectability that situates blacks as morally fit for civic standing.

I also view Obama's support for black cultural pathology melodrama in his My Brother's Keeper initiative. I detail the initiative's connection to black cultural pathology melodrama and show how Obama situates himself as a black symbolic father for people of color. I also assess the pushback to this initiative, suggesting that the "add women and girls" approach, as opposed to full-on opposition, shows the perils of identification where minority candidates, like Obama, are concerned. I argue that the summit on advancing equity for women and girls of color authorized a problematic focus on gender complementarity and infantilized black women.

Turning from a focus on formal politics and toward a focus on melodrama, liminality, and popular culture, Chapter 3 examines Tyler Perry's classic Madea figure in his foundational breakout movie, *Diary of a Mad Black Woman*. Perry is a dominant figure in Hollywood productions featuring black characters and culturally focused narratives. Much of his success depends on the melodramatic storylines he constructs that address "dating panic" (Herzewski 2011, 3) in black communities and "Other" single women (Taylor 2012) by, among other means, promoting heterosexual coupledom as the optimal state for black female self-actualization. Not only does Perry present marriage as an ideal state, he figures narratives of return and self-governance as solutions for black social ills. In this way his movie fits neatly into the neoliberal emphasis on micro-level scales of assessment and action, often found in post-feminist movies and images. Moreover, drawing on psychoanalytic concepts, such as Freud's ideas of condensation, and displacement in dreams, and multivocality in free association and applying them to *Diary*, I demonstrate how Perry's racialized cross-dressing via Madea is tied to his own ambivalent connection to his mother and serves as a mechanism for him to symbolically eliminate black women, and occupy the plenitude and authority associated with stereotypical figures such as the mammy/matriarch. Finally, like Kennedy, I find that post-feminist, post–Civil Rights ideology evokes particular affective responses. Instead of focusing on how such ideologies address white male anxiety, however, I examine various levels of connection through which black audiences identify with Perry's Madea figure and the fantasy relayed in his signature, paradigmatic movie.

Chapter 4 examines with two objectives in mind melodrama in the context of the history of white male rape of black women. First, I consider the relevance of black women and families to US-based American political development by pointing to their importance to social contract theory. I consider the role of blacks in our assumptions about family, gender, and race implicit to the social contract. Second, I investigate the psychological defenses used to ignore or rewrite this US record.

Although this reality is well established by historians and treated extensively in black women's literature, social and political discourse denies, represses, and/or disavows it. I delineate how this denial, repression, and disavowal occur, and how the history of white male rape of black women nevertheless "haunts" US culture and politics. I trace these psychological responses and hauntings in three sites regarding *The Help*—namely, the book of oral histories Stockett uses in writing her narrative, as well as the book and movie version of *The Help*. Although some recent work by women's and gender studies scholars posits that too much of black feminism focuses on black women's experiences as an archive of pain (see, e.g., Nash 2014; Musser 2016), this treatment suggests that we fail to reckon with or mourn black women's sexual violation in particular.

Chapter 5 continues a discussion of melodrama by examining the MeToo movement. More specifically, the chapter examines liminality along two fronts. First, I show how liminality positions black women as abject figures unworthy of concern in terms of sexual harassment or rape. I point out the irony of this reality, given the way that black women have been so important in the history of resistance to rape and harassment, in the context of enslavement to the present day. Second, I assess two important case studies, one focusing on transnational business masculinity (Connell 2012) and the other on black cultural pathology melodrama and celebrity. The first case study centers on the explosive international drama involving accusations of rape by Nafissatou Diallo, a black female immigrant housekeeper, against Dominique Strauss-Kahn, the once politically and internationally powerful former head of the International Monetary Fund. I discuss Strauss-Kahn as an exemplar of transnational business masculinity and point to the particular vulnerabilities of black women immigrants, like Diallo, who are framed as abject in the structure of liminality. The second case study examines liminality in terms of black cultural pathology melodrama's central role in Bill Cosby's public persona, as a super minority role model. As Dr. Huxtable on *The Cosby Show*, Bill Cosby presented a model of upper-middle-class patriarchal respectability. This imagery was part of the dualism or splitting function of liminality, where models of respectable citizens are juxtaposed to abject black others in need of tutelage and rehabilitation to deserve public embrace. I also show how black cultural pathology melodrama explains his deriding of the black poor and his

TABLE I.1. Summary of Chapter Themes

Topic (Repressed/ Disavowed in Politics)	Lessons on Black Liminality Respectable vs. Abject Blackness
Chapter 1 Conservatives	• "All skin folk, ain't kin folk": no monolithic black community. • Representationally, even conservatives can be figured as liminal (split) subjects. • Identification, especially regarding racism, can short-circuit critique of class and other ideological commitments.
Chapter 2 Gender	• Deracialization is an insufficient explanatory frame; must consider "cross-cutting" (Cohen 1999) issues, such as gender. • The Moynihan Report is an urtext for post-politics: focus on stability of family, self-regulation, social relations, and splitting (e.g., super minorities/magical negroes vs. endangered black males and their mothers). • Black symbolic fathers, like Obama, escaping robust accountability.
Chapter 3 Revenge	• *Diary of a Mad Black Woman* is prototypical black post-feminist, post-racial fantasy (i.e., the black version of *Bridget Jones's Diary*). • Perry enacts revenge on black women and men perceived as falling short of gender ideals, through Madea and other characters.
Chapter 4 Rape	• White male rape of black women is foundational to the US social contract. • *The Help*, a celebrated post-politics film, shows how the history of white male rape of black women is denied, disavowed, and repressed, even as this history "haunts" (Rashkin 2008) this narrative. • This history must be mourned (Flax 2010) through speaking.
Chapter 5 Harassment/ Sadomasochism	• As abject others, black women raped or harassed are not sufficiently recognized or seen as representative figures (e.g., in the MeToo movement). • Advocates must attend to: —Transnational and domestic business masculinity —Destructive "père-version" (Wright 2013) or self-fathering (authoring) —Sadomasochism as key frame and lessons from whistle-blowers/feudal power

attempt at self-fathering or "père-version" (Wright 2013). I argue for the importance of sadomasochism as an analytic in assessing sexual harassment and explore parallels between victims of harassment and rape and whistle-blowers.

For further emphasis I encapsulate major arguments and themes from each chapter in Table 1.1.

The Conclusion offers a metaphor from the physics of flow for understanding the form (methodology) and substance in this book. As opposed to laminar flow, which has a more or less linear or unidirectional force, turbulent flow exemplifies dynamic, sometimes explosive, variation in movement. The turbulent flow of politics needs an approach that can match its character. The interdisciplinary exploration of post-politics, liminality, and melodrama can provide an uncomfortable ride for those who tend to labor in largely set scholarly parameters or discourse communities, and in such cases I ask for patience. Interdisciplinarity was necessary to capture the full measure of what is at stake and what has transpired in the development of post-politics. After discussing turbulence, the Conclusion recaps key insights from the book. And, in hopes of provoking additional work on post-politics, I discuss recent examples of it, namely Barack Obama's continued support for My Brother's Keeper; Michelle Obama's memoir *Becoming*; 2020 presidential candidate Kamala Harris; and the reaction to the documentary *Surviving R. Kelly*. Among other issues, the Conclusion pays special attention to the way in which post-politics explains the surprise some experienced at the ascension of Donald Trump, arguing that post-politics is best seen as a range of competing fantasies that still vie for public attention and action, all designed to undermine collective efforts at progressive social change.

A Coda speaks to the COVID-19 crisis. I discuss how this crisis is a symptom of capitalism under neoliberalism, the same neoliberalism that uses the production of liminal subjects and melodrama as its handmaidens to give it life. The Coda speaks to the need for revolt to secure a future beyond the deadly character of late capitalism.

1

Splitting Condi(licious)

Condoleezza Rice and Melodramas of "Closeness" in
US National Community Formation

We must rethink the sentiment that "all women" are good
for democracy and consider that some are an affront to
democratic principles.
—Wendy Smooth (2018)

In the fall of 2015, New Jersey elected Bonnie Watson Coleman to
Congress. In several settings, individuals suggested that people should
vote for her, indicating that, if she won, she would be the first African
American congresswoman from the state of New Jersey. Of course, as a
longtime public servant, Bonnie Watson Coleman is a well-established
Democrat, known for progressive politics. Still, the shorthand promotion of her election's historic significance as a political "first" was
assumed to be beneficial for black communities and for the state more
generally. When a friend mentioned her historic win, proudly indicating
that she was the first black woman from her state elected to Congress,
I noted that the same could be said of Mia Love of Utah. As a black
female, her election was also historic (Wineinger 2019). As a black Mor-
mon conservative member of the Republican Party, however, she and
Bonnie Watson Coleman could not be further away from each other
politically.

I note the irony of these two historic wins to highlight a few basic
points suggested above, namely: descriptive (or identity-based) representation does not necessarily translate into substantive (or ideological)
representation, and although public opinion among blacks suggests a
sense of linked fate across economic status (Dawson 1995) and most
blacks who vote are registered democrats (Pew 2018), there is diversity of thought and ideological complexity among blacks (Cohen 1999).

Voting tendencies notwithstanding, blacks are socially conservative relative to the general population (Philpot 2007, 2018; Lewis 2013). Moreover, black conservatives, while fewer in number, have gained greater visibility since at least the 1970s, and the Republican Party has courted black conservatives aggressively as well (Jones 1987). Why then is there relative scholarly inattention to black conservatives or Republican political women?

As I noted in the introduction, the protocols of race direct attention to culture and politics that are seen to openly challenge racial oppression and discrimination. Claudia Tate (1998) observed that work by canonical figures such as W. E. B. DuBois or Zora Neale Hurston that fell outside of a protest model or did not directly challenge racial oppression were generally neglected. Examining these less popular works is important, however. Tate suggests, in fact, that novels that stand outside of a protest tradition focus on issues that are "repressed," and, therefore, provide a window into "unconscious discourses or implicit narrative fragments that fulfill latent wishes, much like dreams" (12). "They 'make visible,' moreover, 'the ways in which we . . . have circumscribed black subjectivity and black textuality by a reductive understanding of racial difference that has in turn made concepts of race and desire [where desire is understood to encompass a broad range of concerns, not just sexual longings] seem incompatible'" (12).

In a similar way, study of black politics generally focuses on those actors who are identified with liberal or left-leaning politics. Because it does not support a progressive social justice model, conservatism is one of the repressed aspects of black politics, a dimension that, while longstanding and evolving, most ignore or observe with passing interest. Black conservatism and black conservative figures are, nevertheless, important to investigate because they can reveal "latent wishes" not just in black politics but in US politics as well. There are certainly particularities regarding how such latent wishes operate regarding conservatives and conservatism, specifically in black politics. In this chapter, however, I focus on black conservative Condoleezza Rice in order to assess a desire for color(difference)-blind national community formation in US politics as a whole and its expression through a post-feminist melodrama urtext. She is a particularly apt figure to explore those "unconscious discourses," given her political career.

Despite the unprecedented role of Condoleezza Rice in US politics and foreign policy, political scientists and other scholars have generally fallen short in producing scholarship on her public roles. Unfortunately, there has been relatively little work on her, at least in ways that are commensurate with her importance. Although a number of biographies have been written about Rice (largely for popular audiences) (e.g., Felix 2002; Edmondson 2006; Bumiller 2007; Kessler 2007; Mabry 2007) and works that consider Rice's role as an international actor (Lusane 2006), there have been few scholarly treatments from a feminist perspective (see, e.g., Davies 2007; Eisenstein 2007).

In this chapter, I counteract the inattention to black conservatism in black politics and women and politics by examining Condoleezza Rice, a conservative black female political figure. Specifically, I ask how do melodramatic frames, along the political spectrum, construct her alternatively as victor or villain, and what can this tell us about black female political subjectivity? To be clear, I do not see Rice as a black everywoman. Far from it. She is, in some ways, singular in her political visibility and experiences. Although I do examine how the splitting function inherent in melodramas takes on specific raced and gendered resonance for her as a black female political actor, I want to underscore that her class position and courting of white patriarchal power shape her experience of black womanhood.

I assess variants of the dominant storyline of "closeness" that frames the discussion of her as a political actor, specifically in light of what it reveals about the gender, race, and class dynamics embedded in imaginings of community within contemporary public discourse. I demonstrate that the dominant storyline of closeness works both to create and undermine the US national narrative of color(difference)-blind integration.[1] I show how Rice and other conservatives frame her as a victor over oppression, on the one hand, and how this fantasy of idealized integration is unraveled, on the other.

Rice, along with other black conservatives, has been critically important to white conservatives' projection of their version of an idealized racial present and future. This idealized raced and gendered present and future, which Rice is taken to represent, is one where racism and sexism have been practically eradicated and a (US-based) American Dream ideology that promotes notions of success based on individual effort and work trump collective claims for social justice directed at the state. This conservative vision places Rice as an "insider" or a family member within the US national community.

But Rice's position within this community reveals a liminal status, at best; that is, it reflects the status of one, occupying an indeterminate space between social positions, who is alternatively and contradictorily perceived as acceptable and unacceptable, insider and outsider, fully human and subhuman. The dominant storylines that frame our understanding of Rice situate her within traditions of gendered racial paternalism reminiscent of nineteenth- and twentieth-century racism, where whites produce understandings of blacks as trusted servants situated close to and supportive of the seats of power, not in a color- or gender-blind racial present or future. The conservative notion of the insignificance of race (Wilson 1980) and gender are continually unmade as Rice's public representation and reception are freighted with the repressed history of black women's hypersexualization and exploitation. My central argument throughout is that Rice signifies the liminality of blacks in general and black women in particular and that this liminality is contrary to the triumph of integration she is said to and claims to represent.

Traditional examinations of the presidency in political science might focus on Rice as one of several insiders or assume a comparative perspective where Rice and her performance are juxtaposed with those of other comparable state actors, such as Madeleine Albright, Hillary Clinton, or Colin Powell. Instead, in contrast to traditional political science approaches, I utilize an interdisciplinary, Critical Race Black Feminist approach that has two advantages. First, it draws our attention to the narrative dimensions of power and politics, allowing us to see political discourses as texts. Political discourse, and by extension policy and social movements, can be understood as depending and trading on various types of narrativity, in this case dominant melodramatic storylines (Stone 1988), that can be assessed not as taken-for-granted features of politics, but in terms of the strategic effects of their "production and consumption" (Joseph 2002, viii). Second, a Critical Race Black Feminist approach allows us to foreground the importance of black women as cultural signifiers and, hence, make visible the raced and gendered elements of seemingly race- and gender-neutral political developments. For instance, instead of gauging Rice's influence within the insider politics endemic to the presidency, I ask what is invested—what is the political work achieved—in Rice as a black woman being projected as being "close" to the president. I focus in on the unique symbolic dimensions of representations of Rice as a black female.

As it relates to women's and gender studies, I expand our understanding of post-feminism by showing its influence in formal politics, as well as culture, and demonstrate the relevance of race to post-politics. Black feminists have long examined black women in terms of stereotyping or as cultural symbols (see, e.g., Collins 1991; Jewell 1993; Hancock 2004; Jordan-Zachery 2009). I contribute to these discussions by introducing psychoanalytic theory on object relations and splitting. I link splitting to the production of black women and black people more generally as liminal subjects and explain its connection to melodrama.

In developing this argument, I first outline the dominant storyline of closeness as it relates to symbols of black womanhood and its connection to black liminality within contemporary conceptions of national community. Next, I examine melodrama through two competing versions of the dominant storyline of closeness. The first, which I identify as the "Condi" or "like one of the family" version, produces Rice as a signifier of the post-1964 integration ideal that positions blacks within the US national family or community. The second, or "Condilicious," version demonstrates Rice's liminality as a black female political actor. Within this version of the storyline of closeness, she continues to be alternatively constructed as a representation of black female hypersexuality and cultural and political disorder, in ways that affirm essentialist views of black women. I close this chapter with a consideration of Rice's agency as it relates to her public image, as well as the implications of my analysis of black female liminality for our understanding of US politics.

Melodramas of Closeness, Black Liminality, and National Community

On Melodrama and the Dominant Storyline of Closeness and Black Liminality

In examining Rice, I focus on melodramas of closeness. These melodramas bear all of the identifying elements of this political genre. There are, of course, other frames one can identify. The frame of middle-class uplift and respectability, for instance, feeds into that of closeness projected by conservatives and others. The dominant melodramas of closeness I examine feature shifting controlling images of black women that place black women "close to" or complicit with white male power.

In order to understand the controlling images of black women as close to or complicit with male power, it is important to recall the general origins and functions of controlling images in general. More directly, most scholars point to variations of three foundational images of black women—the mammy, the matriarch, and the Jezebel (Collins 1990; Jewell 1993; Cole 1994), and each foundational image is linked to physical and emotional characteristics tied to dominant storylines. These images are powerful symbols whose visual representations come to stand in for and unconsciously invoke the dominant frames and "rationalizing ideologies" (Steinberg 1989, 30 and Chapter 1, generally) with which they are associated. The mammy, prevalent in the slavery era, is generally portrayed as a large, dark-skinned black woman, typically arrayed with a characteristic scarf headdress and bright smile (Jewell 1993). Taken as representing the antithesis of white female beauty and femininity (Riggs 1986), she is seen as asexual, an image that is contrary to the historical reality of sexual exploitation experienced by black women in white slave homes (Jewell 1993, 40; Stephens and Phillips 2003, 8–9). Content in her subservient role within the slave community, she represented blacks' joyful submission to the institution of slavery (Riggs 1986). Although the origins of this imagery were in slavery, variations of it are still prevalent today. Whereas mammy is cast as nurturing of white families, especially children, the matriarch can arguably be seen as mammy's alter ego. As a domineering, abusive mother who emasculates men and usurps their authority, the matriarch is ill fitted for traditional gender roles (Collins 1990, 73–75). The matriarch symbolizes black female chaos and disorder. Through her perceived role in running slave families, or, in a contemporary context, receiving welfare, the matriarch is deemed as being in alignment with state power. The Jezebel, in contrast to the mammy and matriarch, is not only sexualized but hypersexualized, a wanton woman who invites and covets male attention (Jewell 1993, 46). The Jezebel, based on ideas of black female seduction and wantonness, was a projection of the rapacious appetite of white males. The Jezebel figure served to justify rape of black women.

Although each of these controlling images appeared in different historical moments, they continue to insinuate themselves into the present. The mammy, matriarch, and Jezebel figures—and more specifically the constellation of characteristics and dominant frames with which they are associated—have proven to be quite malleable, morphing into related but distinct representations and storylines over time. As black feminist sociologist Patricia Hill Collins (2005, 148) argues, "the controlling images of Black femininity . . . are never static. Rather, they are always internally inconsistent . . . [and] subject to struggle." In the past century, for instance, we have witnessed the rise of the black welfare queen (Collins 1990; Hancock 2004; Jordan-Zachery 2009), the black lady (Lubiano 1992), and more recently, the gold digger, diva, dyke, baby momma, educated black b***h, and traitor images, among others (Stephens and Phillips 2003; Collins 2005; Alexander-Floyd 2007). In each case, these images emerge as a response to specific happenings within everyday politics and work to rationalize political views and actions. The mammy figure justified slavery; the matriarch affirmed black women's inadequacy as mothers and as wives; and the Jezebel functioned as a rationalization for black female sexual exploitation and abuse. The black welfare queen, with its dominant storylines of abuse of government largesse and pathological family life, supported the historic welfare reform law of 1996 (Hancock 2004; Jordan-Zachery 2009). The Black Malinche or traitor figure, an adaptation of the matriarch and Jezebel images, is a response to black feminism and public critiques of black male sexism (Alexander-Floyd 2007, Chapter 4). The Malinche, with its trope of the black-woman-as-traitor, is a recurrent theme that appears especially, although not exclusively, among critiques of black feminism. These images are deployed in connection to, and indeed in shorthand form embody, dominant narratives regarding race and gender.

The melodramas in which Rice is situated invoke storylines of closeness, drawing on coded racial language tied to iterations of this dominant symbolic imagery of black women. Indeed, as I demonstrate below, melodramas of closeness link Rice to variants of the mammy, matriarch, and Jezebel figures. The notion of black women being close to or complicit with dominant white power is significant because it constructs black women as liminal figures within the national community. Black women are marked as insiders in the most perverse way—namely, as traitors who are conduits of upheaval within black communities. At the same time, their inclusion is framed within notions of closeness based on long-standing controlling images. These same images, and their derivatives, are deployed to critique their actions or positions, including by some of those who are liberal or on the political left.

The "black woman," like monolithic notions of black people generally, proves to be an unstable sign. As Linda Zerilli (1994, 2) relates, "Woman is not a being, but a signification—wholly arbitrary and fundamentally unstable because dependent for its meaning on the relational structure of language. She is a complex, discursive site of sociosymbolic stabilization and destabilization, a site of cultural meanings that are constructed and contested across a wide range of signifying practices." In this context, Rice as a black woman is produced as a "discursive site of sociosymbolic stabilization" in terms of envisioning a postgender, post-racial national community, as well as "destabilization" in signaling entrenched racism, sexism, and class inequality.

This instability can be seen as a hallmark of splitting within a psychoanalytic context. Object relations theorist Melanie Klein (1946 [1975]) posits two "positions" critical to early human development (i.e., originating within the first year of life), namely, the paranoid-schizoid position and the depressive position. In the paranoid-schizoid position, a child defends against a perceived threat to its life. As Klein explains,

> We are, I think, justified in assuming that some of the functions which we know from the later ego are there at the beginning. Prominent amongst these functions is that of dealing with anxiety. I hold that anxiety arises from the operation of the death instinct within the organism, is felt as fear of annihilation (death) and takes the form of fear of persecution. The fear of the destructive impulse seems to attach itself at once to an object—or rather it is experienced as the fear of an uncontrollable overpowering object. (4)

The child defends against this anxiety in some basic ways. Most especially, the child splits its mother into "part" objects that are either good or bad. It idealizes and internalizes the good part object, typified by the whole "good" breast, and externalizes or projects the bad object, which is seen as being "in bits." The suckling of the good breast is countered by aggressive action toward the breast in early fantasies, so the breast is perceived as disintegrating.

If all goes well, the child assumes the depressive position. In the depressive position, the child is able to see both good and bad within the mother/caretaker and feel remorse for its fantasies of destruction visited against them. This leads the child to make "reparation" or amends. The depressive position is so called because the child may fear that its reparative action may not be enough to rebuild the mother, upon whom the child depends and develops genuine care and concern. The position is significant for at least two reasons: it supports integration and wholeness of the ego and provides the basis for our understanding of morality.

These positions remain important throughout our lives. As political theorist C. Fred Alford (1989) observes in *Melanie Klein and Critical Social Theory*, for Klein, positions are "structural" as opposed to "chronological or developmental" (33), that is, they tell us about where we stand in relationship to perceiving and responding to ourselves and to the outer world. Alford notes that Klein in her later work sees the depressive position as "a developmental achievement that must be constantly defended and regained throughout life in that stress, as well as depression itself, reinforces defenses associated with the paranoid-schizoid position" (33). Although the paranoid-schizoid position in adult life is not necessarily linked with psychosis, the extremes of this position, particularly in terms of splitting and projection (or what she terms "projective identification"), are what form the foundation of schizophrenia. Conceptually, Klein's paranoid-schizoid position, and its attendant splitting, idealization, and projective identification, are helpful in understanding the production of liminal subjects.

We can understand the paranoid-schizoid position as the mechanism through which systems of domination mark "Others" as part objects that are conceived as polar opposites, all "good" or all "bad." As noted in the Introduction, liminal subjects in general and black women as liminal subjects in particular are unstable signs, caught between representations of "good" or acceptable behavior and "bad" or morally or politically objectionable conduct (Entman and Rojecki 2001, 50–51). This liminality is serviced through the codes of US racial thinking where, as Morrison (1997, x) writes, "illogic, contradiction, deception are understood to be fundamental characteristics of blacks and in judging them there need be no ground or reason for a contrary or more complicated view." Morrison further elaborates, "When race is at play the leap from one judgment (faithful dog) to its complete opposite (treacherous snake) is a trained reflex" (xi).

The dominant storyline of closeness discussed above in relationship to stereotypes of black women is significant because it constructs black women as liminal figures within the national community. Although her liminality is in some measure reflective of the ambivalent construction of blackness as a whole, Condoleezza Rice's symbolic meanings are informed by significations or dominant storylines particular to black women. In what follows, I trace the contradictory melodramatic storylines of closeness in which Rice is interpolated as a good or virtuous figure set within the family-cum-nation as well as a bad or villainous figure who is cast, because of her political views and identity as a black woman (particularly a single black woman) as incompetent, domineering, or hypersexual, at best, and as bestial or nonhuman, at worst. Before I discuss the specifics of the conservative melodrama of closeness, however, I must first provide context regarding the importance of integration to conservative political thought in the post–Civil Rights era.

Rice and the Conservative Integration Ideal

Conservative ideology on race and gender is conditioned by the dictates of the post-1964 political terrain. The movements for social justice, which climaxed in the 1960s and 1970s, forced a reordering of the language and frames through which conservatives press their agenda. As noted in the Introduction, as part of the backlash to social justice movement activity, conservatives fashioned a politics that displaced attention to inequality by offering alternative readings of the causes of poverty and racial and gender injustice. In this new conservative America, a breakdown in cultural values was deemed to be at the heart of US deterioration, particularly emanating from underclass black America. Instead of looking at macroinstitutional structures, conservatives focused attention on the microinstitution of the family. This emphasis was in keeping with neoliberal politics that reads public priorities into private spaces. Family disintegration within black communities, something that seeped into and tainted the rest of the population, was said to account for the plethora of challenges facing African Americans. Racism and sexism, now legally challengeable through new legal protections, were things of the past. All that stood in the way of racial and gender progress and class mobility was the lack of the cultural bona fides of previously disenfranchised groups.

Part of this backlash against the social movements of the mid-twentieth century featured a cadre of black conservatives who were touted as embracing conservative US values, such as hard work, individuality, and self-reliance, and rejecting the victim mentality that conservatives associated with women and people of color who pressed claims against the state. Most importantly, their identity as blacks deflected critiques of the racial politics of the Republican Party specifically, and for the conservative movement more generally, and the conservative machinery maximized this benefit by promoting them as spokespersons for the larger black community (Jones 1987). Black conservatives, then, formed the cornerstone of conservative identity politics in which blacks symbolized idyllic progress in terms of race, class, and gender in the US national community.

The life course of Rice, who was born in Birmingham, Alabama, to a middle-class family staunchly committed to ideals of racial uplift (T. F. Reed 2008), fits well into the narrative of triumph over racism, sexism, and class oppression supported by contemporary conservative ideology. Rice, for her part, has affirmed conservative notions of family, uplift, and racial triumphalism. She has done this in a notable way throughout her career, including in speeches at national Republican conventions, interviews, and books. One of Rice's (2010) memoirs, for instance, is subtitled *A Memoir of My Extraordinary Ordinary Family and Me.* In it, she touts the efforts of her parents and their defiance of Jim Crow through the values of hard work and excellence, rationalizing, among other things, her father's decision to not join King in civil disobedience in her hometown of Birmingham. This middle-class prescription for integration identified with Rice in particular and conservatives more generally trades on a related frame of respectability that dovetails with the melodrama of closeness. Rice, in her success and assimilation into the highest corridors of power, represents the road to ultimate middle-class integration for blacks in terms of the imaginings of the conservative US community:

"As a Black woman in high political office, she represents herself, and is represented, as challenging—perhaps even subverting—traditional institutional inequalities" (Holmes 2007b, 67). As a high-ranking official, she was arguably the poster child for diversity in America—conservative style. The first black female to serve as national security advisor, she was also the first black female to occupy the position of secretary of state, third in command from the president—a position, before her tenure, held only once before by someone who is black (Colin Powell) or female (Madeleine Albright). Of course, as Lakshmi Chaudhry (2007, 13) reminds us, "Over the course of his presidency, George W. Bush has appointed women to some of the most prominent positions in his Administration—all the while working to undermine women's rights across the board. So it is that we witnessed a fierce assault on women's reproductive rights even as Condoleezza Rice became the first African-American woman to make Secretary of State." This "politics of visibility," absent policies that support substantive equality, highlights the disconnect that can occur when we equate descriptive and substantive representation or emphasize notions of "symbolic empowerment" (Simien 2016), as a means of increasing political participation.

Nevertheless, many people, regardless of how they feel about Rice's ideological views, see her promotion to high levels of the international relations infrastructure as a boon for women, and in ways that position her as a victor over racial and gender inequality. The cofounder and former director of the Center for the Advancement of Women, Faye Wattleton, for instance, argues that the high public profile of women such as Rice is "an important social progression," as "'it moves us toward a time when we can attack someone like her [i.e., Rice] because of what she stands for and not because she is black or a woman, because we already know that the country won't go up in smoke because we had an African-American woman from Alabama as Secretary of State'" (Chaudhry 2007, 13). Chaudhry also notes that Laura Liswood, one of the founders of the White House Project, sees Hillary Clinton and Condoleezza Rice as exerting what Laura Liswood, White House Project cofounder, calls the "'power of the mirror,'" mirroring to young US citizens a different vision of women's place in society and politics (Chaudry 2007, 13). From this vantage point, some women are inspired by and even proud of Rice. Her appointment to important public roles in government, particularly those that made her visible on the international stage, and her projection as someone who is close to the president work to stabilize or affirm our understanding of the US national community as being based in racial, gender, and class equality.

Although Rice sees herself and is seen as embodying the idea of black integrationism central to conservative notions of national community, she can also signify contradictory meanings of race and gender, and this has to be carefully negotiated; the melodrama of closeness serves this purpose well. In some sense, Rice is potentially disruptive of conservative agendas: The fatherhood and pro-family movements are fueled, in no small part, by a reaction to "second-wave" feminism and the challenge that this has presented to the "marketplace model of masculinity" (Gavanas 2004, 7, 70–72), particularly in white middle-class communities, where manhood is based on breadwinning and patriarchal family roles. As an intelligent, assertive, single, childless woman, Rice represents aspects of a model of womanhood that conservatives have long been working against. Figuring Rice as being close to the president, however, mollifies the threat that her power as secretary of state could otherwise represent in the public imagination. Why? Because, as I delineate below, even though she was a key operative for the most powerful country in the world, her public role was reread and reinserted into private space: She was defined through a familial relationship with a man—George W. Bush.

The Dominant Storyline of Closeness and Projection of National Community

The melodrama of closeness typically emerges amid a common narrative structure in news articles and other stories about Rice. Not all (or, in some cases, any) of these elements may necessarily be present, but the general outline remains the same, and Rice is depicted as a superwoman, able to conquer racial and gender adversity. Aside from (and typically prior to) any focus on the substantive parts of her job function (promoting "transformational diplomacy" in the Middle East or answering for national security mishaps before Congress), most stories focus on Rice's personal attributes and background. There is generally a recounting of her origins as a black girl from Alabama, with mention of, and personal tidbits about, her father, John Rice (the Presbyterian minister who was once a football coach), and mother, Angelena Rice (Condoleezza received her love of clothes from her mother) (Dowd 2005, 47). These details present a "family romance," to borrow Anne duCille's term (1996, 11), that situates Rice as a child prodigy—the brainchild of her parents, who raised her to be impervious to the impact of the cruelty of segregation and the limitations that some would present to black women in the United States. Aside from her origins, the common narrative structure in stories produced about Rice (and that, in turn, themselves produce storylines concerning her public life) feature a list of her considerable achievements (e.g., beginning college at fifteen, serving as provost of Stanford), excelling in competitive endeavors and art (she is a concert-level pianist and once figure skated competitively), her dedication to exercise (she plays tennis and wakes at 5 A.M. to work out), and her penchant for wearing fine clothes. Finally, she is presented as someone who is unusually disciplined with an impossibly busy schedule, one that by implication leaves her with little time for a personal life, although she is rumored to date on occasion, particularly football players, such as Gene Washington. Although the specific contexts and foci may change, most stories are anchored by this basic narrative structure (see, e.g., Dowd 2005; Butler 2007; Samuels 2007).[2] They present Rice as a "super minority," an idealized, respectable citizen—a concept I explore more fully in Chapter 2 regarding Barack Obama.

Rice is also often noted as having been introduced to Bush by his father, George H. W. Bush. As one source relates, "By the late '90s Rice had again been a witness to history, having advised the first President Bush on the Soviet Union just before the fall of the Berlin Wall. The senior Bush was so impressed with Rice's talents that he cooked up a rendezvous with her for his son at the family retreat in Kennebunkport, Maine" (Dowd 2005, 48). This narrative gesture implies a type of homosocial bonding between father and son, where a woman is exchanged (here in acquaintance) in order to strengthen their connection as men (Bird 1996). Rice and Bush's relationship is forthrightly defined as being "close," and then details that track the development of this closeness or give clues to its dimensions are discussed. They are both putatively Christian and often talk about faith as being personally significant and even relevant to their decision-making and functioning as public officials. Both Rice and Bush love football and exercise, for instance (Dowd 2005, 48). She was reportedly so close to the president and his wife, Laura, in fact, that she would often spend time with both of them at home, sharing "dinner with the Bushes on Sunday nights and sometimes watch[ing] movies with the first couple before they [would] go to bed" (Samuels 2007, 50). As one story noted, "now colleagues say she is *so close* to W that it's hard to tell what's his idea and what's hers" (Dowd 2005, 48 [emphasis added]). Another states that "in Washington, nothing matters more than access to and face time with the President. What distinguishes Rice from her predecessors is her personal and professional *closeness to* George W. Bush" (Butler 2007, 87 [emphasis added]).

Condoleezza Rice is positioned so close to Bush, in fact, that she is often described as being akin to a "family member." Africana studies scholar Carole Boyce Davies (2007, 72) notes in her examination of Condoleezza Rice that "Numerous examples . . . abound regarding Rice's relationship with and service to the Bush family. Bob Woodward in *Bush at War* reports that after her parents died, George and Laura Bush became in effect Condi's family." Ann E. Butler (2007, 87) observes, "[Rice] is a politically astute performer with a brilliant mind and a keen sense of diplomacy, which has helped her maneuver into the heart of one of conservative America's most powerful families, the Bushes." In fact, Butler suggests that Rice is Bush's "work wife," a counterbalance to his "real wife," who stands in as a model of respectable, traditional womanhood (2007, 90–92). This characterization is not without import: her singleness or high-powered career did not present a problem for US conservatives who are set on reaffirming women's roles in private space, because Rice was part of a family—Bush's family.

Although it is tempting to think of Rice's relationship with George W. Bush as idiosyncratic, it constitutes a melodrama of closeness that draws on long-standing notions of black women who work in intimate spaces—specifically black domestics—as being like one of the family. Davies (2007, 72) makes this connection of Rice being "like one of the family," as well, pointing out that "the 'like one of the family' option for black subjects has an entirely other interpretation and history as it relates to the hierarchy of domestic service in white households, and generally to black service to white dominance." Domestic service was a form of labor that black women generally understood as exploitative and oppressive. The stereotype of the mammy, however, draws on a storyline of closeness that suggests, among other things, that black women are supportive of white families and neglectful of their own.

To the extent that Bush's clan stands in for conservative imaginings of national community, Rice's role as being like one of the family (again, implicitly as a mammy figure) constitutes a powerful ideological message for blacks and women: Embracing color(difference)-blindness is the path to acceptance and integration. It is a means for conquering—being a victor over—class-, gender-, or race-based inequality. It is a form of post-politics, because it sets discrimination as something that is in the past, suggesting that, now, unfettered by the chains of legalized discrimination, Others can obtain freedom at home, in the family, and in the nation. They can operate in celebration of democratic values.

Significantly, Collins (2006, Chapter 1) documents the idea of the black domestic as "like one of the family"; the designation "like one of the family" captures the patronizing attitude of whites to those blacks constructed as close to whites, but as outsiders who enjoy a dubious position of belonging within the institution of the white family. Collins's exploration is drawn from Childress's fictionalized stories about black domestics. These characterizations are echoed in the oral histories, as well, of black domestics, a point to which I return in Chapter 4 when I discuss *Telling Memories among Southern Women: Domestic Workers and Their Employers in the Segregated South* (Tucker 1988), the book of oral histories Kathryn Stockett (2009) used to write *The Help*.

Just as black domestics as servants are seen as being close to whites, but outside of the legitimacy and full membership of the family, so too is Rice constructed not as a political insider but an outsider-within (Collins 1990)—that is, a black female who affirms hierarchical relations of the nation-cum-family. As Collins (1990, 11–13) explains, the vantage point of the outsider-within is that of one who is invited or allowed into particular spaces or contexts (here, the nation or family), but whose status is marked as different or Other. Thus, far from being a marker of unfettered inclusion, Condoleezza Rice's public, political role is framed within historic roles of black female subservience in private, domestic spaces.

Destabilizing the Color(Difference)-Blind US National Community

Although the conservative or "Condi" melodrama of closeness positions Condoleezza Rice as representing the US integration ideal—where race, gender, and class exploitation are fading relics of years gone by—left-liberal melodramas of closeness focus on Rice as a warrior princess or neo-Jezebel, Black Malinche figure, as I discuss shortly. This often hypersexualized, "villainous" or "bad" version of Rice, read through political cartoons and other cultural artifacts, codes her variously as mammy, matriarch, and Jezebel in ways that affirm essentialist notions of black female identity. Rice is viewed in the paranoid-schizoid position, as both good and bad object, in other words. To be clear, I do not mean to suggest that critiques of Rice, her politics, and particularly her involvement in the 9/11 wars are misplaced. On the contrary, there is a need to deeply explore and illuminate her political career, including her role in masterminding US foreign policy. My analysis here is meant to do four things, in particular: (1) critique the facile idea that color- or gender-blindness is an achieved ideal, that is, that we live in a "post-identity" society; (2) emphasize that Rice, as a black woman, is only comprehended in the context of long-standing tropes associated with black women; (3) discuss the extent to which discursive formations of Rice as bad object are symptomatic of repressed ideas about black women's rape and exploitation; and (4) think about the implications for black women as political actors in formal politics. I demonstrate, through analysis of cartoons and other cultural artifacts, that these essentialist notions mapped onto Rice cast her not as a tentative insider but, in contrast, as part of the constitutive outside (Butler 1990) of the white US national community.

Rice's portrayal in cultural sites such as cartoons is important, because cartoons serve as an important source of symbolic and political meaning. As Beth A. Ferri and David J. Connor (2006, 76–77) relate, "Political cartoons are cultural artifacts that offer a glimpse into various points of view operating during particular times and places. . . . In a cartoon, even complex issues can be reduced to a single image with minimal writing. As such, cartoons have the ability to convey meaning in an extraordinarily concentrated manner." Because of the limited space of cartoons, cartoonists often condense meaning into ideological scripts that convey suggested interpretations. These suggested interpretations are not uniform in their effect, because their reception can be and is challenged and reinterpreted in myriad ways (Ferri and Connor 2006). Still, the particular conventions of cartoons' form, such as labeling, captions, and balloons, along with images, produce ideologically significant meanings and systems of significations that not only mirror but, indeed, generate raced and gendered concepts and perspectives (79–85).

In the warrior-princess melodrama of closeness, for instance, Rice is figured as politically affirming of US power at home and abroad. This theme is particularly prominent among liberal to left-leaning cartoonists or proponents, and is often showcased in political dialogue via the Internet. In one cartoon, Rice is shown as a vulture identified with the United States (Cartoonstock.com 2007). This representation pictures Rice, stern-faced and somewhat sullen, as a vulture perched along a dead vine. At the tip of the vine is a US flag, signifying her as a faithful envoy of US political interests that require her to be pressed into service to feed off slain or dead political enemies. In a second representation, displayed on a left-leaning blog, Rice is portrayed as a female Klingon who is "Admiral of the Klingon Empire" (Ablogalypse Now 2005). She stares pensively into the distance, one hand wrapped around her chin with fingers suggestively shaped as talons. Dressed in a Klingon-issued uniform, she is shown with long hair and pronounced vertebraelike ridges displayed across her forehead characteristic of Klingons. This image is significant for a number of reasons. First, it constructs Rice as a warrior, given that Klingons (whose aircrafts are described as "birds of prey") are a people skilled at war and who live ready to die while serving to carry out their missions. Second, this image, in line with classic notions of scientific racism, depicts Rice as fundamentally subhuman. Klingons, like Lieutenant Worf of *Next Generation Star Trek* fame, are typically portrayed as noble savages who are given to explosive anger and violence. Notably, Rice is also shown in a sexually suggestive manner, with her cleavage bared. She arguably becomes a sexualized warrior princess (Eisenstein 2007), who dominates others, in part through her sexual prowess. A third image, titled "Condoleezza Rice Is a White Man," depicts her shaking hands with Fouad Siniora, the Lebanese prime minister (Sparx 2007). This image was released after US-backed bombings occurred, and it positions Rice as not only supportive but also facilitative of US hegemony in the region. Overlaying the picture are words written in various shadings: "what is the enemy," "power is the enemy," "whiteness is the power."

Some might argue that these images, displayed on private blogs or websites, are not indicative of mainstream sentiment, but such a view misunderstands both the importance of new media and modes of cultural production and the significance of these images as constitutive of symbolic meaning. As our forms of communication have radically shifted, so too have communities of assessment and types of cultural production and political discourse. Moreover, these images are not merely reflective but are constitutive of the left-liberal melodrama of closeness; that is, they must be read as politically relevant cultural phenomena that instantiate Rice as a political neo-Jezebel, warrior figure, or both.

Whereas the aforementioned images pictured Rice as "close to" or supportive of US power in ways that were not necessarily sexual, other left-liberal melodramas of closeness suggest a sexual or more intimate connection indirectly or directly. These constitute neo-Jezebel, or Black Malinche versions.

The neo-Jezebel and Black Malinche figures are related representations of black womanhood that cast them as hypersexualized or traitorous, respectively. The Jezebel figure, in its original manifestation, portrayed typically light-skinned African American women as vixens. They lured men with their primal sexual powers. The neo-Jezebel figure may trumpet black women's sexual allure, casting it as a form of sexual freedom, or drawing heightened attention to accoutrements of femininity, such as shoes or stylish clothes or modes of dress. It also lies implicit in depictions of mammy as I discuss later. The Black Malinche, as I discuss elsewhere (Alexander-Floyd 2007, Chapter 4), casts black women as traitors to black communities. The Chicana figure Malinche (or Malintzin) was said to become the sexual partner of her oppressor, aligning herself with colonizers and working against the best interests of her people. Likewise, Black Malinche refers to the trope of the black woman as traitor, that is, the black woman who uses sexual power to her advantage and to undermine the perceived interests of black men and communities. The Black Malinche figure is a recurring one. In 2013, for instance, Russell Simmons (2013) released a video online that depicted Harriet Tubman, the famed abolitionist, as being the willing sexual partner of her white slave owner in order to manipulate him, downplaying the history of white male rape of black women.

In this vein, several noted cartoon representations, for instance, symbolize Rice as a mammy figure. In perhaps the most prominent of these cartoons, titled "Condoleezza Rice in the Role of a Lifetime," Jeff Danziger shows her sitting barefoot in a rocker, holding and feeding an aluminum tube (ostensibly a weapon of mass destruction, or WMD) and speaking in pidgin English (Ampersand 2004). In the cartoon, Rice echoes the lines Butterfly McQueen made famous playing Prissy, a maid (or mammy) to Scarlett O'Hara, in the movie *Gone with the Wind* (Fleming 1939) ("I don't know nothin' 'bout birthin' no babies"),[3] stating, "I knows all about aluminum tubes! (Correction). I don't know nuthin' about aluminum tubes. . . ." Rice is shown, as well, with several tubes to her right and one lying across the floor to her left. This image is important because here she signifies black womanhood that is close to and supportive of state power. It alludes to her role in affirming the presence of WMDs in Iraq as justification for initiating the US war against Iraq, on the one hand, and the inability of the United States to produce evidence about such WMDs, on the other. Rice's role here as nurturer of the WMD argument to legitimate the war parallels her support of US international objectives.

The mammy figure, as noted, situates black women as happily serving existing power arrangements and nurturing of white masculine authority and implicitly suggests sexual affinity as well. Here, the aluminum tubes stand in for the ideological narrative of the state in fostering destabilization in the Middle East. Although most receive mammy as an asexual figure, it is important here to unpack the underlying meaning of this symbolic representation. As Barbara Christian and others have noted, the representation of mammy as asexual distorts the reality of black women's sexual subjugation at the hands of white men in slavery. As Christian notes, in the documentary *Ethnic Notions* (Riggs 1986), the diaries of slave mistresses speak to the distress caused in slaveholding households because of the predatory nature of white men toward black women within the context of slavery. I interject this historical context here in order to make sense of the depiction as mammy. These symbolic images work in part as codes that are implicitly linked to a body of ideas, meanings, and storylines. Here they get marshaled within a melodramatic "sense-making system" (Brooks [1976] 1995, xvii) that sets black women as the always-already-available entry point for undermining progressive politics by aligning with white patriarchal power. By setting mammy within a historical context, we can detail the underlying sexual meaning embodied in this important image: Rice is both neo-Jezebel and Malinche in this representation.

The notion of sexual desire and involvement embodied in this left-liberal melodrama of closeness is made explicit in other cartoon images and songs about Rice. In his popular *Doonesbury* cartoon series, Garry Trudeau, a regular contributor of editorial cartoons for major media syndicates, suggests that Rice and Bush are romantically or sexually intimate. In the cartoon, he shows balloon captions above the White House, without directly showing Rice or Bush. In the captions he writes,

> [BUSH:] Condi, what if I nickname Clarke "stretcher." You know, because he's stretching the truth?
>
> [RICE:] Not strong enough Mr. President . . . I mean, this guy is the *king* of lies! Sir! Do you know what he wrote about our first meeting?
>
> [BUSH:] Of course not—it's in a book.
>
> [RICE:] He wrote I gave him the impression I'd never even *heard* of Al Qaeda!
>
> [BUSH:] Had you?
>
> [RICE:] Oh, like, *you* had!
>
> [BUSH:] Careful, "Brown Sugar." (Ampersand 2004 [emphasis in original])

This cartoon embodies a tangle of contradictory significations, some of which connect to the hypersexualization of black women. It plays on the popular notion that Bush is unintelligent and takes direction from the intellectually superior Rice. Rice here is exerting influence and control consistent with the symbolic image of the black woman as matriarch or Sapphire, a stereotype of black women based on the Amos 'n' Andy character by the same name who constantly berated her black male counterpart (Jewell 1993). Conversely, it also suggests that former National Security Council counterterrorism adviser Richard Clarke is correct in his assertion that Rice was unaware of a critical

US security threat, one of the many indicting statements penned in his controversial book *Against All Enemies: Inside America's War on Terror* (Clarke 2004), about his time fighting terrorism. Notably, his public statement that Rice was ignorant of Al Qaeda blatantly signals Rice as incompetent.

Moreover, the tenor of the conversation between Rice and Bush shifts from what seems to be a professional (albeit trite) exchange to dialogue that suggests Rice and Bush have extraprofessional relations. The discussion is happening in the White House, and Rice repeatedly refers to Bush in formal terms, such as "Mr. President" and "Sir." It is not until the last two frames that the viewer gets the idea that Rice and Bush are having more than a political discussion in the Oval Office. The term "Brown Sugar," popular in the 1960s and 1970s, refers to black women who are the sexual intimates of men, particularly those who are white. Indeed, its most notorious usage in recent history is as the title for one of the most popular songs by the Rolling Stones, one where Mick Jagger celebrates white slaveholders' sexual exploitation of black women. The fact that Trudeau chooses not to physically show Rice or Bush, coupled with the sexually suggestive reference "Brown Sugar," guides the reader to speculate whether Rice and Bush are "in bed" literally or metaphorically in the Oval Office. The cartoon, thus, invokes the Black Malinche (Alexander-Floyd 2007) in depicting Rice as Bush's sexual partner, confidante, and co-conspirator in facilitating the 9/11 attacks.

Others, besides Trudeau, have highlighted the question of whether or not Bush and Rice are intimately involved. Rice, while attending a 2004 party thrown by Philip Taubman and his wife, Felicity Barringer, reportedly had a Freudian slip. She stated, "As I was telling my husb—'" and then quickly changed to "'As I was telling President Bush'" (Schoenemann and Moran 2004). One comedic website recounts this story and accompanies it with a collage of pictures in which Rice and Bush are standing close to one another, in bed, or apparently sharing a kiss (Kurtzman 2004). Significantly, within this scenario, Rice is framed as a black woman who not only desires the president, but also wants to be joined to him within the institution of marriage. She is a signifier of black female desire for white men in particular, and female incompleteness in the absence of sexual and legally sanctioned attachments to men more generally. Black female desire, Oedipally speaking, kills off (presumed) black male or seemingly less powerful suitors, to have access to dominant white patriarchal power.

One music video in particular, "Condilicious" (This Just In 2007), provides a particularly poignant example of Rice's hypersexualization and alignment with US state power. The video begins with her being questioned about the war in Iraq by Senator Barbara Boxer, Democrat from California. Rice's character says, "Man, forget these questions," and breaks out into a rap song video based on Fergalicious, a popular song and video by Fergie, a white female singer, in which she touts her sexual power and authority, including her preeminence over other females and her ability to attract and dazzle men.[4] In like fashion, in "Condilicious," Rice is shown promoting her power and authority in highly sexualized ways, blowing kisses, grooving to pulsating music, and detailing the ways in which she is superior to Democrats and other women. As with other narrative renderings, this video follows the closeness melodrama. Rice is not only supportive of the United States, but also in control of the war in Iraq. As the song relates, "she sends boys to Ir-Iraq" and is generating a military situation "like Vietnam." She serves as a "sexual decoy" or cover for US hegemonic power internationally, as Zillah Eisenstein (2007) argues.

Just as in other contexts, the public anxiety over the "disorderliness" of her status leads to contradictory significations.[5] Some representations of Rice highlight aspects of her personality that affirm femininity, the effect of which is to stabilize a traditional, less threatening gender identity. Her love for shoes is mentioned, for instance. On the other hand, her reportedly ambiguous sexual orientation is highlighted. Rice demonstrates affection for white, male Fox News reporters, and one news story is shown with the caption "Condi Loves Bush." Early in the "Condilicious" video, she says that she is "really manly, but not Rosie," referring to the openly lesbian celebrity Rosie O'Donnell. Later in the video she says, "girl on girl with Mary Cheney," Dick Cheney's lesbian daughter, and is shown suggestively pressing hands with Cheney as they descend out of view. Ultimately, the video is meant to be political satire whose aim is to critique and ridicule Rice's image and her role in supporting the war. From that vantage point, it arguably captures well her neoconservative commitments and her construction as an emasculating neo-Jezebel or warlike figure. Satire, like irony, however, has an ambivalent function in post-politics. People offer or experience it as both critique and a source of enjoyment, often depending on their own political leanings.

Other representations of Rice portray her as being ill fitted for femininity or project onto her fantasies of desire or conquest. On his *The Revolution Starts Now* album, self-described "socialist" (Franco 2007) songwriter Stephen Fain Earle produced a song, "Condi, Condi," in which he confesses his desire for Rice. In one verse, Earle states he has no money, but that his "love" or desire is endless, crooning at the end of the verse, "People say you're cold, but I think you're hot." The second verse is more sexually suggestive:

> Oh Condi, Condi. I'm talkin' to you girl.
> What's it gonna hurt? Come on give me a whirl.
> Shake your body. Let me see you go.
> One time for me. Oh Condi, I love you so!
> Skank for me Condi. Show me what you got.
> They say you're too uptight. I say you're not.
> Dance around me, spinnin' like a top.
> Oh, Condi, Condi, Condi, don't ever stop.
> (Earle 2004)

The song appears amid others that criticize the Iraq War and George W. Bush and, according to one reviewer, "quite sarcastically, praises the feminine charms of Ms. Condoleezza Rice" (Franco 2007). However, as Morris (2004), another interviewer, explains, "Earle concedes that Condoleezza Rice is more of an enigma to him than a target." In the interview, Earle reveals,

> Her [Condoleezza Rice's] whole existence fascinates me. . . . She's exactly my age, and she's black and she's well educated. She's a specialist in a country [the USSR] that doesn't even exist anymore. But all well educated white people who end up being Republican [also?] fascinate me. The Beach Boys fascinate me. I don't know how you get from transcendental meditation to being a Republican. (Morris 2004)

Earle's ambivalence notwithstanding, the inclusion of a love song to one of George W. Bush's key operatives on an album designed to be critical of the Iraq War and Bush's administration can be read as an attempt at irony. But, as I discuss in greater depth in Chapter 2, as Angela McRobbie (2007) suggests, irony is a feature of post-politics that promises to offer critique, but serves to allow us to have our cake and eat it too—in this case, mocking her presumed lack of femininity, while enjoying a fantasy in which Earle and the listener can openly desire and exoticize Rice. Tellingly, after Earle played the song at the prestigious Montreux Jazz Festival, he exclaimed, "I love that b***h!" (Earle 2006).

Others question her romantic involvements. One political cartoon, "Condi Kiss," shows Rice vigorously washing in the shower after brushing her teeth and gargling, leaving empty tubes of paste and mouthwash strewn about. In the rear of the cartoon stands the looming image of a Canadian Mountie, suggesting her purported romantic interest in Canadian Minister of National Defense Peter MacKay (Foden 2007). Elsewhere, in their monologues, comedians joke about Rice's status as a single woman, and her indomitability by, and presumed incompatibility with, the male sex. As Jay Leno remarked, for instance, "It's rumored in Washington that Condoleezza Rice has a new boyfriend. Allegedly, he's Canada's foreign minister [of national defense], Peter MacKay. Since he's a diplomat and he visits her at the White House, he has to have a Secret Service code name. Do you know what his Secret Service code name is? 'Captain Kirk.' You know why they call him that? Because he's going where no man has gone before" (Kurtzman 2007). Likewise, David Letterman stated: "Today is the 54th anniversary of the first man getting to the top of Mt. Everest. Now, if only we could get one on top of Condoleezza Rice" (Kurtzman 2007). He also remarked, "Condoleezza Rice is apparently dating a Canadian politician. It's a proud day for Canada. They're the first nation to put a man on Condoleezza" (Kurtzman 2007). These jokes are typical of rape culture, objectifying Rice and presenting her as a target of conquest.

Importantly, the policing of Rice's sexuality bears connection with common post-feminist themes as it relates to women generally. The focus on shoes and clothes, as in the "Condilicious" video, is especially significant as it represents consumption as a means of enhancing personal value, glamour, and esteem. Relatedly, this policing also reflects a post-feminist obsession with singleness and perceived "dating panic," and an obsession with heterosexual coupling.

The single woman, commentators have noted, is a particularly prominent post-feminist figure because she directly challenges normative understandings of gender. Diane Negra (2009, 62) underscores the ways in which singlehood is seen as "abject" and a form of "social death." Anthea Taylor (2012, Chapter 1), following Negra, also examines singlehood as a form of abjection and lack, further noting heterosexual relationships as an indication of the social soundness that facilitates and instantiates the citizen-subject. She explains,

> Being in a romantic (heterosexual) relationship has historically been conceptualized as the key marker of mental health and maturity in modern societies. . . . [And,] it is still perceived to be one of—if not the—central choices that *all* citizens will make, and indeed that *makes* all citizens. (Taylor 2012, 20 [emphasis in original])

In contrast to other melodramatic storylines that cast her as a victor, the discussions of Rice's romantic involvements or lack thereof reinforce her positioning as an abject figure and challenge her legitimacy as a good citizen deserving of public trust. The fascination with Rice's sexuality—her singleness, her availability, her sexual power, and her proximity to the president—are all reflections of the anxieties that people have with Rice as a "disorderly and disordering" woman (Zerilli 1994, 142), and the dissonance-generating nature of her role as an upwardly mobile black female secretary of state.

Aside from these connections to generally applicable post-feminist themes, there are some ways in which these representations connect to Rice specifically as a black woman. Chillingly, the policing of Rice's sexuality and gender performativity (especially rape jokes such as the one mentioned above applauding Canada for "put[ting] a man on Condoleezza") also echo and call forth black female sexual assault at the hands of white men. These condi(licious) melodramas of closeness mark the return of the repressed history of black women's labor in domestic spaces in slavery and during segregation, and also the sexual exploitation to which they were subjected. The work of psychoanalyst Esther Rashkin is valuable here. Rashkin works to unravel the ways in which cultural happenings or artifacts can be the manifestation of political, cultural, or social issues that exceed the particulars of surface communications.

In *Unspeakable Secrets and the Psychoanalysis of Culture*, for instance, Esther Rashkin (2008) notes that the postwar France obsession with cleanliness and soap was not simply an indication of heightened marketing in the expansion of consumerism during the postwar period or merely a reference to ethnic cleansing of Algerian refugees. She notes in particular that the obsession with cleanliness is also an example of repression of France's shameful complicity in Hitler's plan to kill Jews and rule Europe—to cleanse it of Jewish contamination. She (Rashkin 2008, 7) explains,

> The advertisements for soaps, detergents, and skin creams, and Barthes's exposure of the semiotics of warfare, expulsion, and destruction inscribed within these odes to hygiene, can thus be read as telltale signs of the drama of the Holocaust, which permeated the social fiber, practices, and discourse of postwar France . . . the ads can be read as symptoms of the return of the repressed. They are ciphered signifiers of the nation's struggle—and in large part failure—to come to terms, in the aftermath of the Second World War, with its eager collusion in rounding up and eliminating the Jews.

In a similar vein, the obsession with Rice's sexuality and personal life is a symptom of the repressed history of white male rape of black women. Women who break barriers within different contexts can be hypersexualized in cartoons and other means; cartoon and other depictions of Geraldine Ferraro, the first vice presidential candidate for a major party, is one case in point (Miller 1992). Still, taken together as a whole, the images, songs, films, and other cultural media involving Rice point to a deeper historical resonance specific to black women.

To be sure, it is not necessary to draw on these melodramatic storylines of closeness in relation to Rice, even when generating critique. Carole Boyce Davies, for instance, assesses Rice's political priorities and actions as a case study of a more general approach taken by black and Latino conservatives. Con-di-fi-cation, according to Davies (2007), entails black and Latino conservatives serving the interests of US domestic projects and imperialism, as opposed to progressive politics that may benefit their racial communities. In keeping with post-politics, such collusion with state power invokes race in the service of conservative (and neoliberal) ends, identifying racial harm as something squarely situated in the past. Clarence Lusane provides an in-depth analysis of both Rice and Colin Powell's participation in the 9/11 wars. Lusane (2006) demonstrates that Rice and Powell were both active participants in legitimating, strategizing, and executing US military action in Afghanistan and Iraq. Still, as I amplify more below, that Rice is discussed and represented, as either victor or villain, drawing on well-worn race-gender registers, highlights how liminality functions to frame and distort black women, including in the public sphere.

Conclusion

What are we to make of Rice's framing within white conservative and left/liberal melodramas? What are the implications of these representations for future black women in public office? What is at stake in recognizing the liminality of black women as political actors? What does it reflect, in the final analysis, about the impact of post-politics in the US political system at the beginning of the new millennium?

Within the alchemy of melodrama, Rice becomes a multiply useful political figure. For many, especially conservatives, Rice serves as a model or prototype of how women and minorities in general can stand victorious over any adversity through adopting the appropriate values of middle-class uplift—namely, hard work, perseverance, patriotism, and belief and adherence to the US creed of individual progress. The focus on her as an individual, in particular, affirms post-feminism's neoliberal tendency to reconstruct the self as a mechanism or recipe for social change. Rice is marked as a triumphant defeater of segregation or shamelessly complicit, warmongering traitor. Even some feminists who may not share Rice's ideological views, like Faye Wattleton, quoted earlier, nevertheless affirm the mirroring power of Rice's visibility in traditionally male spaces.

But Rice is not a triumphant figure who overcomes racist and sexist oppression in order to demonstrate the arrival of a color- and gender-blind world. Psychoanalytically, the reality of this melodrama of closeness can be seen as symptomatic of race-gender oppression. The splitting that occurs within these dueling melodramas of closeness reflect a political unconscious stuck in a paranoid-schizoid position.

Where conservatives work to contain US diversity and equality by stabilizing acceptable, nonthreatening definitions of identity, as represented by Rice, for instance, others, including those of left-liberal leanings, assail this project by resorting to essentialized understandings of race and gender. Rice is imagined within fantasies of racial and gender inclusion, associated with and introjected as a figure of maternal goodness where she is seen as being "like one of the family." Other left-liberal critiques use storylines of closeness that develop and trade on villainous melodramatic representations. In these representations, negative parts of individuals' gendered-racial unconscious are split off and projected on Rice. She is signified as bestial, hypersexual, and a "bad" mother, nursing and abetting state power.

One "schizophrenic" rendering of Rice is particularly illustrative of splitting and the paranoid-schizoid position. Film producer Sebastian Doggart created two documentaries based on her life and career. The first, *Courting Condi* (Doggart 2008), he dubbed a "musical docu-tragi-comedy" (Ishikawa 2009). In the movie, Devin Ratray (playing himself) has amorous intentions toward Rice and travels the country ostensibly to learn about Rice, his love object, in order to win her affections. As the film goes along, however, Ratray learns details about her ideological and political commitments, particularly regarding her role in the 9/11 wars, that dampen his affections. A year later, the same producer released *American Faust: From Condi to Neo-Condi* (Doggart 2009), a more traditional documentary that suggests a tracing of a transformation in Rice from conservatism to ultra-conservatism and war mongering after 9/11. Both documentaries, which use some of the same footage, have narrative arcs that show Rice as a "good object" upon whom the producer and viewers can project acceptable parts of the self, including affection or desire, or respect for personal accomplishment via the American Dream, respectively, and then reveal her as a "bad object" of scorn, aggression, and deceit. We see the entanglement of melodrama and splitting, in this case, where critique can only develop with some passage through appreciation and attachment to Rice as a good object.

The diverse representations of Rice from across the political spectrum reflect deep anxieties about refining and reconstituting nationhood in terms of race- and gender-based identity. These anxieties are addressed and negotiated in myriad ways. Far from signaling the triumph of US democracy over racism, sexism, and class barriers of the past, the various meanings attached to Rice, even by those who are politically liberal or left-leaning, emerge precisely because she so deeply troubles long-standing, actively nurtured, and (in some cases) cherished notions of racialized femininity along the political spectrum. These reactions to her point to the persistent liminality in which black women such as Rice are situated and that frame Rice's political career, even as a darling of conservatives.

The question that remains, of course, is what can be done to address the melodramas of closeness or other racialized, gendered essentialist framings of black women in politics? The issue, however, is not whether there is space for agency or not, but how such agency can be directed in ways that progressively challenge the status quo. Condoleezza Rice, for instance, has arguably exercised agency in executing a middle-class strategy of advancement through educational and professional exceptionalism, pursuing power, and acting aggressively on behalf of George W. Bush's administration. This expression of agency, while personally advantageous, has been in the service of state power in ways that do not serve the cause of fighting institutionalized social inequality.

Some would argue that controlling images of black womanhood have impacted her public representation, indicating the symbolic power of these images that in some ways cut across class status. Rice's case is useful in understanding black women as liminal subjects in the United States, but not in ways that essentialize black female identity. To be sure, at a macro level, processes of racialization and gendering that impact individual black women, such as Rice, recursively act to promote essentialist understandings of black subjectivity as a whole. These processes, however, do not flatten black women's experiences as raced and gendered subjects. There is no "Sister Citizen" á la Melissa Harris-Perry's (2011) assessment that operates as a monolith, one that transcends issues of class. At a micro level, Rice is able to utilize her middle-class upbringing and operate within melodramatic codes of closeness to exalt or advance her personal advantage and political commitments.

Paradoxically, Rice is both subject to raced and gendered discrimination, but fully complicit with the power structures that give them life. It is at times difficult for people to withstand this paradox. During one question-and-answer period after a talk on Rice, for instance, one listener stated that "I feel that you are messing with my ability to be critical of Rice." They stated flatly what manifested in some of the other questions and statements, that is, the sentiment that maybe Rice is not so bad after all, or perhaps she is a more complicated figure. This is not the intent of my analysis. If it functions for some in this way, melodrama and the processes of identification I discuss herein can explain it. Racist or sexist treatment can trigger identification. Moreover, this identification can carry with it an assumption that shared experiences will translate into an assumption of "linked fate" (Dawson 1995) or even a shared outlook. But racist or sexist reactions or treatment of Rice do not negate her ideological commitments or political actions, domestically or on the world stage.

Furthermore, to the extent that we see her as signifying some form of representational success, it is important to underscore her actions do little to change the substantive operation of hierarchy and power in the United States or abroad. Historian Marissa Fuentes's (2016) analysis of Rachel Pringle Polgreen is relevant here. Polgreen, a black woman who ran a brothel, is typically lauded for her ability to etch out a unique existence in the context of sixteenth-century Barbados slavery. Fuentes cautions that Polgreen's is a "complicated" agency (Fuentes, 50–51, 67–68). It was personally beneficial materially, but did not undo the oppressive systems in which she operated and that enslaved other black Barbadians (67–68). In this same conceptual vein, Rice's public roles demonstrate a "complicated," individualized agency, at best.

Indeed, however unsettling Rice's visibility upon the world stage as secretary of state may be, she ultimately does not displace the dominant power structure. As Rachel Holmes (2007b, 67) remarks, although Rice is seen as defying forces of oppression, "In truth, her validation and power depend upon her active repetition of this dominant [US] culture and its value system."[6] Rice's personae reflected deeply legitimated conservative political narratives, values, and orderings of national community, which enabled her to achieve the positions and status of national security advisor and then secretary of state. In this light, the supposed beneficial effects of having women such as Rice in high positions of authority because of the mirror effect are questionable: Rice pictures black women assuming status and success by embracing the norms of white male power. As black feminist political scientist Wendy Smooth (2018), whose words provide the epigraph for this chapter, contends, "We must rethink the sentiment that 'all women' are good for democracy and consider that some are an affront to democratic principles."

The notion of closeness does not surely exhaust the registers of essentialized notions of race and gender that people across ideological lines tap into, and which black women officials from whatever ideological camp would have to confront. Other prevalent ideas about black women as unintelligent, hypersexual, or excessive (i.e., representing a lack of boundedness or the wild) arguably informed the political conflict generated by Jocelyn Elders's discussion of autoeroticism (she was cast as fanatical) (Elders and Chanoff 1996) or the failed potential appointments and nominations of black women, such as Johnnetta B. Cole or Lani Guinier during the Clinton presidency (Guy-Sheftall 1995, 20; Harris 1999). Melodramas of closeness, however, are a recurring feature of postfeminist, post-racial US politics, and I examine this type of melodrama in terms of representations of black female–white male relationships in the next chapter in *Crash*, on *Grey's Anatomy*, and in Barack Obama's historic 2008 presidential campaign, as well as in Chapter 4 on *The Help*.

Post-politics, with its convergence of neoliberal and conservative thought on class, gender, and race, presents a difficult terrain for black women to negotiate. One resounding lesson is that, in lieu of a celebrationist approach highlighting markers of formal gender and racial equality, students of black women in politics and US racial and gender politics more generally would do well to continue to map and subvert new manifestations of the gendered racism that continues to define US politics and culture. Another lesson is that students of black politics must be cautious of melodramatic framings of public figures such as Rice as pure victors or villains (the paranoid-schizoid position), as attachment to and identification with these extremes can undermine complicated analyses of such figures' political commitments and impact.

Unpacking President Barack Obama's "Improbable Story"

A Case Study of Gender, Race, Class, and Melodrama in Electoral Politics

I'm in my early 30s, and my friends and I don't sit around and discuss race. . . . We're post-civil rights, post-feminist babies, and we take it for granted we live in a diverse world.
—Shonda Rhimes (Fogel 2005)

I nonetheless stand behind the often unsympathetic portrayal presented here, claiming my right to walk (criticize Obama from a left-democratic perspective) and chew gum (defend him against racial bigotry and outrageous rightist misrepresentation and abuse) at one and the same time.
—Paul Street (2009)

In 2008, for the first time in history, a major political party in its primary had two major contenders who were a racial and gender departure from the historical norm for presidential candidates. In a heated contest, Hillary Clinton's and Barack Obama's quest to win the Democratic Party nomination for President awakened a range of debates, including, but not limited to, the viability of white women and racial minorities for national offices and the mobilization of voters across a broad range of demographics and party allegiances (see, e.g., Guy-Sheftall and Cole 2010). Although Hillary Clinton received a significant number of votes (she famously quipped that, because of her historic run for the democratic nomination, there were "eighteen million cracks" in "the highest, hardest glass ceiling" of the presidency) (Clinton 2008), Barack Obama won out as the Democrat's candidate and went on to win the national election against Republican rival John McCain, senator from Arizona.

Even from Obama's own vantage point, his was "an improbable story." Born the child of a black Kenyan man and white Kansan woman, Obama was reared in Indonesia and Hawaii, where he was educated in private schools. He also attended Columbia University and Harvard Law, where he served as the school's first African American named president of the prestigious *Harvard Law Review* (Obama [1995] 2004). After first serving three terms as a state legislator, and then in the midst of his tenure as a first-time US senator, he made his historic bid for the country's highest office. The United States elected him as its first African American president. The question is, How do the candidates' experiences, informed by not only race or ethnicity, but also gender and class and other factors, affect how they run for office and govern thereafter?

Obama was not the first example of the phenomenon of "crossover" black candidates, only its most prominent and significant in national politics. Indeed, since David Dinkins's election as mayor of New York and Doug Wilders's election as governor of Virginia in 1989, black politics specialists in political science, in particular, have sought to discern what allows black politicians to become successful crossover candidates, gaining votes along a broad spectrum of voters in order to win statewide or national office. Special attention has been given to attempts at "deracialization" (a concept I discuss later in this chapter), as a means to garner votes from nonblack constituents. Obama's election has understandably renewed discussions of deracialization and cross-over strategies, including an effort, most notably by Andra Gillespie (2010),[1] to map the new "waves" or generations of crossover candidates, including not only Obama, but, most notably, Corey Booker, a US senator; former Newark, New Jersey, mayor; and early contender in the Democratic primary for the 2020 presidential election (see also Price 2016). With the strong showing of Frank Gillum and Stacey Abrams in the Florida and Georgia 2018 gubernatorial races in Florida and Georgia, respectively, there is sustained interest in the factors that account for crossover appeal and successful strategies for black candidates vying for statewide and national elections.

I argue that understanding President Obama's ascendancy requires an intersectional analysis that centers post-politics as an analytic. Deracialization, or a sidestepping of a protest model of black affinity, is an insufficient explanatory frame. Deracialization is a misnomer: the term codes race as black, leaving whiteness as an unmarked racial category and fails to account for the racial and other dimensions embedded in candidates' personae, rhetoric, priorities, and politics. Rather, we can ask, "How do gender, race, and class shape elected officials' personal narratives and electoral strategies, not only in terms of issue choice, but also in terms of narrative framing?" This latter question, which is the focus of this chapter, helps us to discern how patriarchy and other gendered, raced, and classed elements are embedded in candidates' self-presentation, ideological formation, and political priorities and actions, even (and, at times, especially) when, they gesture toward post-racial futures. Many highlight the imagery of Obama as a post-racial candidate as meaningful. I hope to signal how Barack Obama's image and ideology undergirding his historic election and subsequent governance drew on neoliberal notions of difference that focused on formal representation and multiculturalism, saw racism and sexism as individual problems and/or episodic, and naturalized class inequality, as a function of personal failure and cultural dysfunction.

Melodrama, in terms of these neoliberal notions of difference, is a critical frame. As I noted in Chapter 1, the liminality produced by melodrama functions through splitting, whereby individuals or groups are seen as good or bad objects. In this context, neoliberal melodramas of difference construct blacks as liminal subjects, that is, on the one hand, men endangered or victimized by black family breakdown and female-headed, single-parent households and, on the other, men who are super minorities and models of respectability that can restore order. Understanding the operation of neoliberal melodramatic frames is critical to unpacking President Obama's improbable story and to re-imagining black people in general and black women especially beyond the binaries of liminal subjectivity. These frames are also relevant for the newest cohort of black political figures more broadly (whatever their gender identification), and enable us to deepen our intersectional understanding of race and ethnic US politics. Where the last chapter looked at Condoleezza Rice and competing melodramas of closeness, and how these challenged liberal notions of equality and assimilation, this chapter examines melodrama, particularly black cultural pathology melodramas, as a backdrop to and context for black and US electoral politics.

My analysis proceeds in three parts. First, picking up on arguments I noted in the Introduction, I show how the Moynihan Report served as an urtext for post-racial, post-feminist politics. I explain its special relevance to the production of blacks as liminal subjects, who are either super (model) minorities or abject figures, such as the endangered black male or black welfare queen. The turn away from the state for social change and toward self-rehabilitation christened by the Moynihan Report became a sign of things to come for the broader society.

Second, I show how neoliberal themes about racism and sexism, as being in the past, episodic, or supplanted by "miscege-nation" (Rowe 2007) play out in the mutually constitutive domains of culture and politics. I explore several themes, grounded in a melodrama metanarrative frame, namely (1) a focus on individualistic interpretations of inequality, (2) rehabilitation of the family and wounded masculinity, and (3) racial and gender redemption centered in "fantasies of miscegenation" (Courtney 2005). I demonstrate that these themes, prevalent in the "nested" or cultural context of the era, manifested in TV shows and movies such as Grey's Anatomy and Crash, respectively, and the 2008 Obama campaign. These two cultural touchstones, Grey's Anatomy and Crash, provide a sense of the ways in which the themes evident in the campaign were in fact part of the everyday commonsense (Gramsci [1971] 2008) shaping people's thinking. Third, I show how the black cultural pathology melodrama played out most prominently during the Obama presidential era in his signature program bridging his last days in office and his presidential afterlife, namely, his My Brother's Keeper initiative. I also assess the black cultural pathology melodrama in relation to the Obamas' summit, "Advancing Equity for Women and Girls of Color: A Research Agenda for the Next Decade," developed in response to criticism of My Brother's Keeper.

Black women, notably, were the demographic most solidly behind candidate Barack Obama (Smooth 2013); therefore, throughout this chapter, I pay particular attention to the implications of these themes for black women and black feminist politics, arguing that they render moot any ongoing critique of normative or hegemonic ideologies and forestall exploration of black women's lived realities and political agendas that could be socially and politically transformative, providing instead an ideologically conservative narrative—that of assimilation.

"Post"-ing Social Movements in Culture and Politics

In order to understand President Obama's improbable story as a successful crossover candidate we have to examine the broad historical context from which his candidacy emerged. President Obama is an ideal post-feminist, post-racial candidate. As I noted in the Introduction as well as Chapter 1, post-politics refers to a broad range of backlash politics from the mid-1960s onward. As Omi and Winant (1986) explain in their important work on racial formation, political contestation takes shape among individuals and groups as they resist or affirm the racial (and I would add gender and class) politics of the state. The sea change ushered in by political activism and Cold War imperatives in the mid-twentieth century forced a realignment of state politics that had to respond to, through various modes of resistance and cooptation, the demands for inclusion and equality presented by New Left, Civil Rights, Black Power, and feminist activism.

An urtext for the new blueprint for state backlash against the social movements of the mid-twentieth century is found in the infamous Moynihan Report. As Moynihan ([1965] 1967) famously explained, with the passage of laws that invalidated de jure discrimination via the Civil Rights Act and laid the ground for formal equality, blacks would now be confronted with the larger task of substantive or economic equality. This goal, Moynihan averred, could not be addressed by government, but could only be met with rehabilitating black families. For Moynihan, black families suffered socially, economically, and politically because they were matriarchal (specifically female-headed, single-parent households) in a society that valued and operated with two-parent patriarchal homes as the gold standard for child rearing. Black males--both child and adult—suffered in this setting, children because they lacked a father's leadership and adults because they were not allowed to "strut." The Moynihan Report anticipated many of the themes we see in post-feminist, post-racial politics, such as a neoliberal turn from the public good to private rescue and self-help and concerns about family breakdown. As previously noted, the 1965 Moynihan Report, not the rejection of the Equal Rights Amendment (ERA), is a more accurate starting point for marking the current trend of post-racial/post–Civil Rights and post-feminist discourse. As an urtext for post-feminist, post-racial politics, the report serves as a template for understanding social and political distress and appropriate goals. In the rest of this section, I talk a bit more about the Moynihan Report and the black cultural pathology melodrama it produced and then discuss its relevance to broader trends in post-feminist, post-racial politics.

My previous work has detailed how the Moynihan Report gave rise to what I call the black cultural pathology paradigm (BCPP) (Alexander-Floyd 2007). This paradigm suggested that family breakdown, not economic and educational considerations, produced poverty and an array of social harms. It served, thus, as an alternative explanatory narrative that facilitated a backlash against the social movements of the mid-twentieth century—social movements that pushed for social justice, and highlighted class, gender, and racial inequities. Moynihan's identification of black communities as embodying the polar opposite of white family norms installed family dysfunction as the primary reason for black suffering.

Here I want to expand my consideration of the BCPP by exploring its melodramatic dimensions. The BCPP's rhetorical move from considerations of the public good to private concerns maps a move from social justice and jeremiadic genres of political discourse to that of melodrama. As I note in the Introduction, melodrama channels public concerns into private domains. Social and political concerns are read as individualistic or relationship-bound. The Supreme Court nomination of Clarence Thomas, which I return to in Chapter 5, provides a case in point. The introduction of sexual harassment into Thomas's confirmation hearings, and particularly the sensationalist, soap-opera atmosphere generated, ushered discussion of the Supreme Court nomination out of the public domain, which is inherently read as masculine, into the private domain of soap-opera melodrama (Grindstaff 1994). There, two warring figures were set in conflict with allegiances formed around normative understandings of good and acceptable behavior for men and women in domestic relations, in the home, workplace, and community. Similarly, with the shift from social justice concerns, which imply demands on the state, public policy intervention, and economic redress, to the BCPP's melodramatic frame, we see a concern for propriety and normative heterosexual gender constructions, and dueling figures arrayed in battle. Models of black male/female respectability are juxtaposed to their downtrodden, urban counterparts.

Indeed, the black cultural pathology paradigm is a melodrama, with vivid characters that embody representations of villains and victims. The black welfare queen (or the black welfare mother) is the single woman who is sexually uncontrolled and produces children while living off of the public purse (Stephens and Phillips 2003, 9–10). Without a proper male mate to keep her in check, she remains morally unfit to raise children. Black male children in particular suffer and are unable to grow into functional patriarchs. They turn to a life of excess—criminal and sexual—and devolve into what in 1996, during a speech supporting her husband, President Bill Clinton, during his second term, Hillary Clinton infamously dubbed "superpredators" (Clinton [1996] 2016). Reared in female-headed, single-parent households, the endangered black male is a boy who never truly grows into a man. This melodramatic shift from the public to the private effects a shift in scale, so that macrostructural issues are sidestepped and emphasis is placed on the microinstitution of the family.

Dysfunctional figures, such as the black welfare queen and endangered black male, are abject representations of blackness that are contrasted, sometimes explicitly, sometimes indirectly, with virtuous, idealized figures of respectability and success. The 1995 Million Man March stands as an iconic representation of the black cultural pathology melodrama and its antidote of respectable public citizenry. According to the organizers, black men, at what was at the time the largest such gathering on the Mall, stood to atone for the sins of the black nation (Alexander-Floyd 2007; White 2017). These men, mostly middle-class, modeled patriarchal manhood for other black men and black communities as a whole. Its ideological underpinnings were identical to that of the historic legislation that would happen just one year later during Bill Clinton's tenure as president—namely, the Personal Responsibility and Work Opportunity Act (commonly known as "Welfare Reform"). Welfare Reform—which shrunk the rolls and decreased social spending for the poor by capping welfare payouts, adding work requirements, and providing block grants to states—held all the markings of the punitive, stereotype-laden black cultural pathology narrative. Even fatherhood initiatives that would come to fruition during the George W. Bush administration, be developed in the Obama years, and sustained under the Trump administration, had its roots in the Welfare Reform authorized by Democratic president Bill Clinton. More importantly, fatherhood initiatives in particular would center in many instances on the concept of proper role modeling for black fathers. As I discuss more below, this impulse to train up boys to be men would also drive President Obama's My Brother's Keeper initiative.

One might ask how the black cultural pathology paradigm or melodrama relates to the country as a whole. The answer is straightforward. With the arrested development of social movement activity in the mid-twentieth century, the black cultural pathology paradigm served as a prime example of melodramatic narrative formations that curtailed analyses of material questions of inequality and social justice frames in general. It is unsurprising, thus, that Moynihan (1996) would point to the decline in patriarchal families in black communities as a harbinger of things to come for society as a whole: black family breakdown is seen as emblematic of the destruction that comes from advances in civil rights for white women and racial minorities. After 1965, popular and political discourse would turn to an emphasis on the supposed excesses or detriments of feminist and civil rights agendas, on the one hand, and the achievements (and, therefore, future irrelevance) of such agendas, on the other. Conservatives, for instance, in addition to engineering Welfare Reform, attacked affirmative action as being patently unfair and amounting to reverse discrimination toward whites, particularly white men (Walters 2003, 126). Additionally, conservatives, most prominently those on the religious right, railed against the feminist movement for disrupting two-parent, patriarchal families more generally (Alexander-Floyd 2007). Lambasting the feminist movement as the source of the problem, conservatives criticized white women's entrance into the public sphere of politics and work as a serious threat to the US way of life. This perceived threat to patriarchal aspirations—a different form of white wounded masculinity—emerged as a significant catalyst for the fatherhood movement and religious groups, such as Promise Keepers (White 2017).

In a related vein, the individualist-centered assessment of racism and sexism would eventually come to dominate political and legal discourse. Discrimination laws that once comprehended both individual acts of discrimination, as well as group harm(s) focused on the disparate impact of seemingly neutral business and government practices, would be circumscribed to encompass only the most egregious acts of individual discrimination that could be subjected to high standards of legal proof. Civil Rights proponents and feminists struggled with articulating a vision of inequality that broadly captured race- and gender-based harm. Feminists in particular argued about whether women should be treated the "same" or as having acknowledged "difference" before the law. This sameness-difference or formal-versus-substantive-equality debate took shape as activists and scholars struggled to implement the legal protections that grew out of social movement activity in the mid-twentieth century (see, generally, Bartlett and Kennedy 2018). Even outside of discussions of black communities, our understanding of race, gender, and class inequality are read as individual or interpersonal issues, or both, shot through with discussions about family and nation formation.

The Moynihan Report, thus, as an urtext of post-politics, gives us a window into neoliberal social and political formation in response to the social movements of the mid-twentieth century. We can see in it the development of blacks as liminal subjects, caught betwixt and between virtuous and villainous figures. And we can see in it, as well, many of the prominent melodramatic themes that emerge post-1965 and that provided the nested historical context out of which Obama as a presidential figure emerges—namely (1) a focus on individualistic interpretations of inequality, (2) rehabilitation of the family and wounded masculinity, and (3) racial and gender redemption centered in "fantasies of miscegenation" (Courtney 2005).

To summarize: As I note at the beginning of this chapter, we cannot understand the political life or broad appeal of crossover politicians, specifically President Obama, without an intersectional analysis. We have to take into account the race, gender, and class politics espoused by the candidate and that shape the nested (historical and cultural) context in which they operate. With President Obama, in terms of both his historic 2008 campaign and his governance, we can see many of the post-feminist, post-racial themes of the era.

I use *Crash* and *Grey's Anatomy* to further illustrate the nested context of Obama's watershed campaign. This method highlights the mutually constitutive domains of culture and formal politics and provides a bridge for feminists, who typically focus on the former, and political scientists, who tend to focus on the latter. In this next section, as we look at the mutually constitutive domains of culture and politics, we see black and white wounded masculinity, questions about family breakdown and efforts to reconstitute it in private domains, as well as on the job, and interracial relationships figured as restorative of national unity.

Melodrama: Defining Inequality

The question of defining inequality in terms of interpersonal, melo-dramatic terms can usefully be assessed in light of two subthemes: (1) multiculturalism marked by racial and gender diversity and rare occur-rences of hostility or structural discrimination, and (2) multiculturalism marked by ubiquitous interpersonal conflict read as homogeneous claims of social harm.

Fantasies of Multicultural Equality

Grey's Anatomy is an important starting point for discussing this theme, because it was the first of several shows, including Private Practice, Scandal, and How to Get Away with Murder, that would form Shonda Rhimes's TV empire, a slew of popular shows that would span over a decade and a half at the start of this century. Although a discussion of each of these shows exceeds the scope of this current work, they all, in some way, trade on post-politics themes discussed herein (see, e.g., Brüning 2018 on Scandal). Grey's Anatomy is the foundation of "Shonda-land"; since it first aired in 2005, it has met with critical acclaim and high viewership for well over a decade. Although medical TV shows are stan-dard fare, the show boasts a particularly impressive multicultural cast. Set in "Seattle Grace," a topnotch hospital in Seattle, Washington, the show in its earliest seasons centers on Meredith Grey, a surgical intern, and a coterie of her friends as they negotiate the grueling demands of a surgical internship. In addition to Meredith, there are more than four other female surgeons who played key roles on the show, including her best friend, Christina Yang, a Korean American. In keeping with tra-ditional casting patterns, where minorities are cast in leadership roles (Entman and Rojecki 2001, 152), there were three African Americans in supervisory positions in the initial seasons, including Dr. Webber, the chief of surgery; Preston Burke, a renowned cardiothoracic surgeon who is one of the attending surgeons responsible for instructing the interns; and Miranda Bailey, aka "Hitler," the resident who is the interns' immediate supervisor.

The post–Civil Rights, post-feminist ideology of *Grey's Anatomy* takes for granted that the goals of social movement activity of the 1960s and '70s, at least at a formal equality level, have been achieved. As the epigraph from Rhimes used at the start of this chapter relates, Rhimes explicitly sees herself as a product of post-politics ("We're [she and her friends] post–civil rights, post-feminist babies"), situating racism and sexism as concerns relevant for a prior era ("we take it for granted we live in a diverse world") (Fogel 2005). From this perspective, there is little room for expansive definitions of gender, race, and class inequality that take into account institutional structures, ongoing processes of engendering and racialization as they intersect with market forces, or even the daily struggles that white women and racial minorities experience in workplaces such as hospitals. On *Grey's Anatomy*, not all of the interns, for instance, hail from economically privileged backgrounds. Still, their varied and humble beginnings, while useful in explaining some of their personality quirks and personal foibles, do not impede their upward mobility in the highly competitive field of medical surgery. Education and hard work, it is assumed, are the great equalizers. This upward mobility is implicitly gendered, as I describe herein, in its reconstitution of patriarchal family in the workplace.

In addition to class, racism and sexism are not seen as significant problems and are instead seen as episodic, that is, as resting in individually directed behavior by a minority of people who are wedded to anachronistic, socially repugnant worldviews. In terms of gender, two trends hold on *Grey's Anatomy*. On the one hand, the lead female characters are surrounded by men (who stand ready to have monogamous relationships), but remain hopelessly afflicted with angst about whether "having it all"—that is, career and family—are possible for women. On the other hand, the female characters enact a "do-me masquerade post-feminism" (Projansky 2001, 82–83) in which they highlight their heterosexuality and demonstrate their "independence" by having numerous and varied sexual partners at work. In terms of race, it was not until season four that racism was addressed directly, even though the cast is celebrated for its diversity. In this episode, racism is cast as a freak occurrence, embodied in misguided individuals whose views are not generally supported. By this logic, racism and sexism are relegated to the past, only to occasionally surface, before being quickly doused by egalitarian moral sentiments.

Fantasies of Multicultural Conflict Resolution

Notably, despite its attempt to address questions of racism and (to a lesser extent) other forms of inequality directly, in the final analysis, *Crash* is also scripted within the political parameters of post–Civil Rights, post-feminist ideology. The iconic Hollywood blockbuster *Crash* (which enjoyed a second life as a television series) is generally hailed as a progressive movie that takes a daring, forthright approach to dealing with the question of racism and prejudice. The movie, which garnered three Academy Awards, including Best Motion Picture of the Year (Mack 2006), focuses in on the multiethnic environment of Los Angeles and the seemingly ubiquitous prejudice that passes viruslike between whites and nonwhites and among various racial and ethnic communities. The film, mostly praised by critics, is shown in "diversity" seminars (Hsu 2006, 134) and is used as a teaching aid in colleges across the country.

Instead of avoiding a discussion of racism, *Crash* seems to take it head-on. The opening scene centers on two black males who seem to be critiquing an assumption that they are to be feared and are likely criminals, after a woman crosses the street and hugs her purse a bit more tightly. The viewer, moreover, is greeted with people of all racial, gender, and class backgrounds espousing prejudiced views, ostensibly to suggest a more complicated picture of racial and ethnic strife (Nunley 2007, 339–40).

Viewers quickly learn that the two aforementioned black males are, in fact, thieves, as they begin to break into cars. This opening scene is especially significant as it broadcasts the importance of irony to the movie and its accompanying storylines. Recall McRobbie's assessment of a popular ad (discussed in the Introduction) in which a model performs a strip tease before entering a car that speeds off. She notes that this ad presumes a certain level of sophistication among viewers, that the audience "gets" that the ad is flaunting, and yet implicitly critiquing, a well-known mode of female objectification. Similarly, in *Crash*, viewers are subjected to a steady parade of ethnic slurs and racist jokes—slurs and jokes ostensibly meant to highlight their inherent absurdity and their use among people of various racial and ethnic backgrounds. These jokes and slurs are ironic, however, because they provide opportunity not only for implicit critique but also delight. As Hsuan Hsu observes, *Crash* uses racist jokes that are "simultaneously offensive and titillating" (2006, 145). The post–Civil Rights subject is expected to take umbrage with these, of course, but is still afforded an opportunity to enjoy and openly laugh at them. This post-feminist, post–Civil Rights proliferation of jokes and slurs normalizes racism and sexism, whereas, under a traditional feminist or Civil Rights paradigm, they would be condemned—and avoided—as passive forms of racism and sexism that support the status quo (Tatum 2003).

In addition to its problematic use of irony, the putatively straightforward approach to confronting racism fails in its proliferation of false equivalencies. The globalization of prejudice that *Crash* exhibits masks an important distinction between prejudicial attitudes and racism, the latter of which centers on not only prejudicial views of individuals but also on institutional racism. Indeed, *Crash* "flattens out asymmetrical power relations as they intersect with white privilege" (Nunley 2007, 340), so that the viewer is invited to make no distinctions, for instance, between a Latina and an Asian woman who exchange ethnic epithets after an automobile accident, on the one hand, and the white District Attorney who abuses the power of his office to coerce a black cop into participating in a racially motivated cover-up, on the other. Moreover, like *Grey's Anatomy*, *Crash*'s underlying assumption is that class and other institutional barriers are largely assailable through hard work and attainment of middle-class status (D. Holmes 2007, 318–19). The movie showcases individuals (largely men), such as a Persian convenience store owner, a black cop, a black television executive, and a Latino handyman, who are striving to overcome adversity through pursuit of the American Dream.

Ultimately, despite their differences, like *Grey's Anatomy*, *Crash* trades on a multiculturalism that positions racism and other social and political harm in the realm of pathos-driven melodrama acted out on and through individuals. *Crash* rehearses the familiar understanding of inequality read through a "melodramatic vision that foregrounds individual suffering" (Hsu 2006, 146), cast in a masculinist mode. It achieves this, for instance, through its focus on reclaiming wounded white masculinity, thereby highlighting "reverse discrimination" (146) against white men. But, as Hsu explains, "As a banal product of history, urban architecture, and state institutions, racism runs on autopilot, without much need for melodramatic acts of hate, intolerance, or malice" (148). By equating prejudice with racism and melodramatic attitudes or actions as the entire scope of racial play, *Crash* undermines the Civil Rights and Black Power imperative to make not only attitudinal but also institutional change and obscures the more mundane elaboration of white, US privilege and power. I use *Grey's Anatomy* and *Crash* as touchstones to gain a general read on the range of post-politics sensibilities in the opening decade of the twenty-first century; I do so because they are part of the nested context in which the Obama campaign took shape, as the subsequent discussion illustrates.

Like *Grey's Anatomy* and *Crash*, the Obama campaign constructed racism and sexism as being relics of the past and equated with melodramatic individual attitudes, stripped of an understanding of asymmetrical power relations. The most striking example of this false equivalency fallacy was represented in Barack Obama's speech on race presented on March 18, 2008, set against the backdrop of Constitutional Hall in Philadelphia, Pennsylvania. Although reaction to Obama reflected prior ideological commitments, liberal pundits were especially keen on the speech. Some thought of the speech as being in the tradition of other momentous speeches in US history, such as Lincoln's "A House Divided" or "Gettysburg Address" or Martin Luther King's "I Have a Dream" speech, among others (Sharpley-Whiting 2009, 6). In "With a Powerful Speech; Obama Offers a Challenge," for instance, which appeared on March 25, 2008, in the *New York Times*, columnist Bob Herbert (2008) remarked, "The speech, which has gotten wonderful reviews, should be required reading in classrooms across the country—and in as many other venues as possible. With a worldview that embraces both justice and healing, Senator Obama is better on these issues than any American leader since King." Joseph Biden, who was a candidate early on in the 2008 presidential race and eventually became Obama's pick for vice president reportedly stated, "'He [Obama] told the story of America—both the good and the bad—and I believe his speech will come to represent an important step forward in race relations in our country'" (Murray and Balz 2008). Even Michael Gerson (2008), who penned "A Speech That Fell Short" for the *Washington Post*, described it in some dimensions as an "excellent and important speech on race in America."

Still other commentators talked about how the speech allowed them to speak about race relations within the context of their own families. Connie Schultz likened the speech to the "beginning of a movement" (Schultz 2009, 104), in fact, noting that the speech allowed whites, like herself, who struggled with relatives who held racist views, to finally find a way to discuss their racist attitudes. For her, the messages in her inbox also told of stories of presumably positive, white racial transformation. She relates,

> At the beginning of Barack Obama's campaign, I could count on one hand the number of white readers who wanted to claim him as one of their own. Now, this is one of the most persistent themes in calls and letters from white readers who continue to weigh in about Obama. As evidence, it's purely anecdotal. But we are in a time when one man's personal narrative has changed the trajectory of an entire nation. His story is now our story. It continues, one anecdote at a time. (Schultz 2009, 112)

Some pondered the extent to which the speech could actually represent a model for others to follow internationally (see, e.g., Thomas 2009). This speech, T. Denean Sharpley-Whiting notes, was one Obama was destined to make, given the centrality of race to US life (Sharpley-Whiting 2009, 6). Judging by polls, the speech effectively met its mark, that is, it quelled the anxiety produced by a controversy involving Obama's African American pastor.

In that controversy, which was the immediate impetus of the speech, Obama was publicly chastised for his longtime association with the Reverend Jeremiah Wright, then pastor of Trinity United Church of Christ in Chicago. During the election, sermon recordings of Wright "damning" the US for its imperialist involvement in geopolitics surfaced and presented perhaps the biggest challenge to Obama's campaign. Obama cut ties with Rev. Wright, but not until after providing what he hoped to be a conciliatory speech in Philadelphia's Constitution Hall. After the speech, the *New York Times* (2008) reported that "Seven in 10 said

Mr. Obama, Democrat of Illinois, did a good job talking about race relations, and as many said he did a good job explaining his relationship with Mr. Wright [in the Philadelphia speech], according to the CBS News poll." Although each of these varied perspectives on the speech constitute genuine reactions, the part of the speech that is interesting for our examination regards its melodramatic mode and its figuring of male leadership.

In his now (in)famous "Philadelphia compromise speech" (Reed 2008) on race in the United States, Obama begins fashioning a melodramatic frame by first drawing a clear distinction between the past, marked by virulent racism, and the present, which is marked by substantial racial progress. For Obama, although those, such as his former pastor Jeremiah Wright, who experienced Jim Crow–style racism, were understandably "angry" about racism, he faulted Wright and presumably others for not fully acknowledging US racial progress. Just as importantly, in his historic speech Obama draws a parallel between the suffering of blacks and that of disgruntled whites who feel harmed through affirmative action (Obama 2008b). Also, in his neglect of questions of sexism as they relate to those of class and gender, he promotes post-feminist, or more directly, a post–black feminist, politics.

What are the implications of this post–Civil Rights, post-feminist ideology for black feminist analyses and politics? As I note in the Introduction, radical black feminist politics operates on a basic assumption that various aspects of identity are "mutually constitutive" (Harris 1999), that is, that the elaboration of identity and politics are inherently raced, gendered, and classed and that this reality must inform any social justice agenda. Post–Civil Rights, post-feminist ideology directly contradicts this basic presumption. More pointedly, because it denies the institutional and complex nature of social inequality, it is not merely inattentive to, but actively works to obscure, the realities of black women's experiences with sexism, racism, and class-based inequality. By way of illustration, it is interesting how the reality of black women in the medical profession is diametrically opposed to the picture of multicultural, post-feminist integration presented on *Grey's Anatomy*. Significantly, the American Medical Association, which established a special committee to study the racial divide in medicine, issued an apology in 2008 for the long-standing history of the organization's discriminatory actions

(Davis 2008). Also, although blacks comprise over 10 percent of the US population, Dr. Nelson Adams, former president of the National Medical Association, notes that "there are fewer African-American physicians per capita to date than in 1910" (Steenhuysen 2008). The Association of American Medical Colleges reports that, as of 2015, only 3 percent of professors at US medical schools were black (AAMC 2016). In her study of black female surgeons, Patricia Dawson relates the experiences of black women as they struggle to succeed in environments rife with "gendered racism" (Dawson 1999, 97). In one case, for instance, Xena, a black female chief resident, had to be hypervigilant in executing her work and lacked administrative backing to fulfill her supervisory role (82). Another black female, Marie, states that "One of the big problems [during residency] was the fact that I was a female and then that I was black. There are stories [or humorous jokes] that go on and on about, 'Your doctor is not only Black, she's female . . . your doctor is not only female, she's Black'" (98).

These aforementioned experiences suggest that, far from the serene, convivial environment projected on *Grey's Anatomy* or the symmetrical experience of suffering on *Crash*, work and social environments, such as hospitals, are spheres of intense conflict—or what Pratt (1992) refers to as "contact zones"—where previously dispossessed, disenfranchised groups interact with the dominant culture and institutions in situations of radical inequality. Black women in these spaces, in particular, deeply challenge the "somatic norms" (Puwar 2004) of medical and other professional environments, given that they embody the antithesis of white masculinity. Although post–Civil Rights, post-feminist ideology embedded within popular representations showcases gender, race, and class hypervisibility as markers of social progress, it renders invisible the discrimination black women, as well as other racial minorities and white women, endure.

These fantasies of multicultural conflict resolution were part and parcel of the cultural milieu of the time. They were also central to the Obama campaign and persona. Far from being a deracialized candidate, Obama mirrored and enacted the prevailing post-politics fantasies of the time, fantasies that have little to do with addressing ongoing inequality. The next section explores another prominent post-feminist, post-racial theme of the era: melodrama and family restoration.

Melodrama and Family Restoration

Countering Feminism and Mending Race and Gender Woundedness: Interracial Romance and the Family-as-Nation

The "family in jeopardy" is part of the "core grammar" of media and cultural productions (Lipsitz 1997, 17). Unsurprisingly, then, narratives of family decline and restoration remain central to US politics in general and black politics in particular. This section of the chapter builds on the enumeration of post-politics themes by examining melodrama and family restoration on both macro and micro levels. On the macro level, we examine interracial romance as symbolic of family destruction on a global scale—that is, as a result of feminism—in the case of *Grey's Anatomy*, and as symbolic of family rehabilitation—as a stand-in for racial reconciliation—in the case of *Crash* and would-be President Obama. This latter form of macro family rehabilitation, where interracial unions serve as a proxy for healing racial strife, is discussed in terms of Carillo Rowe's concept of miscege-nation (Rowe 2007).

Miscegenation, understood as the transgressive violation of interracial sexual boundaries, has been a cornerstone of US popular culture, and provides what is perhaps the starkest, and most politically charged example of melodramatic narrative scripting. Two elements of this scripting are especially important: the use of miscegenation to channel or resolve anxieties provoked through challenges to the established raced and gendered order and the redemption of whiteness through black bodies. First, as Susan Courtney (2005, 16) demonstrates, in fantasies of miscegenation of the modern era, such as *Guess Who's Coming to Dinner* (Kramer 1967), the price of acceptance of racial transgressions—of affirming racial integration—comes only at the expense of, and are indeed constituted through, the reassertion of the approved "dominant sexual order." So, while Sydney Poitier's presence as fiancé-in-waiting for a young white woman is initially unsettling, the white father's concerns give way to acceptance as he embraces Poitier as a Magical Negro figure who would unite in wedded matrimony with his daughter and thereby affirm his liberal racial commitments, even amid the reassertion of gender norms. Second, black characters occupy what Toni Morrison (1993) has referred to as an Africanist presence, that is, the utilization of blackness and black figures to effect the elaboration of white, US identity and racial hierarchy. Similarly, Nunley amplifies, "whether it is the magical Negro trope . . . or the servant trope . . . not only must the white character be redeemed [e.g., the white father in *Guess Who's Coming to Dinner*], but the redemption must also occur upon or because of the discursive terrain of the black body" (Nunley 2007, 344).[2]

In *Grey's Anatomy*, the primary resolution of family crisis can be seen in the life of the main character, Meredith Grey, and takes shape via a fall and redemption symbolized through transgression of the black body via an interracial union. Meredith Grey and Derrick Sheppard have had a fiery, albeit on-again-off-again relationship, perennially hamstrung by her "obvious daddy issues" (*Grey's Anatomy* 2006). This unfortunate state of affairs is owing to an extramarital affair that Ellis Grey, Meredith's high-powered surgeon mother who is now afflicted with Alzheimer's, had with Dr. Webber. This liaison effectively ended Ellis Grey's relationship with her husband. Although Ellis Grey leaves her husband to be with Webber, he decides to stay with his black wife, Adele.

Importantly, the Grey family saga can be read as an allegory that registers a cautionary tale about the impact of the mid–twentieth century feminist movement on white middle-class women, one in which blackness provides the symbolic parameter for elaborating white family distress. Given her age, Ellis Grey would have entered the medical profession when there were not likely as many women in the profession. In her choice to have a career, she set aside traditional family life. Although Ellis Grey is a professional success, she is a distant, emotionally unavailable mother. She also effectively emasculates her husband, driving him away from the family and causing him to abandon his daughter. Her subversion of gender norms that would prohibit her from having a career is inherently racialized. Her transgression of white middle-class gender norms is figured as a transgression of racial norms, literally (in terms of sex), as well as metaphorically (in terms of her symbolic positioning). Kimberly Springer has remarked, "Even when they are not on the screen, women of color are present as the counterpart against which white women's ways of being . . . are defined and refined" (2007, 249), and in *Grey's Anatomy*, black women, read as emasculating Sapphires, are the implicit symbolic register for women who violate gender norms. Most notably, Ellis Grey, as it relates to her husband, becomes symbolically black: as a woman who transgresses the cult of womanhood reserved for white middle-class women, she comes to assume the stereotypical characteristics of black women who are viewed as the antithesis, and indeed provide the constitutive boundaries, of proper femininity.[3] Interestingly, although Ellis Grey is generally stern, often cruel in her verbal engagements, she is calm, happy, and emotional when with Webber, a picture of traditional femininity. As a black man—a "real" man (read: sexually potent)—he is able to tame this otherwise unyielding, tyrannical woman. In keeping with the melodramatic mode, Webber is, in the end, a villainous character. Ellis Grey, we learn in season four, is so distressed by Webber's decision not to leave his wife that she attempts to commit suicide, a pattern that Grey's daughter ineluctably follows.

Season four ends with Meredith coming to terms with her fear of emotional intimacy with Derrick Sheppard by going to therapy and realizing that she can, unlike her mother, "have it all." She tells Derrick she is ready for a family. The black doctor is an Africanist racial presence, in the final analysis, providing the backdrop through which this story of white wounded masculinity and its recovery is actualized and gender harmony restored. This miscegenation is less a rupture of gendered racism, as some might suggest, than an explicitly depoliticized interracial union that implicitly reaffirms white male-female patriarchal family unions.

In the movie *Crash*, amid an epidemic failure of masculinity, where men are unable to protect their women or otherwise affirm their manhood on the job or in the home, the story turns on an interracial rape scene that provides the impetus for masculine redemption. This central element of the plot involves the interplay between two sets of characters, namely two white cops—Ryan, the more senior officer, and Hansen, his junior counterpart—as well as a black, middle-class couple, Cameron and Christine. The characters first encounter each other when Ryan decides to pull Cameron and Christine over without just cause.

Ryan's emotional trigger for making this stop stems from his woundedness as a white male, a woundedness that is grounded in a family history that serves as an allegory for the broader context of black-white US racial history. His father cannot urinate because of a urinary tract infection (a condition symbolic of wounded, white masculinity) (Hsu 2006, 133; Ray 2007, 352), and is denied access to the medical clinic after hours by a black female because his condition is not an emergency. Also, Ryan's father hired black employees for his janitorial business and was "good to them," only to be forced out of business by blacks who received government contracts. In this melodrama that figures white male decline due to black social advancement, Ryan's father exemplifies white liberal commitment to racial reform, situated in the past, that has ultimately failed him and his family; and Ryan, symbolic of the current moment, emerges as a victim of affirmative action who is outraged by its deleterious effects on him and his family, in the first instance for his father's job loss and most immediately in terms of representing the inadequacy of the health care system. Ryan's unwarranted stop, then, is motivated by his wounded white middle-class masculinity.

Ryan seeks to assuage his wounded masculinity via a sexual violation that assaults not only Christine, the black woman, but also her husband, Cameron. Ryan stops the black couple, and proceeds to have Cameron perform a sobriety test and "checks" his wife, Christine, for weapons. Unaware at first of the danger they are in, Cameron proceeds to tell Ryan that he is a movie producer just returning from an awards show. This announcement of his middle-class status is ostensibly meant to distance him from the criminal stereotype of the pathological endangered black male. Christine, who has been drinking, is cast in a classic Sapphire stereotype and "mouths off" at the officer. Under the guise of a weapons check, Ryan rapes Christine, assaulting her by molesting her legs, hips, breasts, and buttocks, and driving his fingers under her dress in what her character later describes as "finger f**k[ing]" (Haggis 2005). From here, the story takes on two modes of masculine redemption. One unfolding of masculine redemption is centered on Cameron's character. After the car stop in which his wife is raped as he watches, he and Christine have a difficult exchange in which she verbally batters him for not saying anything to the officer when she was assaulted. Cameron remarks that he was in a complicated situation. Assumedly resisting the assault could have invited even more and potentially deadly harm to them both. Nevertheless, Christine, affirming the centrality of black wounded masculinity in black politics and culture, avers that the interracial sexual assault on her body was really directed toward Cameron. Here, her character rehearses a familiar narrative concerning black women and rape that focuses on its effects, not only on black women, but also most especially on black men (Projansky 2001, Chapter 5).

In keeping with melodrama's transformation of the villain, sometimes by rehabilitation, the second instance takes on a mode of white masculine redemption. In a later scene, Ryan is called to a car crash in which Christine turns out to be the victim. He enters a vehicle, leaking gas and about to catch fire, in order to save her. Christine, understandably reluctant to be helped by Ryan, relents in order to save her life. As Hsuan L. Hsu observes, this scene depends on "a familiar model of white male heroic agency at the expense of the inarticulate, passive, victimized black woman . . ." (2006, 133).

The scene is not only one of white male redemption in which Christine embodies an Africanist presence that allows white subjectivity to emerge (which it certainly is), but one that represents an increasingly popular narrative trope: the black woman's body as a site for racial reconciliation and restoration. As Hsu (2006, 132–33) notes, the popular movie poster used to advertise *Crash* shows Ryan and Christine in what, in key ways, looks like an apparent romantic embrace. One would certainly not gather from the advertisement that Ryan is a man who perhaps as little as a day earlier rapes her. One critic remarks, "'The burning-SUV rescue, with its body contortions and spilled fluids, operates as a kind of vicarious miscegenation, essentially allowing Sgt. Ryan (and, presumably, the audience) the desired and dreaded coupling that his earlier roadside finger-f*** only hinted at'" (Michael Sicinski, quoted in Hsu 2006, 150). Such popular renderings are fantasies of "miscegenation" (Rowe 2007, 127), where interracial relationships (particularly those involving white men and black women) are the crucible for the production of a new national community that skirts responsibility for structural change to dismantle inequality. Also, as with other melodramatic narratives, it vindicates wounded white masculinity by showing that "the 'villain within' is reformed, or the villain turns out to have been the hero all along" (Grindstaff 1994, 55).

Obama's campaign also depended on addressing wounded masculinity (as noted later in this chapter's segment referencing Jackson) and a melodramatic miscegenation fantasy, where Obama comes to embody the type of miscege-nation that could move the country beyond racial and other problems. Importantly, his 2004 speech at the Democratic National Convention, which catapulted him into the national spotlight and generated buzz about his future potential as a presidential candidate, emphasized the "one America" narrative that subsequently became his calling card. He consistently points out his biracial lineage and positions himself as embodying the type of oneness he discusses in his most notable speeches. Obama, then, symbolically and rhetorically becomes the quintessential representation of the success of miscege-nation, the racial fantasy that "transgression" of interracial sex taboos can signify a deracialized, reconstituted, yet restabilized gender order. Again, the melodramatic emphasis on personal relationships as the locus for change and national restoration is key. Although Obama has railed against the idea that "unity in this country" can be "purchased on the cheap" (Obama 2008a, 240), the substance of his bearing and politics offers just that: a symbolic mode of gendered racial reconciliation rooted in essentialized notions of biological racial melding via coupling. "But, I Voted for Obama" will join the chorus of other rhetorical gestures—like "But, my boyfriend is black" and "I gave money to the NAACP"—designed to identify one's political bona fides. Yet such forms of identification do not undermine race, gender, or class inequalities and did not prevent vitriolic reactions to his presidency.

Miscege-nation fantasies are a raced and gendered aspect of post–Civil Rights, post-feminist melodrama that has profound implications for black politics as a whole and black feminists politics in particular. In *Grey's Anatomy*, *Crash*, and the Obama campaign, black people are objects through which whites usher in new modes of oppressive whiteness and seek to normalize romantic models of white patriarchal relations. These miscege-nation fantasies depend as well on a studied avoidance of the historical and contemporary realities that surround interracial relationships, particularly those that are sexual. It ignores, for instance, the reality that white desire for black bodies has been part of a long tradition of exploitation and abuse or consuming the Other (see, generally, Threadcraft 2016). Most heinously, it contributes to the historical amnesia and political silence we have in the United States concerning the rape of black women by predatory white men, the ongoing truth that sexual access to black female bodies has been a hallmark of white masculinity since this country's founding, a topic I return to in Chapter 4. This seemingly intractable silence solidifies and is a necessary condition for a legal and political structure that positions black women as always already violable, profane, and inhuman nonsubjects before the state. I am not saying here that the legalization of interracial relationships or the relative growth in interracial unions does not signal progress in terms of race and gender in the United States. I am asserting, however, that when we highlight such relationships without an understanding of their potential complex race and gender problematics and dynamics, when we use them to symbolize regressive re-assertions of race and gender and to figure a redemption of white masculinity and femininity in ways that affirm new modes of racial and gender exploitation, these miscege-nation fantasies work to quell our anxieties and transfix our attention on hollow, counterproductive modes of race-gender "comity" (Entman and Rojecki 2001, 11–12).

Resolving Personal Family Crises

As discussed earlier, the focus on the family in jeopardy was elevated by the black cultural pathology framework that Patrick Moynihan anointed in his (in)famous report. This emphasis on the family in jeopardy has become a broad framework with extensive reach. The prior section looked at macro-level concerns in terms of family breakdown and res-toration and how they manifested in popular culture and in formal politics in terms of Obama's breakthrough presidential campaign. This next section looks at melodramas of family breakdown and restoration on the micro level in terms of their importance to the nested context out of which the Obama campaign emerged. In *Grey's Anatomy*, family is reconstituted in another setting, namely, the workplace. With *Crash* and Barack Obama, melodramas of black cultural pathology are central, with the attendant abject and prototypical figures of endangered black men borne of absent black fathers and super minorities, respectively.

Unsurprisingly, and as our discussion of miscege-nation revealed, even as it sidesteps strident critiques of inequality and reformulates representations of characters that in at least some ways downplay those characters' racial identification, *Grey's Anatomy* operates on an implicit (and wayward) assumption that "second wave" feminists have thrown the family in crisis, marking women's professional "ambitions" (Grind-staff 1994, 55) as villainous pursuits. And importantly, as noted earlier, all of the main characters, whatever their socioeconomic status or racial or ethnic background, come from troubled families. Seattle Grace and its doctors are the site, for them, of a different, more stable family unit. As would-be surgeons going through a grueling internship, they all find occasion to cover for each other's failings (as when they stand together and refuse to "give up" Izzie when she essentially temporarily kills a patient, so he can be moved up on a transplant list). They all have deep-seated personality issues and are whipped into shape and mothered by Bailey, the mammy/Sapphire figure. The chief of surgery, Dr. Webber, someone with his own family issues (i.e., his wife at one point wants a divorce), is the consummate father figure. This reconstitution of family stems from the romance of a "traditionalist" white middle-class vision of patriarchy, that is, the promotion of two-parent, male-headed families, based on a male breadwinner model, as the primary solution for sociopolitical ills.

Indeed, although most minorities in authority positions on TV shows do not become intimately involved with their juniors (Entman and Rojecki 2001, Chapter 9), Dr. Webber takes a keen interest in his interns. This transgression of typical boundaries seen in similar TV shows is made possible because the African American chief of surgery is also implicitly the father in chief. In one episode, for instance, when Bailey complains about Cristina getting a light reprimand after her role in hiding Burke's hand injury is exposed, the chief, Dr. Webber, intones, "Look at how she has grown." Here he is referring to Cristina's moral development in pushing aside her feelings for Burke and her desire to gain surgical experience in order to "do the right thing" by exposing her own and Burke's unethical transgressions.

Some might argue that such oversight is typical, that camaraderie is a natural feature among interns, or that a developmental model undergirds medical training, but the nurturing approach bears more resemblance to familial relations as opposed to the hardnosed training expected in hospitals. To be sure, as women of color feminists have pointed out, the family has been a key source of survival for subaltern US communities (Carby 1987; Davis 2000). But the romance of a white patriarchal family model proceeds without any critique or consideration of the family (and specifically its "dominator" model of patriarchy variety) (hooks 2004, 131–32) as a site of exploitation and abuse of women. Their personal family crises, in effect, are resolved through the reconstitution of family in another institutional domain, thus restoring the romance of white middle-class patriarchy that is seemingly threatened in the "real" world and asserting racial harmony (here figured in the black chief of staff) instead of insisting on a critique of the patriarchal romance.

In contrast to the more generalized focus on family breakdown and restoration in *Grey's Anatomy*, *Crash* evinces a special focus on supposed black cultural pathology and breakdown in black communities. The two black men who are in the opening scene of *Crash* are cast as abject black figures—criminal, underclass, endangered black males. They are contrasted, moreover, with two super-minority figures. The super minority, discussed in Chapter 1 in terms of Secretary of State Condoleezza Rice, is an African American (typically, but obviously not always, male) who is presented as being stripped of stereotypical characteristics generally associated with blackness. A regular on the small screen, super minorities—here prototypical blacks—are constructed as "purified exemplars of White cultural ideals that . . . [lead to the] disruption of Whites' normal mental associations" such that these characters are seen as "'not really Black'" (Entman and Rojecki 2001, 222); this move implicitly suggests a liminal super-minority status as a requirement for assimilation. The point is not that black professionals are not indeed excellent or exceptional, but that, as Entman and Rojecki (2001, 159) affirm,

> Inflected as they are with this symbolic freighting [as symbolic figures made even more so, because they typically appear in "superior" positions work-wise], they act less as interesting, complex characters than as inverted prototypes: they incarnate the pure values of the dominant culture in a body and with a skin color usually associated with the opposite.

The espousing of universalism implicitly supports black stereotypes that affirm therapeutic modes of personal rehabilitation in lieu of structural change. Its denial of difference, moreover, forecloses social transformation into a truly multicultural society. Also, to the extent that super minorities are generally defaulted to male, they reinforce a male prerogative within minority communities that displaces black female subjectivity. Finally, the super minority often implicitly serves as an alternative to the endangered black male or black welfare queen or other "bad" (Jordan-Zachery 2009) black female figures.

In the first set of figures within this black cultural pathology melo-drama, Peter, who co-commits a theft of a vehicle in the opening scene of the movie, is contrasted with his older brother, Graham Waters, who happens to be a detective with the Los Angeles police force. We learn that the brothers have a mother who is poor, drug addicted, and an apparent female head of household. When the mother, concerned about the safety of her youngest son, asks her older son, Graham, the detective, to find him, Graham blows her off. The mother suggests the eldest's need to care for the younger brother—to in effect be his brother's keeper. When Graham, functioning as a provider, stocks his mom's fridge with food, the mother assumes that the youngest, Peter, has made the provisions available. Her attitude and actions suggest she is unfit as a mother, overly concerned about her wayward son. She is unappreciative of her eldest son, the super minority against which the younger brother is judged. Graham, we are left to assume, has gained success by his own will.

In the second contrasting pair, Cameron, a black male who is a successful, middle-class TV executive, derides Anthony, the other character in the opening scene. As I discussed earlier in this chapter, Cameron is involved in a police stop that throws into relief his and his wife's vulnerability before the law. Other scenes involving Cameron show the racist attitudes that shape and constrain his role as a TV executive. In order to assuage his woundedness, from the aforementioned car stop and other indignities he suffers at the hands of whites on his job, Cameron resists Anthony, Peter's friend in crime, who tries to steal his vehicle. In a car-jacking gone awry, Cameron repels the theft of his SUV, scuffles with Anthony, the would-be perpetrator, in the car, and eventually wrests away the thief's firearm. Police stop the vehicle, and Cameron has a verbal confrontation with two officers. In this scene, Cameron as the respectable black male swaps places with the actual career criminal in the vehicle, thus underscoring the supposed mutability of class before the illogics of police assumptions about black criminality. One of the cops is actually the "good" or virtuous white cop who was present during the stop-and-frisk the prior evening, involving Cameron and his wife. He is able to diffuse the situation, and, as Cameron is traveling home, he stops to drop off Anthony, his ne'er-do-well, endangered black male companion, noting with a look and tone of disgust, "You embarrass me."

It is unsurprising, then, that we see the themes of family jeopardy and patriarchal restoration in TV shows and movies, as I illustrate above in terms of *Grey's Anatomy* and *Crash*. What is less commonly considered, at least in terms of electoral politics, are the ways in which it shapes electoral strategies in terms of candidate self-presentation and campaign narratives. In this regard, the Obama case is exemplary.

In the historic 2008 Obama presidential campaign, gender is front and center in terms of a focus on family and black cultural pathology melodrama. The family in jeopardy emerges as a key refrain both in terms of Obama's personal biography and his political views. As he often remarks, he is the product of a single-parent family. Of his father he writes,

> At the time of his death, my father remained a myth to me, both more and less than a man. He had left Hawaii back in 1963, when I was only two years old, so that as a child I knew him only through the stories that my mother and grandparents told. (Obama 2004, 5)

He explains his struggle to resolve the conflicted relationship he had with his father and his racial identity development. Typically set in the context of his rendition of the all–too-familiar Horatio Alger story, Obama implicitly suggests the association of single parenthood and poverty, noting that his mother once received food stamps (Scott 2011, 2).

The reality of his circumstances as a son of privilege (being raised by an educated white mother and having access to an elite education) notwithstanding, Obama strategically used campaign rhetoric that fits within the common refrain of broken families in the United States. Notably, the whole question of father abandonment and personal responsibility was placed in the limelight in June 2008 when, during a Father's Day address at a predominantly black church, Obama took black fathers to task for not caring for or assuming material responsibility for their children. In this speech, Obama explains that the "most important" rock is the family, stating that "too many fathers . . . are missing—missing from too many lives and too many homes. They have abandoned their responsibilities, acting like boys instead of men. And the foundations of our families are weaker because of it" (Obama 2008c). This rhetoric, criticized by some in black communities (most notably Jesse Jackson) for essentially blaming the victim, has been a prominent theme within Obama's political career. Indeed, Jackson, in his now infamous "hot mic" debacle, was so bothered by Obama's "talking down to black folks" that he wanted to "cut [Obama's] nuts out" (Hurt 2008).

Jackson is, of course, correct in his assertion that an emphasis on personal responsibility and rehabilitating the black family through the generation of viable black patriarchs amounts to "talking down" to or blaming blacks. However, Jackson's comment also points to another way in which this romance of patriarchy structures not only intimate family relations but formal politics as well. If, as Patricia Hill Collins (2006) explains, the patriarchal model within families indeed comes to structure other social institutions and political arrangements (39–40), then we must interrogate this significance within black politics, particularly in light of black feminist objectives to assert substantive equality for black women. Indeed, what Jackson does not remark on, but is nevertheless embedded in his comments, is how the romance of patriarchy becomes embodied in two patriarchal types, namely: the black symbolic father and the super minority.

The black symbolic father refers to a male figure, such as Jackson, who stands in as a spokesperson for black communities and whose plight can be read metonymically with that of black people as a whole. Jackson's terror is not only at the flagellation of the beleaguered black masses, but, rather, the demise of an approach to black politics that Jackson best represents and embodies. Jackson, who has long occupied the role of black symbolic father in black politics, is reeling from a perceived Oedipal conquest—whereby a son kills his father to assume his patriarchal status. And, utilizing a basic form of Freudian projection, he wanted to do to Obama what he felt had symbolically been done to him. Obama's ascendance, thus, can be seen as a changing of the guard.

Obama's installation as the new black symbolic father also means something more than a changing of the guard. It also constitutes a new epoch for black men, with Obama operating as symbolic father for the black "nation." In "Destiny's Child: Obama and Election '08," Hortense Spillers affirms that Obama's historic showing in the Iowa primaries marked a moment of arrival and transcendence for black men. She writes,

On the campaign trail, Michelle Obama, you will remember, observed that her husband's journey marked the first time that she had felt proud of her country. You will recall that both Cindy McCain and Sarah Palin thought that the remarks of the First Lady To Be were abominable, and in the reactionary Right's own political choreography of idol worship, one is always proud of her country, as anything less than that announces an act of sacrilege. Mrs. Obama was not alone in signing the moment as singular, exceptional, and unique. Random witnesses that now belong to the archival index reported that for the first time they felt like an American; for the first time, like a citizen. And for some, it was not only the renewal of black manhood but more precisely the coming about of black manhood. The pregnancy of time, having reached its maturation, brought forth in a single propitious instant both the maieutic function of midwife and "the most powerful man on earth, now a black man," as Reverend T. D. Jakes thought about it, in the figural economy of Barack Obama. So on his fragile shoulders, then, rests the dream of fathers and sons, as mothers and daughters in this schema are muted. (Spillers 2012, 5–6)

As a symbolic father who stands in for the black nation Obama arguably serves as a black male who steps fully in as the idealized, super-minority citizen and symbolizes black male potentiality and achievement.

The black symbolic father, in Obama's case especially, is not only community spokesperson, representative, and instantiation of idealized, virtuous black manhood as it relates to the larger US community, but he also serves a "model" father for those within black communities. In this regard, the symbolic father functions in several ways: (1) as a point of identification and idealization of black manhood, (2) as a surrogate for the "absent black father," and (3) as an enforcer of patriarchal norms. This inward-looking, modeling mode of Obama as black symbolic father is especially evident in his interactions with audiences that are mostly black. As others have also pointed out (see, e.g., A. Reed 2008; Harris 2012; Price 2016; Purnell 2019), Obama adopts an authoritarian, castigating posture in interacting with black audiences. One of the most ignominious representations of this happened in his first presidential campaign in a speech he gave in Beaumont, Texas. After encouraging folks to focus on educational uplift in their homes, Obama turned to a critique that more directly framed parents as irresponsible. Obama states,

We can't keep on feeding our children junk all day long, giving them no exercise. They are overweight by the time they are 4 or 5 years old, and then we are surprised when they get sick. I know how hard it is to get kids to eat properly. But I also know that if folks letting our children drink eight sodas a day, which some parents do, or, you know, eat a bag of potato chips for lunch, or Popeye's for breakfast. . . . Y'all have Popeye's out in Beaumont? I know some of y'all you got that cold Popeye's out for breakfast. I know. That's why y'all laughing. . . . You can't do that. Children have to have proper nutrition. That affects also how they study, how they learn in school. (BET-Staff 2008)

He swipes at ne'er-do-well parents who are improper role models: they lack appropriate priorities, unable even to make basic healthy food choices for their children.

Tellingly, even when speaking in Africa, either at the African Union or in his father's homeland of Kenya, Obama adopts a similarly castigating stance, focused on changing "culture" and "habits," as with his US-based culture of pathology melodrama. I quote his Kenya speech at length to illustrate:

Now, I wanna be clear, corruption is not unique to Kenya. I want everybody to understand, that there's no country that's completely free of corruption. Certainly, here in the African continent there are many countries that deal with this problem. And, I want to assure you I speak about it wherever I go, not just here in Kenya. So, I don't want everybody to get too sensitive. But, the fact is, too often, here in Kenya, as is true in other places, corruption is tolerated because that's how things have always been done. People just think that that is sort of the normal state of affairs. And, there was a time in the United States where that was true, too. My hometown of Chicago was infamous, for Al Capone and the mob and the organized crime corrupting law enforcement. But what happened was that over time people got fed up and leaders stood up. And, they said we're not going to play that game anymore. And, you change the culture and you change habits. Here in Kenya it's time to change habits and decisively break that cycle, 'cause corruption holds back every aspect of economic and civic life. It's an anchor that weighs you down and prevents you from achieving what you could. (Obama 2015)

Even in the international context, when speaking to people of African descent Obama focuses on the corruption of culture that must be rehabilitated in order to break "cycles" of derelict behavior that undermine their achievement as full democratic subjects.

Other political scientists have also noted the derision with which Obama greets black audiences. In his discussion of "respectability as public philosophy," Frederick Harris, for instance, suggests that, during the 2008 campaign especially, this focus on respectability when speaking to black audiences eased white anxiety and aligned him with the black community as one who could administer "tough love" (Harris 2012, 104). In *The Race Whisperer*, Melanye Price (2016, 64–65, 68–70) also examines Obama's use of tough love when speaking to black audiences, underscoring how Obama is often inattentive to the ways in which his scripting of black cultural pathology will read with nonblack audiences. I agree that, when speaking to black audiences, Obama is especially keen to "code-switch," or adopt what he deems to be a communication style particularly suited to black audiences (Price 2016, 62–63). One can see this in his choice of language—his phrasing and imagery—as well as his dependence on cultural allusions, particularly to references familiar to black church audiences. Obama has consistently adopted the flagellating posture afforded by black cultural pathology melodrama throughout most of his public career to great effect. His public life and ideology are far from deracialized. Obama, rather, is the quintessential post-politics politician, benefitting from and trading on post-feminist, post-racial fantasies to great effect.

Later in this chapter I further my exploration of Obama as a post-politics politician. I explore what his My Brother's Keeper initiative represents not only in terms of his support for black cultural pathology thinking but also especially his positioning as a black male spokesperson for this paradigm. His opening speech, and other speeches in support of his initiative, focus on black audiences but are presented to broader audiences. As has been long established (see, e.g., Lubiano 1992; Legette 1999; Hancock 2004; Alexander-Floyd 2004; 2007; Jordan-Zachery 2009), black cultural pathology thinking has been a mainstay of US politics as a whole, including within black communities.

Significantly, black materialist feminist Rosemary Ndubuizu illustrates the political capital gained by black elected officials' authoritarian positioning vis-à-vis black mothers and families. In "(Black) Papa Knows Best," Ndubuizu (2014) notes the way Marion Barry, a stalwart of Civil Rights–era politics, remained relevant as a political figure, even among the emergence of the latest cohort of crossover candidates, like Obama and Cory Booker, then mayor of Newark, New Jersey, who fall outside of the protest model of black politics. Ndubuizu demonstrates that, by criticizing black single mothers and working to rid public housing of their pathological influence, Barry was able to sustain visibility in the milieu of Washington, DC. politics. This authoritarian impulse is exactly what Obama, in a different mode, delivers before black audiences.

Obama's castigation of black audiences has everything to do with his strained and ambivalent connection to his own paternal heritage. His biological father's absence is something that Obama has readily admitted and theorized about at length, impacting him so much so that it was the focus of his first book. Although he suggests a level of closure or reckoning with the father absence that impacted him and the feelings of abandonment as well that he may have felt when his mother left him with grandparents, while she engaged in professional pursuits, it is interesting to assess the lingering effect(s) on Obama as a person and politician. His notably calm bearing, even in the face of stark opposition, is one case in point. Some observe that the cool reserve he demonstrates is required for minorities who are read as angry or dangerous. Others, such as Hortense Spillers (2012, 12–15), suggest that this lack of reaction to critics or failure to show a range of emotions has something to do with the absence of a sustained relationship with his biological father.

One psychoanalyst, Justin Frank, writes that one can understand Obama's approach psychoanalytically. Frank (2011, 81–83), more specifically, claims that Obama's cool exterior and reserve are functions, among other things, of his having to suppress his feelings of abandonment and rage at both of his parents. He notes, however, that this rage finds outlets, such as, but not limited to, the assassination of Bin Laden (84) or his supporters at times (139–40). One outlet, I argue, is talking down to black audiences. It is in this mode, interacting with black communities, that Obama channels his supplanted rage. Black people, even if only at an unconscious level, stand in for the father whom Obama really did not know, that father who was "at once more than and less than a man" (Obama 2004, 5), as previously noted. Frank also provocatively observes that, for people like Obama who are not in touch with their anger in terms of openly acknowledging and expressing it, one loses the ability to recognize and respond to danger; further, it is in this way, he avers, that Obama may not have always truly recognized (or at least early enough) the negativity, hatred, and resistance visited upon him by Republicans and their constituents (132–34).

Obama also negotiates his disappointments with his own father by being a model minority or super minority. His image as a super minority is polished to a high shine, as Obama is greeted as an exceptional figure—politicos, for instance, such as his vice president Joe Biden, comment on his "articulateness" and describe him as "clean"—who defies the associations of dysfunction and inferiority typically aligned with blackness. It is unsurprising that Biden and Obama develop a bromance during Obama's two terms; their interracial relationship arguably functions as a form of miscege-nation as well. Obama is such an idealized super minority—some, in fact, dubbed him Barack the Magic Negro (Ehrenstein 2007), alluding to a standard trope in cinema, in which a black (again typically male) character who possesses "special powers" (Kempley 2003) or extraordinary abilities saves the day and facilitates self-actualization for whites. The super minority is a victor within the melodramatic framing of black liminality, a prime example of the respectable, idealized citizen who triumphs over any obstacles to personal success and approximates normative culture.

Also noteworthy is what some would describe as Obama's "deracialized" approach to formulating his political platform. As black political scientists Joseph McCormick Jr. and Charles E. Jones (1993) explain, deracialization has become a political "strategy" (76) used by politicians aiming to reach beyond black electoral bases to garner white support in election to mayoral, gubernatorial, and now presidential offices. More specifically, "*as an electoral strategy*," deracialization entails "avoiding explicit reference to [black or] race-specific issues, while at the same time emphasizing those issues that are perceived as racially transcendent, thus mobilizing a broad segment of the electorate" (76 [emphasis in original]). McCormick and Jones focus on deracialization as an electoral strategy, but acknowledge it as "an agenda-setting strategy" as well (73).

Certainly, there are elements of his policy proposals, such as Obamacare, that have a disproportionately positive impact on black and minority communities. But, in contrast to previous generations of black politicians who foregrounded black misfortune and in keeping with attempts at "deracialization," Obama's breakthrough presidential campaign supplanted issues of racism with a universal appeal to broader constituencies. Furthermore, as in his Philadelphia Speech, Obama positions racism and racist views as something in the past (see, e.g., Obama 2006). Such moves are consistent with the ideology of post-politics.

In this melodramatic theme of family restoration, we can see, once again, the confluence of culture and politics. Cultural representations, media representations, and formal politics all draw upon similar themes of family distress and restoration of wounded masculinity. They function in separate spheres, but in ways that reinforce and mutually influence the current political milieu. In the following section, I continue examining Obama as a post-politics politician by looking at how melodrama and the black cultural pathology paradigm played out in one of President Obama's signature efforts during his time in office and one of the few explicitly earmarked for minorities: the My Brother's Keeper initiative.

My Brother's Keeper and Black Cultural Pathology Melodrama

President Obama's My Brother's Keeper initiative—along with the White House Council on Women and Girls' summit on women and girls of color, developed in response to critics of My Brother's Keeper's lack of gender inclusivity—is a direct outgrowth of the black cultural pathology melodrama. My Brother's Keeper, in particular, positions black and Latino boys as in need of repair. It promotes an uplift philosophy for black communities, undermining blacks and Latinos as citizen-subjects and civic members. Furthermore, the summit on women and girls, as I discuss shortly, exemplifies a problematic, regressive gender complementarity.

President Obama kicked off his My Brother's Keeper initiative on February 27, 2014, signaling its importance by making his presentation in the White House. Surrounded by young black men and other proponents of black male crisis ideology, President Obama took the better part of an hour to explain the initiative's importance.

In the speech, Obama rehearsed familiar themes about black pathology, the impact of father absence, and the need for personal and community responsibility. Significantly, he centered himself in the framing of his initiative, positioning himself as an example of what can happen to young, fatherless men at risk, given the right attention and encouragement. I quote him at length to illustrate the importance of this connection:

> So as Christian mentioned, during my visit, they're in a circle and I sat down in the circle, and we went around, led by their counselor, and guys talked about their lives, talked about their stories. They talked about what they were struggling with, and how they were trying to do the right thing, and how sometimes they didn't always do the right thing. And when it was my turn, I explained to them that when I was their age I was a lot like them. I didn't have a dad in the house. And I was angry about it, even though I didn't necessarily realize it at the time. I made bad choices. I got high without always thinking about the harm that it could do. I didn't always take school as seriously as I should have. I made excuses. Sometimes I sold myself short. (Obama 2014)

Obama at times spoke about giving all children the opportunities he had, but his dominant point of reference remained black and Latino boys. The universal framing and his description of harm to black and Latino boys as "national issues" signals a desire for broad support for an agenda meant to assist the perceived impact of father absence and ostensibly broken homes.

In keeping with neoliberal rollback of government support, Obama suggested the government take a back seat in the effort to assist young men of color. He opined,

> And, in this effort, government cannot play the only—or even the primary—role. We can help give every child access to quality preschool and help them start learning from an early age, but we can't replace the power of a parent who's reading to that child. We can reform our criminal justice system to ensure that it's not infected with bias, but nothing keeps a young man out of trouble like a father who takes an active role in his son's life. (Applause) (Obama 2014)

Everyone, according to Obama, including "parents," "teachers," "business leaders," "tech leaders," and "faith leaders," will have to play their part (Obama 2014). This emphasis is in line with black cultural pathology thinking and prior policies and initiatives.

As previously discussed in this chapter, the black cultural pathology paradigm that grounds Obama's post-politics has long served as a type of urtext for neoliberal melodrama. It was the basis for the historic 1996 welfare reform, which sought to rehabilitate lazy black welfare queens thought to be raiding the public purse. It also provided grounding for fatherhood initiatives. Championed across several decades and administrations, from Al Gore's support during the Clinton administration to its development under George W. Bush to its solidification under the Obama and even the Trump administrations, fatherhood initiatives focus government resources on rehabilitating fatherhood, particularly in low-income, black communities. Support for fatherhood initiatives stemmed from black male crisis ideology championed among churches, represented in male-only schools and community programs, and anointed by the Louis Farrakhan– and Nation of Islam–led historic 1995 Million Man March, at that time the largest gathering on the nation's Mall (Alexander-Floyd 2007).[4]

Since the patriarchal macho and bootstrap self-help politics of black cultural pathology melodrama provide one of the dominant, if not the most dominant, frames in black and US political discourse, when Obama hails his My Brother's Keeper initiative, he is not doing anything particularly fresh idea-wise or ideologically risky. Instead, he is trading on a political paradigm that serves as the basis of US nationalist longings (whether associated with the state or black cultural nationalists): abject victims or national outsiders are rehabilitated and disciplined into model, worthy citizens—at least that is the hope. The My Brother's Keeper (MBK) initiative and summit on Advancing Equity for Women and Girls of Color trade on the same themes that animated the nested context (represented by *Grey's Anatomy* and *Crash*), out of which Obama's ascendancy to the presidency took shape. Obama's identification as symbolic father to children—in particular, one who models a transition from abject, fatherless subject to anointed, prototypical father and super minority—is especially salient. Obama and his signature MBK initiative crowning his eight years in office represent the maturation of the black cultural pathology melodrama. To be sure, although Obama suggests the death of Trayvon Martin (a youth gunned down by George Zimmerman, a white vigilante, and whose murder sparked Black Lives Matter) was part of the impetus for his initiative, it does very little to help young men like Trayvon. As Tanya Ann Kennedy (2017) pointedly states, "However empathetic President Obama has been to a young generation of black activists, his rhetoric and the policies legitimated by that rhetoric share more in common with the post-racial, post-feminist discourse of the mainstream media and conservative critics of the black family than with Black Lives Matter" (115).

Significantly, there has been pushback to Obama's My Brother's Keeper initiative, but it has focused on complementarity, as opposed to full-scale critique. In the months following the initiative's introduction, feminists and legal activists, led by noted black feminist Kimberlé Crenshaw, forged a multipronged strategy of critique, including op-ed placements and social media commentary and the circulation of two open letters to the president, one on behalf of black men and other men of color and one on behalf of women of color. In her *New York Times* op-ed titled "The Girls Obama Forgot," Crenshaw (2014) chastises President Obama for his exclusionary policy focusing on black male crisis ideology. Noting Obama's efforts to support women, she points out that, nevertheless, "My Brother's Keeper highlights one of the most significant contradictions of his efforts to remain a friend to women while navigating the tricky terrain of race. It also amounts to an abandonment of women of color, who have been among his most loyal supporters" (Crenshaw 2014). Crenshaw invokes the language of "mothers" and "sisters" who are left behind, gendered language that evokes sympathy and connection in terms of the language of family. She points out that a focus on black men, while certainly not original, finds a stark contrast to prior policy in recent memory. She also offers a blistering critique of black male crisis ideology, pointing out the ways that black girls and women also have issues on many of the same markers as black boys and men, and a varied, different set of issues as well, such as domestic abuse. If black males are the canary in the mine, as is often suggested in justification of black male crisis ideology, she insists, then we must tend not only to the canary but to the miners as well. She in the end adopts a tricky balancing act of challenging black male crisis ideology, but ultimately leaving it moored.

A May 28, 2014, missive, "Letter of 250+ Concerned Black Men and Other Men of Color Calling for the Inclusion of Women and Girls in 'My

Brother's Keeper'" (2014) struck a similar note regarding expansion of the president's initiative. The letter, couched in ameliorating terms emphasizing the group's support for President Obama, expressed "surprise" and "disappoint[ment]" at the exclusion of women and girls. For these signatories, My Brother's Keeper narrowly focused on black men and boys, excluding the ways in which entire black communities were harmed by a range of issues, issues that were implicitly framed as individualized and stemming from a "'culture of pathology'" (Letter of 250+ 2014). The letter argued that a "denunciation of male privilege, sexism and rape culture" should be "at the center of our quest for racial justice" (ibid.). It also emphasized throughout that male-centered initiatives should not be stopped. The letter paralleled the have-your-cake-and-eat-it-too approach to critique found in Crenshaw's op-ed. It forwarded a more radical agenda in language and did not challenge the core of the My Brother's Keeper initiative. "We cannot 'save' only black males from a house on fire" it said in its conclusion (ibid.), echoing the imagery of black women and girls being left in a distressing structure, in the same way Crenshaw's letter did. The women's version of the open letter had over a thousand signatories and featured such cultural and political luminaries as Angela Davis and Alice Walker, and senior and more junior academics, such as Beverly Guy-Sheftall and Brittney Cooper. Titled "Why We Can't Wait: Women of Color Urge Inclusion in 'My Brother's Keeper'" (2014), this open letter offered support for the letter written by black men and supported inclusion of women and girls, as its title suggests. Like the op-ed by Crenshaw and the letter written by the men, this letter critiqued black male crisis ideology, offering a profile of the ways in which black girls and women, and to a lesser extent Latina and Native American girls and women, suffer harm. It also hearkened to the legacy of the Civil Rights movement's community-wide effort toward social justice; utilizing metaphors, such as the canary in the mines, it emphasized a "shared fate" for black communities (ibid.). "To those who would urge us to settle for some separate initiative" the letter stated, "we need only recall that separate but equal has never worked in conditions of inequality, nor will it work for girls and women of color here" (ibid.). Still, although it argued for "inclusion" of girls and women and extension of the My Brother's Keeper frame beyond black male crisis narratives, a separate initiative is exactly what the Obama administration put in place in order to assuage its My Brother's Keeper critics.[5]

What is problematic with this strategy? Is it not better than not having any response at all? The answer lies in a different set of questions, namely: What norms are we ultimately upholding? What vision of politics and of the future are being authorized and supported? By this standard, of normative ends and political vision, the reformist strategy is profoundly lacking. The My Brother's Keeper initiative and the Advancing Equity for Women and Girls of Color effort pursued under the auspices of the White House Council on Women and Girls are essentially antidemocratic in character. Students of black politics have seen in the move from "protest to politics" (Rustin 1965) the hope and opportunity of previously disenfranchised civic members to be treated as citizens with all of the rights and opportunities theoretically attendant with that status. Black voters, as part of constituencies, can vote, agitate, and otherwise influence the political system in line with their and society's best interests in mind. Accountability is also basic to our understanding and expectations of democratic practice. Politicians ought to be held accountable by their constituents, and constituents should be unfettered in their efforts to exercise their prerogatives to make themselves heard.

With the complementarity or reformist model, however, we get a semblance of democratic practice without the political process or change with which it is ideally associated. First, regardless of his protestations to the contrary, President Obama is identified and idealized as a "black president," one who was seen, particularly while in office, as beleaguered by those uncomfortable with his identity in his role as president, despite his often high public opinion ratings. Opposition to a black president, then, is seen as potentially damaging. Paul Street (2009, xiii), quoted in the epigraph for this chapter, says it best: "I nonetheless stand behind the often unsympathetic portrayal presented here, claiming my right to walk (criticize Obama from a left-democratic perspective) and chew gum (defend him against racial bigotry and outrageous rightist misrepresentation and abuse) at one and the same time." The idealization of and identification with Obama for many foreclosed this option. In this way, the closing-ranks approach of protecting someone closely identified with black communities (Alexander-Floyd 2007) would likely prohibit strong support for actions seen as opposing the president. The impulse to close ranks and the likelihood of resistance to critiquing President Obama are some of the strategic reasons for choosing a "constructive critique" approach in raising questions about the My Brother's Keeper initiative.[6] The cost of this reformist/complementarity model, however, is the loss of a genuine ability of black constituencies to hold black elected officials accountable.

The complementarity/reformist model used to critique the My Brother's Keeper initiative is antidemocratic as well, because it supports the devolution of responsibility for the social good from the federal government or the state, regarded as the First Sector, and toward the private sector and civil society, or what are commonly known as the Second and Third Sectors, respectively. Black communities have traditionally been forced to turn to the Third Sector of civil society and community organizations for self-help (Alexander-Floyd 2007). This is nothing new. The promise of the Civil Rights movement in situating blacks as full voting citizens is, among other things, to make demands on the state, as others do. Obama's My Brother's Keeper initiative and Advancing Equity for Women and Girls of Color effort turn attention away from the state and toward the private sector and civil society, that is, the exact opposite of what a robust political approach would prescribe. This is why focusing on the fact that "X" amount of dollars is dedicated to these initiatives misses the point that, however much is allocated, it will never match what the federal government can provide and lets it off the hook in doing so. Moreover, as Lester Spence (2016) observes, although some might see private foundations as testing ideas that can be used more broadly, with Obama's black cultural pathology melodrama, government is exactly what people will not turn to, even if that is what is necessary. He writes: "When he says that this [My Brother's Keeper initiative] is not a big government program, he in effect makes it incredibly difficult for it to *become* a government program . . . [as] they'd actually have to fight *Obama* before they ever even got to Congress" (Spence 2016, 103 [emphasis in original]).

Finally, the add-women-and-girls approach leaves squarely in place the problematic ideological edifice of respectability politics as an antidote to black pathology. My Brother's Keeper emphasizes role modeling, as noted earlier. Identification is important and can be a healthy means of personal development, especially for the young. Identification, however, is not a solution for social problems. The emphasis of My Brother's Keeper places the liberal politics of identification front and center. The affirmation and institutionalization of "women and girls" as a framework for studying social problems or political issues is also seriously problematic. To be sure, much attention should be paid to the plight of young girls, and scholars such as Ruth Nicole Brown (2013) have long pointed out this fact. But the locution "women and girls" posits an equation of the two, compounding the unfortunate historical reality of infantilizing grown women and adultifying girls. The reverse usage, "girls and women," tries to at least get the developmental sequence correct but is insufficient to dislodge the general equation of these categories. The resulting impact of the complementarity strategy is to include "girls and women" in a problematic, fundamentally neoliberal frame for black and Latino politics specifically and US politics more generally. For the aforementioned reasons, although I was privileged to participate in a lively, daylong strategy session to respond to My Brother's Keeper, which eventually included the aforementioned op-eds and statements, I elected not to circulate or endorse the statements written.

Conclusion

Understanding the improbable story of President Barack Obama requires an intersectional analysis. The analysis in this chapter demonstrates that deracialization is, at best, an insufficient frame. Scholars must attend to melodrama as a political genre and the production of black liminality to capture the post-racial, post-feminist context that shapes popular culture and formal politics, including elections.

The melodramatic mode, with its attention to exaggerated emotion and its figuration of the social and political within interpersonal relations, marked by villains and victims, proves ideal for the post–Civil Rights, post-feminist political formation that has taken shape in the United States since the mid-1960s. This chapter's analysis of Barack Obama, including the nested context out of which his candidacy emerged, and his abiding commitment to black cultural pathology melodrama, signals common trends and developments within popular culture and political discourse that work to normalize simplistic definitions of equality as residing principally in formal signs of representative equality and undermine efforts at substantive institutional change. It leaves people with a dulled awareness of ongoing realities of inequality and oppression, as I discuss more in the book's conclusion. These narratives reconstitute familiar raced and gendered codes and stereotypes in ways that are palatable for new generations, rendering our vision of US politics and culture into something we, as viewers and as citizens, want to hold onto—namely, a meritocratic and unified US body politic, functional political institutions and social relationships, and the image of universalism. Of course, they circulate even as other narratives—relaying what some might consider more direct, overt forms of racism—remain. These post-feminist, post-racial melodramas offer a repertoire of fantasies that can make it difficult for some to apprehend the wide range of antifeminist, racist, and class-based elitism still present in US society.

The next chapter builds on our understanding of black women, melodrama, and post-politics by moving from a foregrounding of formal politics to a focused look at popular culture. In it, I explore black liminality and melodrama in the post-feminist, post-racial work of Tyler Perry, thus far one of the new millennium's most prolific and influential directors. There we see how the narratives of return and self-help strategies common in post-feminist popular culture take on new meaning in black communities, where the black cultural pathology melodrama is used to assuage wounded masculinity through the figure of an iconic female figure, Madea. Black women are counseled on relationships and proper femininity, and the cultural symbols of black womanhood (e.g., the mammy) are marshaled by masculinist prerogatives, through the figure of Madea, to do so.

3

Diary of a Mad Black (Wo)Man

*Tyler Perry, Wounded Masculinity, and Post-Feminist,
Post-Racial Melodrama*

Nobody's telling me I'm special. Nobody's telling me what
I can do, and here you are on television [Oprah]. . . . You
say [during that show, that] it's cathartic to start writing. I
started writing down all of the things that happened to
me. . . . It was a chain reaction.
—Tyler Perry ("Tyler Perry's Traumatic Childhood" 2010)

In an interview on *Our World*, a nationally televised cable show about
current events and politics in black communities, Spike Lee shared with
the show's host Ed Gordon his concern that black popular culture displayed traditional stereotypes of black people. Although Lee affirmed
the right of cultural workers to produce their own distinct creations,
he noted that shows such as Tyler Perry's *Meet the Browns* "harken[ed]
back to 'Amos 'n' Andy'" (Gane-McCalla 2009). Spike's critique was
particularly devastating given the derision with which *Amos 'n' Andy*
is typically viewed by black studies scholars and social critics, such as
Donald Bogel (1973) and Herman Gray (1995), among others. A radio
program and then TV show, *Amos n' Andy* featured black stereotypical figures, including Sapphire Stevens, a smart-mouthed, emasculating
black wife. Predictably, then, Spike Lee's comments touched off controversy surrounding black film and television viewership, and became so
heated that Perry stated in a press conference that Spike Lee could "go
straight to hell" ("Tyler Perry to Spike Lee" 2011); he also noted that
Lee has criticized others, such as Whoopi Goldberg and Oprah Winfrey
(Reeves 2011). Perry maintains that his characters reflect the reality of his
and other black people's experiences ("Tyler Perry to Spike Lee" 2011).
His most popular character—the subject of this chapter—is Madea.

A brash, gun-toting matriarch whom Perry plays in drag in each of her appearances, she skirts and violates the law, while protecting her family and dispensing her special brand of home truths.

The controversy between Lee and Perry illustrates that some of the same types of paradigm shifts displayed within formal politics are also holding sway in black popular culture. As noted in Chapter 2, within formal politics, a new wave of politicians, such as Barack Obama and Cory Booker, signaled a shift away from a protest model associated with Civil Rights activism. Likewise, within black popular culture it is possible to note a shift to a post-politics that strays away from protesting black inequality via racism or sexism, in service of emphasizing undemocratic forms of self-help politics. A successful, iconic filmmaker in his own right, Spike Lee, who emerged in the late twentieth century and continues to make films, is well known for using his work to expose and address US racism, as well as class and caste conflict within black communities. Although certainly not without his own critics (most especially within black feminist circles), in films such as *Do the Right Thing* and *Malcolm X*, and more recently *BlacKkKlansman*, Lee fashioned a model of filmmaking that sought to challenge social inequality in the United States. Perry's film, television, and theatrical productions, conversely, exhibit no such thematic emphasis on exposing racial animus or the effects of white supremacist ideology within black communities. Thus, although many have celebrated Perry's most recent triumph at the time of this writing—that is, opening a new, major movie production company in Atlanta, the first of its kind owned by an African American (Trubey 2019)—if it centers on Perry's work, it will prove a pyrrhic social victory.

Perry's opening of a new production company is not especially welcome, given the ideological content of his labor. More pointedly, Perry's films contrast sharply with prior filmic efforts focused on exposing racism or presenting nonstereotypical images; instead, his films embrace a post-feminist, post-racial ideology that actively stands in opposition not only to antiracist film traditions, but also black feminist perspectives on the family and critiques of cultural symbols of black womanhood. For decades, as noted in prior chapters, black feminists have exposed the devastating impact of the "controlling images" (Collins 1990) of the mammy, matriarch, Sapphire, and other symbols of black womanhood, not only culturally but also in terms of social policy; to be sure, they have been especially critical of suggestions that black women are emasculating black men or that female-headed, single-parent households, as Moynihan and others have suggested, are the scourge of black communities (see, e.g., Jewell 1993; Hancock 2004; Alexander-Floyd 2007; Jordan-Zachery 2009). Although affirming the family as an institution that has been critical to black survival, they have also criticized "dominator" models of patriarchy (hooks 2004, 131–32). They argue for a redefinition of this cultural space (see, e.g., Alexander-Floyd 2007), one that eschews Western models of female domesticity or "marketplace masculinity" (Gavanas 2004, 7, 70–72), where manhood is equated with men fulfilling a breadwinner model within black families.

Against this backdrop, Perry's films, which center on and romanticize patriarchal family models, play on stereotypical images of black women and feature narratives of self-help or personal life makeovers that stand in sharp opposition to radical black feminism. As Stephanie Allen (2016, 79) remarks, "We cannot simply dismiss his [Perry's] stereotypical representations as humor or claim uncritically that they are basic truths about black life. Stereotypes have real-life consequences for black people . . . so we must seriously consider the impact of the material reality of these negative images on black lives and on Black women in particular." Through their representations of the mammy and matriarch, or the good and bad black mother, respectively, Perry's films produce black post-feminist subjects by presenting dominant patriarchal fantasies infused with melodramatic frames shot through with pathos.

In Perry's work, black women and black people in general appear as liminal subjects. In terms of individual characters, black women are split between acceptable and unacceptable forms of femininity and motherhood. As Manigault-Bryant, Lomax, and Duncan (2014, 11) observe, "By distinguishing what is supposedly 'normal' from what is supposedly 'abnormal' and thus what is 'acceptable' from what is 'unacceptable,' 'splitting' places black women and girls within a murky set of cultural representations, theories, and meanings that have over time produced a sea of reductive 'facts' and artifacts." My work affirms their observations. Melodramatic splitting, as I demonstrate here, is reproduced and circulated in Perry's productions. In terms of depicting black communities as a whole, his films consistently portray victims and villains who overcome social problems through personal transformation and triumph, not protest or formal politics. Given his embrace of black liminality, this chapter examines the competing representations of the mammy and matriarch in Perry's films that function ideologically to affirm regressive modes of femininity and masculinity, support hegemonic gender ideology, and undermine political efforts to influence the state.

My analysis centers on the first of Perry's films, *Diary of a Mad Black Woman* (Grant 2005) (*Diary*), which introduces Perry's ever-popular Madea character, a mainstay of his most successful ventures. I begin here because it is his breakthrough film and, in many ways, reveals the themes that will come to define much of his work (Kelly 2016, 118). As I discuss further, it provides a "fantasmatic" (Tate 1998) or template for his body of work as a whole. It demonstrates, moreover, the role of melodrama as a context for supporting post-feminist, post–Civil Rights thinking. I expand my exploration of melodrama, moreover, by examining the operation of desire. The unconscious desires driving the melodramatic action in these films reflects a cultural ethos that privileges a neoliberal self-help orientation. This neoliberal self-help orientation is often seen in films—most iconically, *Bridget Jones's Diary* (Maguire 2001). In the book and film by the same name, Bridget Jones works to transform her physical appearance and life in a desperate struggle to be coupled with a man. As I discuss in this chapter, *Diary of a Mad Black Woman* can be seen as black culture's answer to the Bridget Jones Diary phenomenon and the "dating panic" with which it is associated. In this way, examining melodrama reveals aspects not only about Perry as a writer, director, and producer, but, most importantly, about the culture of the audiences that consume his work.

As previously noted, in my exploration of *Diary* I seek to discern the "fantasmatic" (Tate 1998) or unconscious thematic structure at play in Perry's work. The idea of a fantasmatic is taken from the work of Jean Laplanche, the famed French psychoanalyst, known, among other things, for his translation of Freud's work from German to French. Tate, drawing on the work of Laplanche, explains, "The fantasmatic is not only an internal or masked thematic that determines a subject's unconscious associations; it is also a dynamic formation that seeks conscious expression by converting experience into action" (Tate 1998, 50). There is a reason we see the repetition of a complex interplay of loss, attachment, alienation, and plenitude at work in Perry's films. I am, thus, concerned with Perry's biography or psychic struggles, particularly as they signal those elements of his personal narrative and his productions that bear commonalities more broadly with black viewers. More specifically, Perry's experiences of emotional, physical, and sexual abuse, as well as his sense of wounded masculinity (Alexander-Floyd 2007) and potential ambivalence toward women, animate his pathos-driven plots. Most of his Madea films center on self-help makeover narratives for women and support traditional Western notions of patriarchal family structures. These themes are part and parcel of a long-standing fixation in black and mainstream US culture not only on traditional notions of the family, but also on taming emasculating black female matriarchs and bolstering black male authority in the home (i.e., part of the legacy of the Moynihan Report as urtext, as discussed in previous chapters). In this regard, I lay out the connection between the psychic and the social, how the personal in fact becomes cultural and political in its expression and impact, existing in dynamic, co-constitutive relationship with various realms of influence and discussion. I am concerned as well about explicating why certain conscious or unconscious desires regarding loss, abandonment, and "plenitude" (Tate 1998, Chapter 1) are appealing to viewers in this neoliberal moment.

As I have noted throughout, neoliberalism gears our public consciousness to think in terms of undemocratic definitions of self-help—that is, where social problems and their solutions are read in terms of micro-institutions, such as the family, as opposed to macro-level structures or a broader set of political and social forces. In this context, it is unsurprising but significant that melodramatic narratives, such as *Diary*, that focus on issues such as coercive control (Stark 2007) as the outcome of individual choices, as opposed to a prevalent form of abuse that is undergirded culturally and politically by a dominator model of patriarchy, are so popular. Neoliberalism's depoliticization of socioeconomic and political problems allows such challenges to develop unchecked by democratic forms of social protest and political contestation. Melodramatic narratives such as *Diary* are important to study. They allow us to see how conscious and unconscious desires can serve to translate macro-level concerns into micro-level sites, such as the family or interpersonal relationships, that are commonly associated with melodrama.

My exploration of melodrama, post-feminism, and post-racial ideology proceeds in two parts. First, I elaborate, with various degrees of emphasis and sometimes at some length, several bodies of scholarship that are important to understanding the prevalence and function of the mammy and matriarch in popular culture during the current era. Specifically, I detail the connection between post-feminist subjectivity; black female subjectivity, as represented in the images of the mammy and matriarch; minstrelsy; and psychoanalysis, explaining how these theoretical threads help us understand melodrama and post-feminism as they relate to father absence and anxiety about rates of marriage, themes that are particularly resonant within black communities. Second, I examine the competing, split images of the good or lost black mother (mammy) as well as the bad black mother or matriarch in *Diary*, represented in the figure of Madea, as well as in the main character, Helen. Examining these images allows me to uncover the underlying structure of Perry's thematic productions. Doing so will help me to explain several aspects about desires (conscious, unconscious, or both) fulfilled by the figures of Madea and Helen, namely: how people take pleasure in a derogatory, stereotypically based image of Madea as mammy; how black men who gender cross-dress in service of comedic performances arguably occupy the plenitude associated with the mammy or good black mother and in so doing reassert male patriarchal authority; and how the censure and rehabilitation of the bad black mother gets mapped onto the storyline portrayed by Helen, one of the movie's central characters. I use insights from Freud about dreamwork, specifically the concepts condensation, displacement, and multivocality, and from object relations theory, regarding perspectival free association, to assess themes in the film. I argue throughout that these images of the black mammy and matriarch serve a powerful disciplining function by authorizing acceptable forms of femininity, and relocating complex social problems into the realm of personal address.

Understanding the Black Mammy/Matriarch in the Neoliberal Era

As we have seen in preceding chapters, the post-feminist subject is uniquely suited to meet the demands of contemporary neoliberalism, a cultural and economic system that reintroduces and reproduces liberal notions of the individual subject. Individual subjects under neoliberalism are free to decide about their own happiness, needing only to adjust their personal outlooks, ambitions, or priorities. As Diane Negra (2009, 5) observes, "Over and over again the post-feminist subject is represented as having lost herself but then (re)achieving stability through romance, de-aging, a makeover, by giving up paid work, or by 'coming home.'" This focus on self-recovery and transformation fits neatly within neoliberalism's emphasis on individuals' choices and actions as the proper scale of change. Individuals, too, however, become commodities in a neoliberal political and cultural economy that preys upon this notion of autonomy. Cultural consumers' attention, moreover, is set on developing in them those habits of being that will encourage economic consumption and deflate efforts to shape national governments in any way that will exceed what is necessary for maintaining international circulation of goods and services (Goldberg 2009). Individuals and marginalized communities become directed over and over again to read their dissatisfactions in terms of personal failings and choices, as opposed to resulting from prevailing ideologies and practices regarding class, gender, race, and sexuality via culture, the state, or both.

Narratives of return, where protagonists travel back to their hometowns or reconnect with family and community, and of self-reinvention are common within post-feminism, but are especially resonant within African American communities. Specifically, because of the Moynihan Report's legacy of viewing father absence and disproportionately lower rates of marriage as the sources of black inequality, there is an even greater emphasis on family formation and a push for traditional, Eurocentric notions of patriarchal families. Indeed, for decades, scholars and pundits alike have commented on the difficulties that inhere in black male-female relationships (see, e.g., Hare and Hare 1984). The notion that black women hold high (read: unrealistic) standards for mates is a persistent, hegemonic narrative explaining the sources of "strife." That is, black women are said to look for qualities in men, particularly in terms of financial capacity, that are both undesirable and untenable, because they signal a materialistic focus on income and wealth as markers of success, markers that are impossible for black men to meet given their historically low un- and underemployment rates (Walton and Smith 2001).

Jimi Izrael, author of *The Denzel Principle* (Izrael 2010), for instance, argues that relatively low marriage rates among black women are not a function of a lack of eligible black men, but, rather, black women's misplaced priorities on career success, as opposed to romance, or an insistence on finding a "perfect" match via education or economic status, among other factors. Black women, in reality, might appear superficially to match these narratives, since, in most age groups, the numbers of black women who have never wed can be higher than that of other women (see, e.g., Kreider and Ellis 2011, 2–4). Against this backdrop, it is unsurprising to find a heightened attention in black post-feminist narratives (authored principally, although not exclusively, by men) detailing what constitutes desirable models of femininity, and emphasizing the shoring up of male leadership in the home (see, e.g., Harvey 2009). Throughout various post–black feminist narratives, women are shown as failures in light of hegemonic norms of femininity, and stereotypical images of black women, such as the mammy and matriarch, are used as mechanisms to ridicule black female independence and black women as authority figures in the home.

Psychoanalysis proves vital to understanding the persistence and function of these overdetermined representations of black womanhood: the black mammy and black matriarch, that is, the good and bad black mother. As discussed in Chapter 1 regarding former Secretary of State Condoleezza Rice, the mammy is generally seen as a black woman who is supportive of white families and white racial ideology and enjoys existing in a subservient role. The matriarch is her closely related opposite: an abusive, poor mother who usurps the proper role and authority of black men in the home and community. These images are not static, however, and are often used inconsistently, wherein the various characteristics constituting one stereotype blend with those pertaining to the other. (Indeed, the mammy, even in some of its earliest articulations under slavery, bore elements of the matriarch; she was loving and nurturing toward white families, but abusive toward her own [Riggs 1986]). The repetition of the mammy and matriarch "controlling images" (Collins 1990) signals their pliability, but more than that, their connection to deeper processes of unconscious desire that take shape within cultures dominated by white, Western models of patriarchal thinking, and that drive our cultural fixation on competing representations of the maternal and its symbolic—and, by extension, to femininity writ large. Psychoanalysis provides critical insight into what accounts for why the good and bad black mother emerge at particular historical junctures as ubiquitous and politically expedient cultural representations and types.

In Freud's famed Oedipal complex, young children grapple with shifting attachments to mothers and fathers as they develop in early life (Freud [1955] 2010). In the initial stages of development, both male and female children bear strong attachments to their mothers, associating them with sustenance, caring, and affection. Conflict arises, however, as children develop and grow. Boys see themselves competing with their fathers for rights to the mother, and, as in the Greek myth for which the complex gets its name, imagine themselves killing the father so they can possess their mothers as sex objects. Boys eventually come to grips with their inability to have their mothers (due to the castration complex), and postpone satisfaction of desire as they look forward to the day when they will have a woman of their own and become the father. Girls, on the other hand, according to Freud's theory, vie with their mothers for their fathers' attention, and struggle as well with the realization that they have no penis, a symbol of sexual potency, and social authority, hence, harboring "penis envy." They resign themselves to one day being able to have a man of their own and produce a baby. The baby, in this paradigm, replaces the penis or phallic power (Freud [1955] 2010).

Although Freud sees this as a real biological development, Jacques Lacan, in his rereading of Freud, understands the Oedipal and castration complexes in terms of discourse or structural linguistics. Lacan reads the pre-Oedipal period as a mirror stage in which children perceive themselves (wrongly) as a unified subject. The Oedipal moment forces a detachment of both sexes from the mother, and invites male and female children into their position in language or the law of the father. As Elizabeth Wright explains,

> Though the child tries to identify with the mother's desire, the Father as the figure of law (unlike Freud's natural father) insists that the child take its place in the order of language as "he" or "she." The possessing or not possessing of the phallus (not the biological organ) determines the way

both sexes assume their lack: both have to give up being the phallus for the mother. According to this theory, then, castration is a symbolic event suffered by both sexes, irrespective of their biological sex. (1992, xiv–xv)

This reading of sexual difference as a product of language has been useful for many feminist analysts, although not uniformly so (xv), as it does not easily point to the disruption of sexual difference and its political effects (xv–xvi).

Of course, it is worth underscoring that, for some, the sexist, racist, or colonialist limitations of Freudian, Lacanian, or other psychoanalytic theory and methods may place them beyond the realm of usefulness. Freudian and Lacanian theory are produced within highly racialized and gendered worlds of heterosexuality, and may seem particularly ill-fit for assessing post-politics. Moreover, mainstream psychoanalysis as a method and cultural mode of critique has generally not engaged questions of racism and sexism—not to mention an intersectional approach.

As noted in the Introduction, however, my work draws from and builds on a tradition of black intellectual engagement with psychoanalysis (see, e.g., Tate 1998; Spillers 2003; Ahad 2010). As a Critical Black Feminist, psychoanalysis is a significant and necessary interpretive tool. Claudia Tate's classic essay "Freud and His 'Negro': Psychoanalysis as Ally and Enemy of African Americans" (1998) provides particularly important guidance for those of us utilizing psychoanalysis for social justice. For Tate, psychoanalysis is an interpretive mode that must be wrested from the limitations of its birth and marshaled to assess racist and other forms of domination. She deftly uses psychoanalysis to examine, among other things, Freud's use of a joke where a lion eats a "negro" or black person, arguing essentially that Freud positions himself with dominant social power in the figure of the lion to hide his own anxiety surrounding his Jewishness. Through using psychoanalysis to lay bear the levels of racial, gender, and class politics embedded in Freud's use of this joke and his ideas more generally, Tate both acknowledges the problematic origins of psychoanalysis, in some regards, and demonstrates its ability to unpack contemporary modes of domination (1998, 61). Psychoanalysis, for Tate, can be "reformulated" to account for the race, gender, and class politics of its genesis and targeted toward assessing culture and society (61). She states, "While such a regrounded psychoanalysis will neither be a cure for all social ills nor a grand narrative of Enlightenment, it can nevertheless be a powerful tool for analyzing, for example the deep origins of racist, ethnic, and gender displacements in contemporary Western culture" (61). Here, in my study of Perry's Madea figure, I use psychoanalysis from a Critical Black Feminist perspective. I examine the ways in which this figure of Madea ties into the complicated ideas about desire, power, and authority that many black people experience in contemporary US society.

For my purposes, I am, thus, less concerned with the putative phallocentric nature of Lacan's work, the biological determinism of Freud's, or the suggestion that either of the aforementioned theorists smack of essentialism, although such arguments are valid and important (see, e.g., Thompson [1950] 1964). Rather, I am more concerned with the explanatory value of Freud's and Lacan's formulations in mapping the ways in which unconscious desire manifests itself in black culture and politics.

In this regard, Freud's Oedipal complex (its significant limitations notwithstanding) can be seen as a representation of the West's dominant white, middle-class, patriarchal family romance and the backdrop against which black cultural pathology melodrama takes shape. Furthermore, Lacan's rereading of Freud is particularly useful, as it detaches Freud's theories from the biological realm, and signals the way that unconscious operations of desire operate through language. My analysis is influenced by Lacan's orientation in this regard, and elaborates how psychoanalytic constructs, such as the phallus and lack, get played out in the process of discourse and representation. Finally, following Žižek, I am also concerned about the way that fantasy reveals desire (Žižek 1989). Here, we see, through the melodrama-laden fantasy played out in *Diary*, a range of desires driven by black male experience of lack, and the cultural primacy in black communities on achieving traditional masculine and feminine roles within patriarchal family systems.

Importantly, however, as it relates to the family and as previously noted, black feminists, such as Angela Davis (2000) and Hazel Carby (1987), have long argued that black and white women's relationship to the family critically differ, given the family's central role in survival for blacks throughout US history. Although I do suggest a reworking of our understanding of intimate relationships and conceptions of family, such a project necessitates that we first assess the limitations of prevailing pernicious patriarchal models as they are currently conceived. Black feminist appropriation of Freudian and Lacanian psychoanalytic theory is, in many ways, best suited for this task.

Freudian psychoanalytic theory, for instance, helps us to understand how women are framed within dueling representations of the good, omnipotent mother, associated with the pre-Oedipal phase, and the bad mother (already perceived as castrated, because she lacks a penis), symbolized by Oedipal conflict. The good mother represents maternal plenitude and sustenance. Children view the mother here as an idealized image of protection and nurturance. This connection is severed during the Oedipal stage (J. Mitchell [1974] 2000). When circumstances occasion feelings of ambivalence toward one's mother—as, for instance, when a mother who is loved because of her care and sacrifices on behalf of her family is nevertheless resented or despised because she also abuses or allows her children to be abused or is seen as morally lacking—children may idealize and feel the need to make reparations, not to the father, as is generally the case upon Freudian readings, but rather to the mother (see, e.g., Tate 1998, Chapter 2 on DuBois).

I suggest that a different relationship between infants and the mothers within black communities may lead to different gender identity formation within the family. The focus on black father absence and the symbols of the mammy and matriarch suggest a lack of patriarchal rite or "father law" in black communities. In some cases, this lack of patriarchal rite or father law generates hostility and feelings of abandonment that can be displaced onto black mothers—and by extension, to black women in general, as well as, as in the case of President Obama and discussed in Chapter 2, to black communities as a whole. By patriarchal rite I mean more than is commonly perceived as "father absence," but, rather, the prohibitions produced during enslavement that disallowed the correlating development of the black family along the lines of the white family. As Hortense Spillers (2003, 204) observes,

> According to Daniel Patrick Moynihan's celebrated "Report" of the late sixties [sic], the "Negro Family" has no father to speak of—his name, his law, his symbolic function mark the impressive missing agencies in the essential life of the black community, the Report maintains, and it is,

surprisingly, the fault of the daughter, or the female line. This stunning reversal of the castration thematic, displacing the name and the law of the father to the territory of the mother and daughter, becomes an aspect of the African-American female's misnaming.

In a context where African American families do not conform to the "name . . . law . . . [or] symbolic function" of the father—where matriarchal rite or mother law prevails or, rather, is *perceived* to do so—the castration complex for men and penis envy for women arguably take on heightened importance and different manifestations than in mainstream, white culture. Men and women, then, may struggle with ambivalence that they channel either through making reparation to (or attempting to inhabit) an idealized maternal imago of a lost mother seen as the good mother or through remaking, disciplining, mastering, or even eradicating the lost mother who appears as the bad black mother.

The ambivalence and heightened levels of anxieties produced, I argue, are translated into unconscious psychological mechanisms, such as the condensation and displacement found in "dream work" (Freud [1955] 2010, Chapter 6) and the multivocality that can occur in free association in psychoanalytic sessions (Bollas 2009, 16–18). With condensation and displacement, repressed feelings are either compressed and symbolized via one seemingly unrelated one or placed onto another object, respectively (Freud [1955] 2010, 296–99, 322–26). Multivocality, on the other hand, refers to an analysand's unconscious expression of ideas and viewpoints reminiscent of their earlier selves or other people who have influenced them (Bollas 2009, 16–18). I examine these mechanisms of displacement, condensation, and multivocality here in terms of Perry's depiction of Madea and Helen.

These mechanisms of displacement, condensation, and multivocality come into play, I suggest, because some black men arguably experience both contradictory feelings of greater veneration, as well as negation, of their mothers and heightened levels of castration anxiety as a result of gendered racism. Again, generally speaking, when boys confront the Oedipal complex, they desire their mothers and fear castration from their fathers. Their anxiety or fear of castration from their fathers is allayed when they accept their symbolic castration, but this is only temporary. They do so realizing that they will one day have a woman of their own in place of the mother. In a situation where black men are either absent or perceived as being men dominated by women of their same race, several things arguably hold. First, since the mother is the sole parent or perceived as being dominant even when a man is present in the home, there is arguably a stronger attachment between mothers and sons. This attachment is vexed or conflicted, however, since women are seen as lacking a penis and lack the position authorized as powerful within the broader society. Women are not supposed to have authority over men, so men in this situation can be narrativized as castrated and, thus, effeminate. Second, although one might propose that the lack of a father in the home or the perception of black women dominating black men would prevent the castration anxiety that typically accompanies the Oedipal situation, the opposite may actually occur. The black father may appear as a desired love object and the imposition of racial stigma and race-based discrimination and inequality in the context of white supremacy mark white men as patriarchal or societal father figures. "[A] dual fatherhood is set in motion," Spillers (2003, 228 [emphasis in original]) explains, "comprised of the African [American] father's *banished* name and body and the captor [or white] father's mocking presence." Thus, the social practice, common under legal segregation, of white men referring to black men as "boys" is not an innocent act, but rather marks and effects a disempowered social (masculine) status for black men vis-à-vis white men, who symbolically serve as a superior class of patriarchal authority.

It is significant, as well, that black men who were lynched suffered castration and were often erroneously accused of desiring white women sexually. The myth of the black male rapist as a justification for lynching bears striking resemblance to the Oedipal drama in which a "son" or person of lower social status is seen as desiring the "mother," that is, in this symbolic context, white women. If we read the psychoanalytic dimensions of white supremacy, we can see that white communities made real the threat of castration implied in the Oedipal drama by moving beyond the imaginary and literally castrating black men who were lynched. This practice undergirded the idea of the white male as the most powerful "Father." Finally, as I discuss elsewhere (Alexander-Floyd 2007, especially Chapter 2), women may be seen as occasioning the disappearance or weakness of male father figures or despised for a perceived condition of emasculation.

Black women, likewise, may experience ambivalent feelings toward mothers—and fathers as well. Because they are already deemed castrated, women confront penis envy as opposed to anxiety over castration. From a Freudian perspective, which outlines a heterosexual matrix of positions for male and female, a female's desire for a penis and the phallic power it can represent is deferred until they have a man of their own and have a child, which replaces the penis.

Of course, this psychic imaginary is not an abstract, universal construct; hence, what we must discern is how it changes and evolves, according to temporal and social contexts. With this in mind, we can consider how this scenario bears several interesting implications for black women in the early twenty-first century in the United States, given the fact that they never marry in greater numbers or marry later compared to other women (Raley, Sweeney, and Wondra 2015). First, black women may see having children as a means of having authority and love, but such feelings or attachments may in fact be intensified in those cases where a male co-parent is not present. Second, the absence of a father figure for women may intensify their desire for affirmation from men. It is not simply having a child that provides relief for penis envy, but, indeed, having a man to replace the father. This desire of course may be amplified in cases where women have failed or nonexistent relationships with their fathers. Finally, as with men, women may blame their mothers for the absence or inadequacies of their fathers, or both.

Against this backdrop, we can better account for the seeming ubiquity and diverse meanings of representations of the good and bad black mother—the mammy and matriarch—in contemporary black culture, including their relationship to comedic gender cross-dressing by black men. Black male actors who comedically cross-dress as black women often enact a complex interplay of desire or attachment and appropriation. For many, the fear of castration that forces the boy child to abandon the mother's love and align with the father and the father's power is disrupted. They align themselves with their mothers and admire and desire the maternal plenitude and perceived power she is said to occupy (Tate 1998). At the same time, black men may perceive themselves both individually and on the whole as castrated and deprived of the position and authority of patriarchal rite in black communities. This state of affairs is generally attributed, in no small part, to the position of black matriarchs. Cross-dressing in this comedic context is not necessarily an act of effemination, but rather a means by which men can occupy the goodness and plenitude assigned to the good black mother or mammy, as well as the power and authority assigned to matriarchs.

Given the gross caricatures that are also involved in comedic cross-dressing, we can see the derogation and cultural violence visited upon black women through such representations.[1] Here I draw a distinction between cross-dressing in general or gender performance and Perry's comedic cross-dressing. "Perry as Madea," Gene Kelly (2016, 129) explains, "isn't a trans* portrayal, and certainly is not on par with classic drag queen movies in the queer canon." Perry's comedic cross-dressing, which centers on stereotypes of black women, is pernicious and bears resemblance to minstrelsy. Minstrelsy provides a critical framework for understanding Perry's *Diary*, in general, but particularly in terms of representations of the good and bad black mother. Whereas society suggests women ought to be demure and silent or behind the scenes, Madea's character seems to embrace the sassiness and brashness often associated with black women who are deemed Sapphire figures. Her brandishing and use of a firearm also affirms her ability to protect and defend herself and those she loves. Beyond this initial level of representation, there are several questions relevant to a consideration of melodrama, race, and post-feminism raised by this much-loved character, namely (1) Its stereotypical basis notwithstanding, why did Tyler Perry choose to portray this character himself, as opposed to allowing a woman to play this role, and to what effect? (2) In a society where black men are often seen as emasculated, particularly at the hands of black women, why would a man fashion a role where he plays a female character? and (3) To what extent do figures, such as Madea and Helen, the lead female character, represent the interests, conflicts, and anger not of black women but rather of black men? Black men who adhere to a notion of their emasculation by black women, to be sure, may be seen as having a decided interest in reclaiming their position of authority vis-à-vis black women.

To answer these questions, it is necessary to understand Perry's Madea figure in light of what critic Joseph Roach (1992) refers to as "genealogies of performance" both in terms of, first, black male comedy and, second, blackface minstrelsy. As Roach observes, genealogies of performance (or performance genealogies) constitute "the transmission and dissemination of cultural practices through collective representations" (1992, 462). In this light, it is significant that the gender cross-dressing of a popular comedian in a film inspired Perry's development of Madea. Perry relates that he got the idea for Madea by watching Martin Lawrence and Eddie Murphy play female matriarchs in drag in their hit movies, *Big Momma's House* and *The Klumps*, respectively (Perry 2020). He has remarked, moreover, that Madea is a fusion of his mother's "wisdom" (Kloer 2006) and his defiant aunt (variously referred to as Mayola or Jerry)'s strength (Kloer 2006; Eng 2009; "Tyler Perry's Traumatic Childhood" 2010). Eddie Murphy, in turn, is part of a line of other black comedians who have dressed in drag as part of the effort to solicit audiences' laughs. Noted comedians—including Murphy's contemporaries, such as Arsenio Hall, Jamie Foxx, and, again, Martin Lawrence—have all portrayed stereotypical renderings of black women to great commercial effect. And, earlier comedians, such as Richard Pryor and Flip Wilson, of course, preceded them. Wilson's "Geraldine," a sassy, Sapphire figure, in fact, remains one of comedy's most noted drag personas. Significantly, we do not have a similar genealogy of performance concerning well-known examples of black women comedically cross-dressing as men. Black women are already seen as hypermasculine and occupying the role of heads of household. This is viewed as being contrary to the desired social norm. Presuming they could have access to the means to do so, black women ridiculing black men through comedic dress would, therefore, not have the same purchase. Society is open to black men dressing as black women for denigration and parody, ridicule and domination, as they are the "other of the other" (Wallace 1990). Further, as I argue later, there are particular political stakes: with Madea, Perry, and by extension viewers, occupy and reclaim the plenitude associated with the mammy and assertiveness associated with the matriarch.

In addition to the more temporally immediate connection of black comedians in drag, the Madea figure and other black male drag performances are also connected to blackface minstrelsy in terms of nation-building and community formation, on the one hand, and subjugation through exoticism and appropriation, on the other hand. As Michael Rogin (1996) has observed, minstrelsy was critically important in terms of nation-building, because it melded heretofore ethnically identified groups, particularly the Irish and Jews, into white American identity and the assimilationist paradigm. Rogin notes, by way of comparison, that in Germany, nationalism centered on emplacing Jews as an out-group against which membership in national community was defined. "Anti-Semitism united the disparate nationalities and classes of Central Europe," according to Rogin (1996, 63). Similarly, in the United States, blacks served as the "constitutive outside" (Butler 1993) against which white America and inclusion were set. Rogin explains: "Whereas Jewish outsiders created immigrant insiders in the Hapsburg Empire and the Weimar Republic, in the United States African Americans performed that function" (1996, 63). By participating in the racial ideology of minstrelsy, Irish and Jewish newcomers could assert a sense of belonging, as they affirmed the US sense of national self or identity (56). Of course, gender, sex, and class also mutually constituted these racial elements.

Blackface minstrelsy solidified blacks' outsider status by presenting monstrous, dehumanizing caricatures of African Americans and making blacks the target of cross-racial desire that was appropriated or "mastered" by whites in service of their personal pleasure and affirming a black-white divide. Blackface minstrels—whites (typically) who blackened their faces with cork and performed as "blacks"—presented African Americans with wildly exaggerated physical features—exceedingly large lips, bucked eyes, corked black skin—and acted out storylines centered on servitude and featuring blacks as unintelligent, savage, and hypersexual. Such depictions were powerful cultural productions that rationalized the enslavement of blacks and mistreatment of free slaves (Riggs 1986).

Blackface minstrelsy also centered on the cultural appropriation of black culture and white male desire and fantasies regarding black masculinity. As noted historian Lawrence (Larry) Levine argues in *Ethnic Notions* (Riggs 1986), a documentary on black stereotypes and their cultural production, whites projected their racial fantasies onto minstrels' performative bodies, allowing themselves to "emote" as black, to inhabit, as it were, the stereotypical personae associated with minstrel figures. Eric Lott, author of *Love and Theft: Blackface Minstrelsy and the American Working Class*, elaborates on this point: "To wear or even enjoy blackface was literally, for a time, to become black, to inherit the cool, virility, humility, abandon, or *gaite de coeur* that were the prime components of white ideologies of black manhood" (1995, 52).

Notably, Lott (1995, 53) also observes that white men's coming into patriarchal manhood, associated with puberty, generally involves this "turn to black," and that white minstrelsy performers were in some way indulging in a reliving of this adolescent field of eroticized racial play, one that not only featured dominant modes of heterosexuality, but also homoeroticism. Indeed, like other "Bohemia[n]" practices, minstrelsy did not involve uninterrupted gestures toward patriarchal heterosexuality, but operated through "ambiguous sexual definition" (53). Quoting Eve Sedgwick, Lott (1995, 53) relays that for some, this ambiguity was part of the general rite of passage white Bohemians made en route to a "'repressive, self-ignorant, and apparently consolidated status of the mature bourgeois *paterfamilias*.'" Nevertheless, blackface performers' cross-dressing at times, while not easily equated with homosexuality, did relay and/or invite homoeroticism. And, for some, minstrelsy's association with black heterosexual hypersexuality was used to mask same-sex, interracial desire (Lott 1995, especially Chapter 6).

In my view, this attraction—or love, in Lott's words—is best seen not as a counterbalance or point of contradiction to the "theft" or (mis)appropriation of black culture and representation, but, rather, as an intrinsic element of the cultural and material mastery minstrelsy involved. By mastery I mean the ability to name and inhabit socially constructed identities, to commodify and commercialize them, and to use them in ways that facilitate social control of minoritized groups. Minstrelsy as a genre reified stereotypical notions of blackness and objectified blacks in ways that affirmed and undergirded their social and legal status as property in the antebellum period—their literal objectification—and their second-class citizenship thereafter. White exoticization of black bodies and social constructions of blackness are a constitutive element of white supremacy. White male desire for black masculinity is no less a sign of "brotherly" love than Thomas Jefferson's or another slave master's desire for female slaves is a sign of romantic entanglement.

Of course, some might emphasize that blackface minstrelsy was produced in working-class culture that challenged social hierarchy or that racial cross-dressing productively highlights the constructed nature of racial boundaries. In his work on blackface minstrelsy, for instance, Lott (1995) emphasizes the working-class background of minstrels, averring that their appropriation of black stereotypical imagery and storylines, though problematic, also masked desire for blackness and served as a tool for critiquing and resisting the planter class or bourgeoisie. In another vein, the focus on gender performativity, particularly among women's and gender studies scholars, might suggest that minstrelsy highlights the constructed nature of racial categories. As Judith Butler (1990) has indicated, gender cross-dressing highlights the malleability and constructed nature of gender identity, and then creatively "troubles" the received gender matrix within society.

Arguments surrounding working-class connections to minstrelsy or performativity in the production of identity have to be set within historical and cultural contexts that account for both the power and differences associated with race. First, blacking up, as Rogin (1996, 37) reminds us, was not only a theatrical practice, but was something whites did as they rioted and attacked blacks. Second, blackface minstrelsy not only did not facilitate cross-racial or class alliances, but instead served as the mechanism for racial aversion and white worker racial animus. Indeed, "Blackface did not engender a single interracial political working-class alliance" (38). Finally, and most interestingly, Rogin, drawing on David Roediger's work, underscored that desire (or what Lott would call "love") did not "subvert domination . . . but rather required it" (Rogin 1996, 38). David Roediger (quoted in Rogin 1996, 38) explains, "'The white working class, disciplined and made anxious by fear of dependency, began during its formation to construct an image of the Black population as "other"—as embodying the preindustrial, erotic, careless style of life the white worker hated and longed for.'"

Although cross-dressing can challenge conventional understandings of gender performativity, with minstrelsy, it worked to solidify, not challenge, racial boundaries. Butler (1990) observes that, within the logic of gender, cross-dressing challenges the notion that humans are "either" male or female, forwarding a "both/and" proposition instead. Minstrelsy, by contrast, worked to affirm and produce racial binaries, instantiating a both/and framework that was anything but liberatory. "Although both/and sounds more radical and inclusive than either/or" as it relates to blackface minstrelsy, "its racial history points in quite the other direction. Slaves were both human and property in pro-slavery thought; the primitive trying to become civilized was made fun of as both man and animal" (Rogin 1996, 32). This history demonstrates the contextual variability of performativity and masquerade in destabilizing or affirming social boundaries and political standing.

Thus far, I have explained the relevance of the mammy and matriarch figures in terms of a psychoanalytic frame and drawn parallels to comedic racialized, gender-crossing á la Madea to blackface minstrelsy. In the next section, I tie these two threads together by detailing how Perry recovers and masters the black matriarch, through Madea and other characters, and enacts revenge on failed black manhood. Through a narrative of return for the lead female character in *Diary of a Mad Black Woman*, Perry provides a post-racial, post-feminist fantasy that seeks to rehabilitate the black family and community, by redeeming a traditional model of black male patriarchy.

Mastering the Lost Black Mother, Romancing the Black Male Patriarch

Diary of a Mad Black Wo(man)

Before getting into the details of the film *Diary of a Mad Black Woman* (*Diary*), I want to underscore why it is important, both to Perry's commercial success and its connection to neoliberal melodrama and liminality. Without question, since his first major motion picture, *Diary of a Mad Black Woman*, debuted in 2005, Tyler Perry has ushered in a brand of visual representation that has yielded financial success and been generally embraced by black moviegoing and television audiences. The movies Tyler Perry directs have grossed over a billion dollars (Box Office Mojo 2019). In fact, aside from revenue from films such as *For Colored Girls* and *Acrimony* that do not feature his signature Madea character, "eight films in the Madea franchise [alone] have grossed an overall total of $502 million worldwide" (Dicker 2018). Before hitting the big screen, Perry honed his storytelling craft in plays he wrote and produced, and his filming of these plays have also generated considerable DVD sales. In time, he expanded his brand to include a *New York Times* bestselling book, *Don't Make a Black Woman Take Off Her Earrings: Madea's Uninhibited Commentaries on Life and Love* (Perry 2007), which also "claimed two Quill Book Awards," and television shows, including *House of Payne* and *Meet the Browns*, which set records as the first- and second-"highest-rated first-run syndicated cable show[s] of all time," respectively (Kenneally 2011). Although one reviewer remarked that "Perry has been led out to critical slaughter so many times, it might seem a wonder that he continues to make movies" (Dargis 2010), generally speaking, he is loved and supported by his largely black—and predominantly black female—audience, as his robust movie receipts suggest. Critics notwithstanding, Perry is a dominant figure in Hollywood.

Although the popularity and continuing growth of the Perry brand alone make it worthy of consideration in terms of black popular culture, of particular interest are the ways in which the characters and themes fit perfectly within the melodramatic frame in their focus on family, pathos, victors, victims, and villains. As noted in the Introduction and Chapter 2, melodrama is typically used to channel social anxiety and public problems into the private domain, particularly in the context of family and interpersonal relationships (Brooks [1976] 1995). Almost without exception, Perry's plays, films, and sitcoms focus on family life in black communities in general and male-female romantic liaisons in particular. Also in keeping with the genre, his works are pathos-driven narratives, highlighting extreme emotional or physical suffering. His pitiable characters typically confront their inner failings on the way to triumphing over the villains in their personal lives. As previously noted, given the popularity or hegemony of the black cultural pathology paradigm in black and US politics and culture (Alexander-Floyd 2007), these melodramatic narratives often feature emasculated black men and hypersexualized or emasculating women as well. They hold out the family (patterned along white Anglo-European conceptions) as the key for advancement and wellness in black communities, as opposed to political claims or policy initiatives.

What I want to suggest first is that Perry's focus on familial, interpersonal melodramas stems from his own background, representing an unconscious effort to resolve certain tensions and dilemmas within his own personal narrative. Second, I seek to underscore that such tensions and dilemmas as Perry showcases—surrounding the idea of emasculating black women, angry black women, father abandonment or abuse, and the black family in jeopardy—are issues that are ubiquitous within US black culture and politics.

Tyler's own experience is one that he describes as a "living hell" ("Tyler Perry's Traumatic Childhood" 2010). In his youth, Tyler endured growing up in a household with an emotionally and physically abusive father, and being sexually abused by three different men and one adult woman before the age of ten. He describes his mother, Maxine, and aunt Jenny as his only sources of support. Although his mother was "passive," and unable to defend Tyler or herself, she exposed him to church life, where he gained exposure to a faith that he credits with sustaining him. His aunt Jenny, in contrast, proved to be a source of defense for Tyler. After one particularly brutal beating, Tyler ran to his aunt's house, after which she picked up a gun and proceeded to threaten Perry's father. She counseled Tyler's mother not to leave the child alone with his father. Significantly, and particularly as it relates to *Diary*, Tyler acknowledges watching an Oprah show, specifically where she discusses the healing that can be derived from journaling and the self-discovery and awareness it affords, as a transformative vehicle that facilitated his freedom from his past. Tyler has focused on forgiving his father and undoing the damage from his early life experiences, hoping, through his life and work—and especially his transparency about his abuse—to bring healing to others in black communities ("Tyler Perry's Traumatic Childhood" 2010).

Perry's focus on family dynamics in his work is understandable, given his personal narrative, but as discussed in the Introduction and Chapter 2, this attention to the micro-institution of the family also resonates with broader discourses in US society. The black cultural pathology melodrama as an urtext that has defined this contemporary moment relentlessly focuses attention on the putative breakdown in black families and a focus on female-headed, single-parent households and their attendant maladies. Consequently, as I have discussed, public attention as it concerns dilemmas facing African Americans has shifted from critiques of racism and sexism and its effects or the impact of economic concerns to notions of black cultural pathology as the source of what ails black communities. Beyond the immediate issues that present themselves in Perry's work, its impact also registers in terms of issues of scale, that is, the framing of problems in micro- as opposed to macro-level forms of analysis. That is, because the focus of his work is on black people and their habits of being, as opposed to macro-level issues or their connection thereto, the framing function of his work again centers our attention in ways that undermine progressive or broad social change. Spike Lee, to be sure, is correct in his assertion that Perry's work is based on black stereotypes—essentially a form of cooning.

The movie analyzed herein, *Diary*, centers on a character named Helen, played by Kimberly Elise, who struggles with issues of faith, forgiveness, and independence following a separation from her husband. It focuses on a lot of the same themes encountered elsewhere in post-feminist work, namely, self-transformation and a return narrative that identifies this woman's issues as being all of her own making. After eighteen years of marriage—on the night of their anniversary, in fact— Helen begins her return "home" after her husband, Charles (Steve Harris), kicks her out of their family residence, having arranged a U-Haul truck to carry her and her belongings wherever she would like to go. As the character states at the outset of the movie, her husband, a successful attorney, is good at appearances: he is applauded and recognized for his work professionally, but in private, he is an unfaithful husband who routinely beats his wife. Helen goes to her grandmother Madea's home, and begins to rebuild a life for herself that would resonate with most viewers as a fairy tale of black romance.

On one level, *Diary*'s conscious discourse or apparent social plot, one that focuses on exposing domestic abuse and documenting an abused woman's journey of self-reclamation, offers a marked contrast to much of contemporary popular culture. For example, the latter not only fails to draw attention to black female suffering, but in many cases trades on or even glorifies it. Celebrated films such as *Hustle & Flow* (Brewer 2005), for instance, which focuses on the "struggles" of a black male pimp, highlight endangered or struggling black males whose quest for triumph comes at the cost of black female exploitation, in this case, the prostitution of black women.

As with other post-feminist films, *Diary* incorporates feminist concerns even as it reasserts traditional forms of femininity, focused on self-help. Although black women suffer intimate partner violence, as Kimberlè Crenshaw (1991) and others have observed, this issue has yet to be embraced as one of general concern to black communities. Perry's *Diary*, then, usefully exposes the process of isolation from family that often accompanies coercive control in abusive relationships, where isolation from family and surveillance of communication, relationships, and finances, among other things, serve as key mechanisms of abuse that control or curtail women's freedom (Stark 2007). Moreover, it draws on the well-known theme of forgiveness associated with Christian doctrine in general. Inclusion of Christian themes, such as forgiveness and reconciliation, highlights culturally relevant factors tied to resilience for many in black communities, but that are seen as absent from elite culture (see, e.g., Lee 2015, 65–66).[2]

Diary's general exposure of domestic abuse, however, is accompanied by a corollary discourse that emphasizes self-help and a retreat narrative as central to Helen's recovery. Just as a novel's "figurative" elements, such as clothing or context, reveal its underlying ideological dimensions (Tate 1998, 26–27), so in film, figurative elements, such as clothing, language, and self-presentation, fulfill this same function. In *Diary*, for example, these elements emphasize the class positioning and shifting class associations and aspirations of the characters. After being kicked out of her family home on pain of assault, Helen arrives at her grandmother Madea's home with all of her earthly belongings in tow. Madea, played by Tyler Perry dressed in drag, notes the first morning after her arrival that Helen does not have any "regular" clothing. Helen bears an upswept hairdo with straightened hair, is fully made up, and has perfectly manicured nails, all of which signify her upper-middle-class lifestyle. Throughout the story we learn that Helen desired to marry a rich lawyer, signaling her ostensibly misplaced middle-class aspirations. That Helen's husband leaves her for a fair-skinned African American woman further symbolizes, within the logic of the film, an equation of middle-class achievement with a desire to distance oneself from black communities.

Importantly, as Helen secures employment for the first time in her life and works to rebuild her life, her hair, makeup, and dress change as well. She dons a uniform in her job as a waitress and assumes a shorter, curlier hairdo. This transformation is accompanied and further actualized for Helen by a romantic relationship with a working-class steelworker named Malcolm (Shemar Moore), who showers her with attention and works to help her overcome bitterness borne out of her negative marriage. This transformation reflects the post-feminist subject's obsession with self-recovery through romantic entanglements, retreat to home and family, and rebirth through physical and personal transformation. But this emphasis on transformation also ostensibly underscores the Oedipus complex's operation in the lives of heterosexual black women in terms of heightened desire for and interest in marriage, a desire that may lead them to make less than desirable choices in terms of mates.

Attention is subtly redirected away from Helen's abuse at the hands of her husband, and onto Helen and her choices. Indeed, what is implied throughout is that Helen's fate, including her abuse, is owing in no small part to her desire for the trappings of middle-class white society, including a marital union with a "rich lawyer." Her redemption and remaking lie in a retreat to the black community, here symbolized as authentically working-class, vis-à-vis her family and newfound working-class love interest. Shayne Lee (2015, Chapter 2) contends that Perry's work, including *Diary*, embodies a populist critique, an indictment of elite blacks' abandonment of folk wisdom and resources found in working-class black culture. Although it is certainly true that Perry figures both Helen and Charles as returning to working-class black culture for renewal and redirection, *Diary* is firmly set within post-feminist, post-racial framings. The structure of neoliberal emphasis on self-fashioning and patriarchal family formation is still in place. Black liminality is still at play. The post–black feminist subject is impelled to reject aspiration to middle-class status, associated with whiteness, thereby maintaining racial boundaries but still patterning the black family after a hegemonic, white patriarchal model. In this way, black men can attain masculine status through marriage and alignment with patriarchal power taken as ideal in mainstream society. Helen's choice allows for the allaying of the anxieties associated with castration: men can imagine that they, too, like their fathers, will have access to a woman. At the same time, women's anxieties about access to men are also allayed, as Helen overcomes supposedly poor choices by retreating to the community where she finally finds romantic, marital bliss.

Connecting self-fashioning and successful romantic relationships with a critique of middle-class financial success is a particularly potent combination within black communities, given debates about the demise of black heterosexual relationships and controversy about marriage rates among African Americans. Although the general discourse on domestic abuse and corollary discourse on self-remaking center most directly on the central black female character and by extension black women in general, the unconscious discourse of *Diary* reveals black male aggression and castration anxiety resolution, brought on, as previously discussed, by the Oedipus complex's unique discursive elaboration in black communities. On a basic level, Perry's Madea character appears as an outlaw figure, that is, one who appears heroic because he or she transgresses societal norms in ways that contradict the supposed limitations assigned by society. Movie critics have explored characters from Blaxploitation films, such as *The Mack*, for instance, as male figures who achieve heroic status because they reject the meager options presented by society for black men and instead self-fashion their own, albeit illegal means of achieving the American Dream or financial gain and status (see, e.g., Quinn 2005). Upon this reading, being "bad" is read as being "good" or desirable. One can understand Madea's appeal, accordingly, for other male and female audience members, as she sidesteps the often painful, everyday negotiations that blacks generally and black women in particular have to make in US society. Some (e.g., Knouse 2016) see her as a complex, potentially subversive character, and one analyst of Perry's films, Shayne Lee (2015, 80–81), even suggests that Madea models madness as a pathway to agency, tutoring Helen and others in resisting conditions they find stultifying or oppressive.

Aside from whatever Madea's character may putatively model for black women characters, however, we see in black comedic gender cross-dressing, such as that found in Perry's depiction of Madea, black men recovering their position as patriarchs by symbolically usurping the omnipotence and plenitude of the black mammy or good black mother and the position and authority of the black matriarch or bad black mother. With Madea, elements of the mammy and matriarch figures are melded, so that Perry and film viewers ostensibly celebrate the strength and authority of Madea, the gun-toting assertive mother who, like the mammy, is embraced as a symbol of plenitude and support. But this portrayal betrays an unconscious death wish as well. The black woman is symbolically eliminated or killed and a man comes to inhabit her literal and figurative "plenitude" (Tate 1998, Chapter 1). Perry and many viewers occupy the position of authority that matriarchs are also regarded as denying to black men (i.e., the rightful heads of households). Black women are considered bad precisely because they usurp authority and a role that does not or should not belong to women—in fact, that takes black women out of the category "women." If, as Hortense Spillers contends, "'Sapphire' [here appearing as the matriarch] enacts her 'Old Man' in drag," then the "'Old Man,'" through Tyler Perry's Madea, "becomes 'Sapphire' in outrageous caricature," in order reclaim social authority for men (2003, 204).

Indeed, we can outline several important parallels between minstrelsy and comedic racialized gender cross-dressing à la Madea. The first parallel concerns the stereotypical degradation of the subjects of their minstrelsy, in this case black women. Madea's image is that of an overweight, matronly black woman, with buttocks and breasts reminiscent of those depicted of the "Hottentot Venus," a moniker associated with Sartije Baartman, a South African woman taken from her home and placed on display for crowds throughout the world. As scholars have documented (see, e.g., Holmes 2007a; Willis 2010), Baartman's buttocks and breasts, considered "large" within European notions of beauty, were seen as symbolizing black female hypersexuality. Baartman endured objectification and abuse throughout her life and in her death (a replica of her body being left on display for many years at the Musée de l'Homme in Paris through much of the 1970s and her remains kept by the French until being buried in 2002 in South Africa) (Renold, Chechi, and Renold 2013). Her treatment symbolizes the dehumanization of black women within the West (for an extensive set of analyses, see, generally, Willis 2010). That Madea's visage takes on the corporeal likeness of representations of Sartijie Baartman is striking. That most audiences, including black audiences, laugh at comedic black male drag with her likeness without broad public critique of this association is a stark reminder of the deeply embedded gendered racism endured by black women.

The parallels in terms of how this type of racialized gender cross-dressing, like blackface minstrelsy, relate to nation- or community-building, in this case black nation-building and the forging of black community, are also instructive. With the racialized cross-dressing of Madea, for instance, the black woman as family leader, although an object of desire for her perceived strength, is figured as that which threatens, and, thus, is positioned outside of an idealized racial community and whose power must be diminished. The black matriarch, imbued with power in the family in ways that usurp the position of the black patriarch, becomes the subject of ridicule. With blackface, minstrelsy arguably involved "'love' and theft'" (Lott 1995), that is, a desire for the presumed attributes assigned to black men, and a theatrical or cultural claiming or mastering of this "essence" and its attendant powers. Likewise, with black comedic gender minstrelsy, black men not only affirm their position within an imagined black community, they also project both desire and mastery through their caricatures of black women.

Finally, just as, for most of minstrelsy's history, whites in blackface curtailed black creative agency by controlling representations of blackness and steering the means of creative production, so too does the Madea figure and the narratives in which she is embedded eviscerate black female agency. Madea assumes black women's voice. Through Madea, a black man shares folk wisdom that amounts to telling black men and women what they ought to be and do in their respective roles within heterosexual, patriarchal relationships. The accompanying cast of women, moreover, expresses black femininities that strive to set women within bourgeois norms of respectability, where women are compliant with pernicious definitions of patriarchy in black communities.

In the next section, pinpointing the operation of multivocality, condensation, and displacement, I highlight two particularly powerful dimensions of the film in which cross-dressing operates: explicitly in the case of Madea and implicitly in the case of Helen. These characters, I argue, are used not to relay the frustrations or anger of black women, as the movie's title suggests, but that of black men. These characters serve as vehicles through which black men, like Perry, can imagine occupying, through Madea, plenitude and authority, and rehabilitating or refashioning black femininity, on the one hand, and reparation for abuse or abandonment by fathers, on the other.

Angry Black Men Recovering Patriarchal Ideals

Diary's female characters Madea and Helen serve as a means of black male reclamation and reparation via the three devices referenced in a previous section of this chapter: condensation, displacement, and multivocality. For Freud, condensation and displacement are two general mechanisms operating in dreams. The former, condensation, occurs when dream content is compressed and symbolized by "composite structures"—objects, people, or places—that have varied, multiple meanings or representations (Freud 1989, 211). The latter, displacement, operates through "allusion" or "accent" (214). With displacement in terms of allusion, latent elements are transposed onto other representations in ways that make it difficult to readily discern their point of origin or connection (214–15). With displacement via accent, a dream's central meaning is affixed onto seemingly un- or less important representation(s), bringing other dimensions of the dream into greater focus (214). In both cases the "true" meaning of the latent dream is disguised. Displacement, whether through allusion or accent, allows us to sidestep the discomfort we associate with particular people, ideas, or images. Significantly, for our purposes, Arthur Asa Berger points out that displacement is one of the elements of dreams that "are also found in mass-mediated dreamlike texts, such as sitcoms, soap operas, commercials, advertisements, sporting events, spy stories, crime shows, and many other kinds of texts, which helps explain why the media fascinates us so much" (Berger 2012, 94).

In addition to condensation and displacement, the concept of multivocality in free association also helps to assess Perry's films by discerning the mode of address represented by different characters. Object relations theorists have studied the ways in which people free associating or "free talking" (Bollas 2009, 16–18) during psychoanalysis speak from different vantage points. These vantage points can represent their own experiences or those of significant persons in their lives, such as mothers or fathers. Bollas (2009, 17) explains:

> Object relations theory helps us to see how one moment we might be speaking from our Oedipal self to a part of our mother's personality, then talking from our present age to a part of our own adolescent self, before talking to our self in its late twenties. In the course of a week of analysis we will be speaking not only from parts of our personality but also from parts of our mother or our father, each voice engaging some implicit or explicit other.

With Perry, accordingly, we can trace the connections between certain characters—their roles and dialogues—and the ideological content of the film. Moreover, with this insight about multivocality, we can read the dreamlike text of *Diary* as a movie to better understand the underlying threads of attraction for audiences and the work melodrama achieves in fulfilling post-feminist, post-racial fantasies of self-help and self-reinvention.

Condensation, displacement, and multivocality are at work in *Diary* through the figures of Madea and Helen. Recall: according to Perry, Madea's personality combines the "wisdom" of his mother, Maxine, a good mother or mammy figure, and the assertiveness of his aunt Jerry, a representative matriarch who intervened on his behalf in his real life. Significantly, by merging elements of his mother and aunt Jerry's characteristics and concomitant voices, Perry is able to counsel, direct, and incite revenge through the main character, Helen (as Madea herself quips), and, furthermore, on behalf of all black women. Throughout *Diary*, Madea serves as a source of comfort, direction, support, and sustenance for Helen. Other dimensions of her personality, however, also amplify Madea as matriarch, allowing Perry and audience members to align themselves with the power and authority associated with the feisty aunt Jerry. In one telling scene, in fact, Madea drives to the abused wife Helen's family home from which she was dramatically kicked out, barreling through a guarded gate. Madea then accompanies Helen through the home, and, upon finding a closet full of new clothes purchased for Helen's husband Charles's mistress, directs Helen, to "rip" up all of the clothes. As she and Helen do just that, Madea triumphantly shouts, "*This is for every black woman who's ever had problems with a black man.*" Madea expresses, then, what we already know the story is supposed to directly symbolize, that is, Helen as representative of all black women who suffer in romantic entanglements with black men.

Madea's violent, retribution-oriented leanings ostensibly rub off on Helen, as later in the movie she returns to care for her husband, Charles, when he becomes an invalid, meting out emotional and physical abuse to him in the process. In the end, Helen moves to a point of forgiveness with Charles, but not before confronting him about the effects of abuse on her emotionally (i.e., she was so distressed, she became infertile, having two miscarriages and losing weight). She leaves Charles, divorcing him in order to marry her newfound, working-class lover. In one sense, Helen represents mothers, like Perry's, who are victimized and lack a sense of their own agency. Madea allows Perry to assume a composite personality—his mother's wisdom and his aunt's assertiveness and self-protection—that he can use to speak to women similarly situated to Helen.

The foregoing parallels the manifest content of a dream. Multivocality, condensation, and another form of dream-work, that is, displacement via accent, are also important in interpreting the figure of Helen, the abused woman, who serves to channel not only her own but also Perry's retribution. Again, with displacement through accent, the true meaning of a dream is actually displaced onto a seemingly more trivial or less obvious element. With *Diary*, although the conscious level of this movie as text (its manifest content) focuses on the transformation of Helen, an abused, angry black woman, the unconscious dimensions reveal a desire on Perry's part for revenge and resolution directed against his abusive father. In the language of film criticism, though the diegetic or "temporal and spatial" elements of the immediate narrative focus on Helen, Perry's personal narrative provides an extra-diegetic frame (Elsaesser and Hagener 2010), that is, one outside of the immediate narrative, which informs the film's subtext.

Helen, like Madea, I contend, is also a composite figure. On the one hand, Helen represents the injured and abused woman, like his mother, that Perry fantasizes as having a transformation. On the other hand, however, Helen represents Perry himself, who is able to enact revenge on his father through her character. Like Perry, for instance, the main character, Helen, keeps a diary, chronicling and processing what has happened in her marriage, as well as the transformation unfolding as she returns home, meets a new love, and finds employment, all in the process of self re-creation. Madea, as well as Helen's mother (Cicely Tyson), who is convalescing in a nursing home, counsel Helen throughout. Helen's mother begins to play a larger role in Helen's life, helping her move toward forgiving Charles in order to acquire her own freedom from her destructive past. The creation of a new self is both a metamorphosis Perry likely wishes his mother had undergone, and a means to symbolize the revenge he could have taken out on his father vis-à-vis this angry black woman.

Helen's struggle to forgive her husband also parallels Perry's process of forgiveness and the importance of faith in this endeavor, and several of *Diary's* scenes in this movie fulfill this purpose. Strikingly, for instance, in one pivotal scene, Helen's character, mimicking the cigarette-smoking, violent side of Madea, enjoys a cigarette, as she watches her husband gasping for breath in a whirlpool into which she has literally thrown him. The pool and his trial in it serve two functions: it is the site of a sadistic death wish (Charles lays helplessly in the tub, bubbles escaping from his mouth) and as a symbol of cleansing and rebirth. It becomes a birthing space—a womb—in which Helen's husband, Charles, experiences death, then renewal. Helen's husband emerges, in fact, like a child, dependent on Helen for his every need. A subsequent scene, in fact, shows Helen leisurely dining on a verdant salad, while Charles, helpless and inert, watches in tormented hunger, as Helen taunts him. It reaffirms the reversal of the sadomasochism in their relationship: Helen humiliates and exacts pain; Charles is humbled, abused, denied nourishment, emasculated.

The period of abuse, again, gives way to a process of forgiveness on Helen's part, but not before she is able to confront her husband and exact some measure of revenge. Though forgiveness is a long-standing, central principle in black Christian faith traditions, Perry, through Helen, has his cake and eats it too. He forgives, but only after retribution through Helen's character is achieved. Helen is effectively another dimension of Perry. Perry masks his conscious and unconscious desires, then, not only in terms of the character of Madea, but also, even more importantly, in terms of his representation of Helen. In this way, Madea as a literal model of racialized gender cross-dressing is a red herring, as the ultimate importance of *Diary* centers on the implicit "putting on" or implicit cross-dressing Perry occupies through the person of Helen. The cross-dressing happens literally and symbolically throughout the various filmic frames.

Perry's *Diary of a Mad Black Woman*, in the final analysis, is just as much or more so a diary of Perry as a mad black man and, in some sense, other black men who also experience sexual or physical trauma, feel emasculated as men, or hold ambivalent feelings toward their mothers and other women. It is interesting to note, for instance, that Perry has commented that he did not want to reveal the physical and sexual abuse he experienced as a young person, or his mother's abuse, while his mother was still alive ("Tyler Perry's Traumatic Childhood" 2010). He states that he wanted to prevent her from enduring additional pain. After her death, he began to go public with his painful past ("Tyler Perry's Traumatic Childhood" 2010). *Diary*, importantly, was produced while Perry's mother was still alive, pointing to a clear reason for his suppression of these issues in general. But I want to suggest that Perry, through this movie and subsequent films, not only finds a way to deal with questions of sexual abuse that he has experienced in relationship to his own upbringing, but also, on an unconscious level, works to recover his lost mother, the idealized figure or protective mother embodied in his mother and aunt, to occupy a space of maternal plenitude represented by the good omnipotent mother, which Madea as mammy represents, and finally to bring a sense of recovery both to his mother who stood in need of self-transformation and himself. *Diary*'s displacement and translation of Tyler Perry's anger and other emotional issues, then, operate on several levels: inhabiting the power and authority associated with Madea as matriarch, and rehabilitating Helen, a bad black mother.

Helen is a bad mother, not only in spite of but also because of the fact that she does not give birth, which also acts to divert a parallel to Tyler Perry's life. The fact that she loses children speaks at a deeper level to what Tyler Perry felt happened to him; he notes, more directly, that he felt that he "died as a child" ("Tyler Perry's Traumatic Childhood" 2010). Tyler Perry undoubtedly of course loves his mother, but, as might be the case for anyone similarly situated experientially, he arguably at least at some point held ambivalent feelings toward her. In fact, when Oprah asked him directly if he had any resentment issues to deal with regarding his mother, he at first denied the issue and tried not to talk about it, but eventually acknowledged his feelings of resentment ("Tyler Perry's Traumatic Childhood" 2010). Framing a black male recovery of position, authority, and self within the context of a black woman's narrative is especially useful, as it avoids the obstacle of being classified as an angry black man, and directs attention away from black men's sense of alienation and loss of power that drives this quest for recovery in the first instance. Through processes of multivocality, condensation, and displacement, Perry, along with black male and female viewers, is afforded the ability to simultaneously express and hide their rage.

Conclusion

In its rehabilitation of the bad black woman, Helen, Perry's *Diary* presents a hegemonic model of black femininity concerned with a neoliberal focus on the self. The black woman here is figured as having to deal with abuse, abandonment, and lack of fulfillment, because of her own choices. Black women, according to melodramatic narratives offered in *Diary*, can initiate and sustain relationships by first redirecting their attention to working-class lovers and eschewing the values attributed to middle-class advancement, which are read as counterproductive markers of assimilation. Just as with other post-feminist femininities (Gill and Scharff 2011), women are seen as having liberation through self-help, self-discovery, and self-refashioning. Gone is a consideration of the impact of racism on the life chances of black women and communities, or black feminist readings that understand black women's challenges or issues—including issues surrounding marriage and family or domestic abuse—in light of larger structural concerns. This change of focus, from macro-level to solely micro-levels of analysis is a core mechanism of neoliberalism. It is no accident that we see a plethora of narratives focused on self-rehabilitation and channeling social concerns into the realm of the family. The neoliberal focus on self-making and refashioning is an important accompaniment to the retreat of the state that facilitates the expansion of global capital unfettered by government oversight or responsibilities to taxpayers. As discussed in Chapter 2, in the context of black communities, this retreat from the state and toward undemocratic forms of self-help took shape most noticeably in terms of critiques of female-headed households and the ideology of black male crisis (Legette 1999). Accordingly, as an antidote, here, in *Diary*, we see an emphasis on personal relationships and coupling.

Neoliberal-inflected self-help narratives of return and makeover paradigms exist in black culture as they do in mainstream culture. In black culture, however, black cultural pathology melodrama—with its focus on female-headed households, endangered black men, and black family breakdown—uniquely shapes the expression of these self-help narratives. Although most black and white women will marry during their lifetimes, 78 percent to 85 percent, respectively, they do so at different times, that is, black women on average marry later in life (Cohen 2018, 180). Still, public perception regarding black marriage rates heightens the dating panic prevalent in society as a whole. These black cultural pathology melodrama narratives of return and makeovers are geared toward disciplining bad black mothers. In this chapter's analysis of *Diary*, we see this taking shape in Helen's rebirth as a woman firmly grounded in family, community, and working-class values. We witness also the veneration of maternal plenitude in Madea as Mammy, the reparation or tribute to the good, pre-Oedipal mother. At the same time, we see how the distress brought on by black men's supposed castration arguably accounts for the generation of Madea's grotesque image, which symbolizes a fear and critique of her matriarchal role. The disempowerment black men may feel relative to black women who are seen as powerful Sapphires is leveled with demeaning physical images of black women, such as that found with Madea. Indeed, the distress is quelled via Madea as a cis-male figure who occupies and commands the role of matriarch—"The Old Man in Drag." Although Perry may focus on women in some regards, "Black women are merely the means through which to reinstate traditional notions of dominant masculinities in his model of black community uplift" (Tomlinson 2014, 93).

Furthermore, Perry's *Diary* not only functions to rehabilitate and make over errant black femininity in service of reestablishing patriarchal priority in relationships, it uses Helen as a means of cross-dressing implicitly. Perry is able to use the image of the angry black woman to enact revenge against his personal castration or sense of powerlessness, and sidestep the public criticism and fear generated in the hearts of some by the image of the angry black man. With blackface minstrelsy, white men cross-dressed racially as black men in order to inhabit an expression of masculinity that enabled them to feel sexually and culturally powerful. Likewise, with comedic black gender cross-dressing à la Madea, black males can identify with, inhabit, and reclaim a position of authority. In *Diary*, black men, through fantasy, may perhaps turn to the black woman—the Old Man dressed up in drag, either literally as Madea or figuratively as Helen—as a means of expressing their masculinity, in ways not reserved for them by mainstream society.

Embracing Sapphire, not repudiating or usurping her position, is perhaps the best alternative to wresting perceived control from black women and establishment of traditional patriarchal models. Indeed, as Hortense Spillers (2003, 228–29 [emphasis in original]) remarks, the different positioning of black women historically in terms of gender

> places her . . . out of the traditional symbolics of female gender, and it is our task to make a place for this different social subject. In doing so, we

are less interested in joining the ranks of gendered femaleness than gaining the *insurgent* ground as female social subject. Actually *claiming* the monstrosity (of a female with the potential to "name"), which her culture imposes in blindness, "Sapphire" might rewrite after all a radically different text for female empowerment.

This "radically different text" would not situate men as dominating figures, culturally or politically, but rather situate men and women as co-laborers of equal human value (Spillers et al. 2007, 304).

The next chapter utilizes another popular movie, *The Help*, to examine how the different positioning of black women historically in terms of gender relates to US political development, specifically the social contract. It investigates how melodrama and liminality are at work in the willful ignorance, disavowal, and other psychological defenses enjoined to deny the history of white male rape of black women and its connection to foundational notions of domesticity, gender, and race as it relates to the social contract.

4

The Reality of the White Male Rapist

Black Women's Rape, Melodrama, and US-Based American Political Development

A substitution occurred: instead of black motherhood as the generative source for black people, master-cloaked white manhood became the generative source for black people. Although the "bad black mother" is even today a stereotypical way of describing what ails the black race, the historical reality is that of careless white fatherhood.
—Williams (1991, 163)

It always seems that we are re-creating the wheel. . . . You know, there are all these earlier pioneers in the institutional works of the black intellectual. . . . You know, people are going to have to keep doing it, or rediscover it again, or reassert it because the forces of opposition are so forceful and so powerful and they're always pushing against us, they always want to enforce forgetfulness.
—Spillers (Spillers et al. 2007, 301)

The patient does not *remember* anything of what he has forgotten and repressed, but *acts* it out . . . without, of course, knowing that he is repeating it.
—Freud ([1914] 1958, 150 [emphasis in original])

The vulnerability of black women to sexual assault has been a central feature of US racial and gender politics. Historians such as Deborah Gray White (1999a) and Darlene Clark Hine (1989) have documented, and legal scholars such as Adrienne Davis (2004) have emphasized, the centrality of white men's violation of black women as a constituent part of US slavery, as well as the Reconstruction and segregation eras. They remind us that early rape law was designed to police and protect white female sexuality, and that black women, whatever the race of their assaulters, received little protection from the state (Crenshaw 1991). Although many see lynching, particularly that of black men, as a primary representation of race-based harm, the same is generally not true of white male rape of black women (Carby 1987). Indeed, as Toni Irving (2004) underscores, the failure of the state to recognize and address black female violation speaks to the core of how they are situated as citizens and how race and gender shape US national identity.

How can something so ubiquitous as white male violation of black women's bodies be erased from public memory and popular culture? How do stereotypes about black women as asexual mammies or wanton Jezebels shape the ignorance of black women's rape and harassment in workplaces, and generate their social and legal illegibility as victims? How does the pull of melodrama, and its figurations of pure victors and pure victims, operate in narratives involving black women, whose victimization or abuse is generally unrecognized?

Given the critical role of black women's sexual violation within the cultural and economic landscape in the United States, its significance should not be relegated to the deepest recesses of our collective understanding. It must be made salient, so that we may be ever aware of its meanings and effects. In this chapter, I assert two arguments. First, I contend that black women's sexual violation is a central aspect of US-based American political development.[1] I discuss white male rape of black women as symbolic of white patriarchal authority within the social contract. I expose, as well, how the myth of the black male rapist serves, among other things, as a defense mechanism that shields this reality of the white male rapist and its economic, social, and political importance. Second, I maintain that the rape of black women is what can be called an "unspeakable secret" (Rashkin 2008), one that is met with repression and disavowal, two common psychological defenses (Freud 1937; Sandler and Freud 1985; Vaillant 1992).

Toni Morrison (2000), of course, long ago spoke of the traumas blacks experience as "unspeakable secrets unspoken." Psychotherapist and literary critic Esther Rashkin's work on "unspeakable secrets" also underscores that certain traumas remain hidden not because they are in fact "unspeakable or unsymbolizable" (Rashkin 2008, 19), but because "a subject may experience [events] as literally too shameful for words, and as so potentially destabilizing to the psyche that they must be encased in silence and neither assimilated intrapsychically nor verbalized externally." Repression wards off what is objectionable and potentially harmful to the ego's integrity (Mitchell and Black 1995, 118–19), through submersion in the unconscious, while disavowal replaces the pain associated with a given reality with a fantasy that is more bearable.

Chapter 1 discussed Condoleezza Rice as an example of the repression of conservative politics within black political thought and analysis. Chapter 2 focused on gender as a repressed or neglected aspect of assessment of black elected officials, utilizing President Obama as a case study. Chapter 3 examined Tyler Perry's and some members of black communities' repressed antagonisms toward black women. This chapter addresses repression within the context of rape and harassment. It discusses how repression occurs because rape and harassment are acts of violence, which contradict popular values associated with liberalism, such as equality, virtue, and civilization. Repression of the centrality of black women's rape in US-based American political development is part of a system of "enforced forgetfulness" of the type suggested in one of this chapter's epigraphs. But, what is repressed or buried from our conscious understanding never truly disappears. Like all things that are repressed, the reality of black women's historical victimization percolates to our awareness, often in ways that disable our ability to analyze and assess its current political meaning and operation. Hence, as I discuss later in this chapter, when we do see white male rape of black women discussed, it is typically done in the context of highlighting black male suffering or disavowed through fantasies of treason or romance. In this chapter, I use one prominent discursive site as context for discussing black women's history of rape: *The Help* (Stockett 2009)—both the book and movie—featuring the heroic efforts of a white reporter who exposes the injustice visited upon black domestic workers under Jim Crow in which the history of black women's rape is backgrounded. (Note: The name *The Help* refers to the book and to its narrative more generally unless otherwise indicated.)

This is only one of many examples that illustrate either the evasion of black women's experience of rape, particularly by white men, or its insinuation into present claims of rape made by black women. For instance, the renewed interest in and romanticization of Thomas Jefferson's sexual exploitation of Sally Hemings is one such example (see Gordon-Reed 1998). Another is the revelation, upon his passing, of notorious Dixiecrat Strom Thurmond in his teen years fathering a daughter with a black female domestic worker (Washington-Williams and Stadiem 2005; Curtis 2013). Although rumors of his fathering a child with a black woman had long circulated, some openly wondered if this showed him to be a more complicated (read: not-quite-as-racist-as-we-thought) figure, ignoring the fact that sexual access to black women's bodies is a hallmark of white supremacy. The public spectacle surrounding the rape charges made by a black woman against the Duke lacrosse team, of course, provides another context from recent political history. These examples epitomize the pervasiveness of this phenomenon throughout past and contemporary US culture.

Despite the myriad of examples, I focus on *The Help* for several reasons. Domestic labor has long been a dominant terrain upon which black women have had to confront rape and harassment, and *The Help* afforded a specific look at sexual violence in domestic spaces that can help us understand better how the public space is constituted vis-à-vis these putatively private spaces. Also, *The Help* gained incredible notoriety in the public sphere, not only in the United States but internationally. *The Help*, for instance, made the *New York Times* bestseller list for seventy-seven weeks, sold over ten million copies ("Latest News" 2019), and was the first single volume to sell a million downloads on Amazon's Kindle (Kellogg 2011). The movie version was a blockbuster and garnered coveted Oscar awards. *The Help* speaks to, at many different levels, the way people understand rape in contemporary culture, particularly as it relates to race and gender identity.

Finally, *The Help* provides distinctive insights into the repression of black women's rape or its illegibility in post-feminist, post-racial melodramatic framings. To be sure, some may understand the movie transgressively, in some regards. Black women in particular and black people generally could see in this movie a representation of black women's labor that is rarely framed in a positive light. They may identify with the resilience of the black female characters, and the resistance they marshal toward the whites in the movie who exploit them. Jacqueline Bobo (1993), in particular, has argued that black audiences are able to "read through" the ideological text of movies to insert or emphasize their own values or priorities.

Alternative readings notwithstanding, the movie version of *The Help*, as I demonstrate, is a perfect example of the repression of this country's history of black female sexual abuse in white domestic spaces. It is exemplary of the "doing and undoing" (McRobbie 2007) of antiracism, because it renders a view of black suffering that is sanitized of the gruesome elements of coercive control (Stark 2007) and sexual violence ubiquitous in such contexts—and because it effects this repression, in part, by validating and championing a white female heroine over and against a villainous community whose culture is presented as antiquated and decayed. Tellingly, repression is not the only psychological defense *The Help* usefully illustrates. The journey of this narrative's development, from historical accounts to the novel to the movie, reveals a progressive move from black women's experiences of rape to their disavowal and then repression. I expose *The Help* as a post-feminist, post-racial fantasy by comparing three versions of it: the book of oral history upon which the novel was based (which speaks to white male rape of black women), the novel (which refashions this history through disavowal), and the movie based on the book (which represses this history altogether, but is still haunted by it).

In light of the foregoing overview, this chapter has two goals: to explain the centrality of black women's sexual abuse to US-based American political development, and to explore how the melodramatic narrative framings of *The Help* enable this history's evasion. After outlining key elements of black women's rape in relationship to US-based American political development, I assess various iterations of *The Help*, pinpointing how the melodramatic emphasis on pure victims and villains works to assuage guilt regarding racism and sexism, and is used to rehabilitate and vindicate white subjectivity, while performing epistemic violence (Spivak 1988) and facilitating sexual violence against black women. I end with an assessment of recent examples of disavowal of white male rape of black women in popular culture and a discussion of the importance of mourning in addressing the United States' history of black women's sexual abuse.

Black Women, Rape, and US-Based American Political Development

Our understanding of US-based American political development (APD), particularly as it relates to the notion of a social contract, is clarified when we center black women's experiences. Doing so exposes how both a sexual and racial contract undergird the socio-political contract upon which the US has been built.

Political scientists who specialize in American (or more specifically US) politics have increasingly turned their attention to tracing the historical roots of current-day policies, ideologies, interest group formations, and institutions. This special area of focus, generally known as American political development, provides a sharp contrast to the quantitative methods that political scientists typically employ. As an interpretive, historically based approach, APD challenges the positivistic orientation of the discipline and facilitates interdisciplinary analytical thought. Some APD scholars have also argued for an understanding of race, gender, or both as analytic categories foundational to the US political system (Lowndes, Novkov, and Warren 2008; Ritter 2008). There is a need, however, for a Critical Race Black Feminist approach to APD, based on a constitutive model of identity, that is, one that assesses the mutually constitutive nature of identity categories and centers on the experiences of women of color, in this instance, specifically black women.

It is important, moreover, to point out that this race or gender turn in APD as a subfield is predated by and builds on work done by black and other feminists, and race or black studies scholars in other disciplines, including political science. As Lowndes, Novkov, and Warren (2008) note in their introduction to their volume *Race and American Political Development*, the work of black political scientist Hanes Walton Jr. (e.g., Walton 1985) is an important example in this regard. I would add Mack Jones (2014), Robert Smith (1996), and Jewel Prestage (1991) as other examples, to name a few. Likewise, in her examination of gender and APD, feminist political scientist Gretchen Ritter stakes her claim in large part by showing the ways in which existing scholarship by feminists in the discipline is fully consonant with concerns of APD. In order to disrupt the segregation and hierarchy within the study of race and gender that can occur, it is thus important for APD scholars to engage fully the work by others treading similar ground within and beyond political science as a discipline, and to acknowledge and elaborate a genealogy of relevant work that is coterminous with or, in many cases, even predates their own. In the section that follows, I do just that. I pursue this model of engagement by discussing rape and US-based American political development, particularly as it relates to social contract theory, and the production of racialized and gendered notions of masculinity and femininity and their connection to melodrama and the elaboration of power. In doing so, I draw on work produced by historians and feminist scholars in various fields, demonstrating how feminist theory and scholarship on black women cannot only usefully inform but also transform the way we envision US-based American political development; it lifts the conceptual terrain of US-based APD to a new level, bringing it up to speed with scholarship in other subfields in political science and across other relevant disciplines.

Black Women and Slavery in Historical Perspective

Scholars have extensively discussed the history of black women, rape, and slavery, and I do not undertake a detailed study here. However, a brief historical background provides an essential context. I wish to address how slavery and its effects are repressed and disavowed, and to underscore and theorize its relation to social contract theory. As legal theorist Adrienne Davis (2004, 457–61) has demonstrated, slavery is best understood as a sexual economy—that is, one rooted not only in "productive," but also "reproductive" and "sexual" labor. Black women performed both domestic labor and labor tied to agricultural production. But, beyond this, their reproductive labor, that is, the sale and circulation of their children as chattel, sustained the slave economy. Whereas other Western traditions traced the parentage of the child and attendant social status to the father, in the context of US slavery "the rule of *partus sequitur ventrem*" held sway, that is, "a child inherited its status from its mother" (Davis 2004, 459). "This rule proved to be of immense economic and political significance. The South was one of the smallest importers of slaves, but had the largest slave population in the West" (459). The reproductive capacities of the enslaved were commandeered in service of an expanding agricultural economy that positioned the United States as a major player on the international scene (Steinberg 1989).

Black women also performed sexual labor as slaves. White male slave owners, in their enslavement of black women, mastered their sexual capacities, forced themselves sexually on women, and compelled them to have sex with slave family members and with other male slaves (Davis

2004, 459). White men's sexual domination of black women was exemplified in a legal case, in fact, when an enslaved woman, Celia, was convicted for killing her master, who died while she was defending herself; the encounter happened, notably, because Celia, at the prompting of an enslaved black man with whom she had a relationship, attempted to convince her master to stop exploiting her sexually (McLaurin 1991; Jones and Rosen 2020). Importantly, given the ubiquity of white male rape of black women, the image of the asexual mammy is an inversion of the reality that black women faced in the home of white slave masters who sexually abused them. The figure of Jezebel serves, among other things, as a projection of wanton white lust onto female bodies. As scholar-activist Angela Davis observes, the right of sexual access to black women's bodies by their slave owners is akin to the right of the first night practiced in feudal societies, where feudal lords had sex with peasant brides on their wedding nights, thus signifying and enacting their dominant status and control vis-à-vis their subjects (Davis 2000, 92–93). Though similar in some respects, under slavery this right of sexual access to black women's bodies extended to its extreme conclusion. Because blacks could not marry, black men were not able to legally assume the position of patriarch. Additionally, as Adrienne Davis reminds us, aside from the day-to-day rape or exploitation of black women's sexual labor on plantations, black women were also purchased explicitly as concubines (A. D. Davis 2004, 459).

As I discuss more in my treatment of *The Help*, white male sexual abuse of black women continued postslavery, including during segregation. However, we have yet to fully account for the significance of this historical reality to our understanding of US-based American political development. Consequently, the character of our public discussions mirrors the same kind of neglect.

The historical and current persistence and ubiquity of black women's sexual abuse powerfully suggests its salience not only to the United States' economic and social organization, but also its political development, particularly notions of liberalism and the social contract. The notion of a social contract has been central to US political theory. Ritter contends that gender is a key analytic in understanding APD, which helps us to account for the production of subjectivity, "civic membership," and the elaboration of liberal theory, including social contract theory, that undergirds our conceptual political frameworks (Ritter 2008).[2]

Briefly, the social contract refers to narratives produced to explain the creation of society and politics. While not taken as literal, the various narratives regarding the origins of society represent the key values and political dynamics taken to represent legitimate social and political arrangements. As such, these origin stories give us a window into the normative fantasies that informed and continue to shape society and politics. Importantly, as Ritter observes, feminists have long struggled to reveal the gendered nature of liberal tenets and social contract theory. Feminist political theorists such as Carole Pateman and Wendy Brown, for instance, have detailed the gendered nature of narratives of social origins and contract and the importance of norms surrounding masculinity and femininity to the production of political subjectivity, respectively (Ritter 2008). Ritter (2008) also rightly affirms APD's connection to race and other markers of identity. Black feminist political theorist Shatema Threadcraft underscores the privileging of male bodies within social contract theory, even as race-conscious theorists, such as Charles Mills, and Afro-Modern thinkers have reimagined it (Threadcraft 2016). She points to the need to capture the widest range of human concerns including those related to the home and bodily care we would associate with female bodies and the "intimate" or private settings in which we dwell and relate (102–5). From this perspective, what can the rape and harassment of black women tell us about US-based American political development? The answer to this question begins by examining the relationship among race, gender, and liberal theory's focus on the social contract.

The social contract is preceded by and itself enacts a raced and gendered contract. Social contract theory relays a founding narrative in which paternal right is defeated and individuals sacrifice their autonomy in order to enjoy "freedom" in a civil society that secures the greater good of society as a whole (Pateman 1988, 2). In their classic works *The Sexual Contract* and *The Racial Contract*, however, Carole Pateman (1988) and Charles Mills (1997), respectively, relate how the notion of a universal social contract entered into by individuals who lack ascriptive characteristics is an incomplete story. For Pateman, the disappearance of strict paternal rule does not mean the end of patriarchy (1988, 3).

The social contract's creation of civil society is inherently gendered and based not only on freedom, but also on un-freedom or subjugation (2–4). Men enter into a fraternal order of freedom in which they have authority over women in a public realm and equal access to women who experience subjection in a private realm through marriage. Pateman (2 [emphasis added]) explains:

> Civil freedom is a masculine attribute and depends upon patriarchal right. The sons overturn paternal rule not merely to gain their liberty but to secure women for themselves. Their success in this endeavor is chronicled in the story of the sexual contract. The original pact is a sexual as well as a social contract: it is sexual in the sense of patriarchal— that is, the contract establishes men's political right over women—and also sexual in the sense of *establishing orderly access by men to women's bodies.* . . . Contract is far from being opposed to patriarchy; contract is the means through which modern patriarchy is constituted.

Detailing the implication of social contract theory for psychoanalysis is beyond the scope of this current work. Suffice it to say that this "overturn [of] paternal rule" is directly parallel to the Oedipus complex's assumption of a male child's patricide and desire for the mother, and relatedly the "primal horde," where brothers rise to power through vanquishing their father (Freud [1914] 1958). The interplay of the public and private arenas of civil society prove critical to the execution and maintenance of a fraternal order in which men dominate. Women, if even a part of the contract, derive their contract rights from men, and these rights have been subordinate to those of men.

In addition, race dictates rights and the nature of agency under the contract. From Mills's perspective, the social contract is an explicitly racial one, with not only moral and political, but also epistemological dimensions. The social construction of race into hierarchies in which white people rule is central to the social contract (Mills 1997).[3] Mills avers, moreover, that the racial contract comes closest to approximating a factual historical reality, beginning within a specific temporal frame and buoyed by legal agreements, meetings, and political and military happenings (20–21). Although the specific subsidiary contracts, such as colonization and enslavement, manifest in different social and political arrangements where they are in place, the racial contract, nevertheless, enables global domination by whites of European descent (23–27).

Pateman's and Mills's elaboration of the centrality of race and gender to the construction of social contract theory offers a useful analytical framework by which to examine black women and sexual abuse, particularly in considering black women's subjectivity within US-based American political development. Indeed, when we consider the role of black women, taking into account not only the sexual but also the racial dimensions of the US social contract, we find a more complicated picture of civil society, one that is inherently raced, classed, and gendered and where the lines between the two spheres of civil society, the public and the private, are not distinct. Indeed, hierarchies among men and among women mark civil society.

As an example, the US Constitution is a social contract. In its original drafting, not all whites had the same political rights. White men with means, defined as those who owned property, enjoyed political rights within the public realm of civil society not held by others who did not share their wealth, color, or social status. Blacks were considered property, infamously counted as three-fifths of a person during the 1787 Constitutional Convention to appease southern slave owners for purposes of gauging population (the Great Compromise). At the time of the Constitution's execution, Native Americans and others deemed nonwhite had been and would continue to be progressively subjugated—culturally, territorially, economically, and politically—through war and genocide. Even after Emancipation, when the Civil War amendments would at least in the abstract confer citizenship as an attribute of civic membership to black people, it was undone by the practice of racial and gender subordination. The Fifteenth Amendment, of course, (in)famously conferred voting rights to black men, but not black women, prompting political scientist Mamie Locke to quip that black women went "from 3/5ths to zero" (Locke 1990, 45).

Thereafter, women did not have the right to vote until the Nineteenth Amendment was ratified in 1920. However, prior to 1920, particularly during slavery, black women's rights were subordinate to all groups. For instance, in the private sphere, white women were subjugated vis-à-vis white men, but they enjoyed the social, if not always economic, benefits ascribed to the dominant racial class. Their exercise of power manifested itself in their active participation in practices of racial domination. In *Out of the House of Bondage: The Transformation of the Plantation Household*, Thavolia Glymph (2008) emphasizes that white women in slave communities were no mere bystanders in the horrors of the institution of slavery. Instead, they were central figures in meting out violence and in otherwise supporting the slave system.

Mutually constitutive constructions of white and black womanhood were also central to the social contract. Deborah Gray White (1999a, 6 [emphasis in original]) observes, "Black and white womanhood were interdependent. They played off one another. The white woman's sense of herself as a woman—her self-esteem and perceived superiority—depended on the racism that debased black women. White women were mistresses *because* black women were slaves." The cult of true womanhood came to frame white women as idealized, virtuous women given to domestic concerns; it projected white women as frail, nonassertive, and the apex of feminine beauty. The cult of true womanhood, moreover, emerged because black women were figured as embodying its antithesis: the cult of true womanhood versus a fantasy of black female debasement. In this fantasy of black female debasement, black women were viewed as domineering, assertive, masculine (as in the matriarch) and without sexual virtue (as in the Jezebel).

Questions of virtue of course often come up in rape cases, particularly in a contemporary context. As noted legal theorist and activist Catharine MacKinnon (1989, 175) explains in her classic work, "Rape: On Coercion and Consent," "All women are divided into parallel provinces, their actual consent counting to the degree that they diverge from the paradigm case in their category. Virtuous women, like young girls, are unconsenting, virginal, rapable. Unvirtuous women, like wives and prostitutes, are consenting, whores, unrapable." Although it is true that the splitting of women into virtuous and unvirtuous categories in some dimensions applies to white women, the "paradigm cases" are themselves racialized and classed. Black women, for instance, are not the "paradigmatic" inhabitants of the category of virtuous women. Black women and other nonwhite women are generally deemed paradigmatically unvirtuous, a fact underscored by the easy assumption that black women, and even black girls, are hypersexual or prostitutes.[4] This reality has profound meaning for social contract theory.

The practical elaboration of the social contract, which positioned black women as the antithesis of white women and depended on black women's labor in both public and private spaces, gave rise to interdependent frames of the cult of true womanhood and fantasy of black female debasement, frames that can help us to understand rape as a constituent feature of the contract. The cult of true womanhood suggested that "[white] women were either pure or promiscuous, and sexuality [involving white men and women] was either private and marital or public and prostituted" (Sanday 2007, 13). For most of the time since our country's founding, the protection of rape laws covered white women only, in order to protect their purity and because they were seen as the proprietary interest of white men. The question of a woman's virtue has been and continues to figure centrally in determining the validity of claims of rape (Sanday 2007, 13). Just as social policy has often included calculations of who is really the "deserving," as opposed to the "undeserving," poor (Katz 1989), adjudication of rape in courts and in the public domain has centered on virtuous versus unvirtuous women—the deserving, true victim or Madonna, on the one hand, and the undeserving, impure woman or the whore, on the other. However, black women have never been seen as virtuous, and the rape of black women has been downplayed culturally and before the law (Crenshaw 1991, 1271). This is why black women are especially vexed in public discussions involving rape. To the extent that people still search, if only implicitly, for virtuous victims, black women, who are deprived of this possibility, are denied acknowledgment of their victimhood.

Put differently, the social contract does not simply involve a fraternal brotherhood that grants orderly access to (virtuous) women's bodies, but provides access to "disorderly qua sexualized wom[e]n" (Zerilli 1994, 7) within and outside of marriage, as a means to construct and regulate female and male behavior. The prevalence of rape and the failure to prosecute it underscores its importance as part of the construction of male identity in civil society. Peggy Reeves Sanday (2007), the author of *Fraternity Gang Rape: Sex, Brotherhood, and Privilege on Campus*, offers important insights on this point. She writes, "Within the context of this sexual culture, the male projects his own sexual tension on to the female, fetishizing her desire as being reducible to 'wanting it'" (18). She suggests that this desire for "'it,'" often taken to indicate penis envy by Freud or a central lack by Lacan, is a product of ideology, "a cultural doctrine that functioned to give men a stage on which to socialize one another for power. The *it* embodied (stood for) the male power which women were denied solely because they were female" (18 [emphasis in original]).

Tellingly, group initiation processes enact Oedipalized dramas, according to Sanday, where men bond, through their ritualized group experiences, including rape. Group rape or "pulling train" is also a means of both fulfilling and repudiating "homoerotic desire"; men displace their homoerotic desire onto female victims in group rape and, at the same time, assert heterosexual, patriarchal dominance (Sanday 2007, 42). Pulling train sheds light on how the Oedipal drama is implicated in the social contract. It also starkly demonstrates the projection of desire onto women that nullifies the notion of consent, particularly as it relates to women constructed as unvirtuous.

In this light, the figure of the wanton, unvirtuous black woman or Jezebel is central to constructions of white male authority constitutive of the social contract, as it best personifies the notion that women desire rape or sexual domination by men. The Jezebel stereotype is the ultimate archetype that both shapes and enables male, and particularly white male, sexual terrorism as it supports male dominance. Although women who are raped are often leveled with the charge "she was asking for it," because the Jezebel frames black women as inherently base, wantonly lustful, and given to seduction, she becomes the quintessential representation or embodiment of phallic lack—generally the least powerful hierarchically and, therefore, most desirous of the penis. Against this backdrop, rape is critical to US-based American political development because it is a means of marking and solidifying male authority.

Given the role that rape plays in authorizing dominant male authority, it is unsurprising that discourse on rape and race—specifically the alleged rape of white women by black men—would take shape in a concerted way during the postslavery context (see Giddings 1984, Chapter 1). As scholars have long observed, the myth of the black male rapist served as an ill-founded rationale for lynching and violent retribution for blacks (see, e.g., Davis 1981). On one reading, the public face of this discourse centered on the white female body as a terrain of putative struggle and ownership between men. Blacks' assertion of agency and quest for freedom was interpreted by white men and communities as a threat to displace the racial hierarchy among men, and this battle was represented, culturally at least, in narratives surrounding protecting white women from rape by black men (Giddings 1984).

I want to rather provocatively suggest, however, that this is only part of the story and that the myth of the black male rapist has its origins embedded deeply in the reality of white male rape of black women. Some identify lynching as a manifestation of what Heidi Nast terms "racialized oedipalization," a response of white male fathers to protect white feminine (maternal) purity. Nast (2000, 226–27) explains: "White supremacist fears were spoken through an idiom of violence that attempted to reassert the singularity of a racially superior fatherhood: Black men, historically infantilized as 'sons,' were well positioned psychically to carry a symbolic burden of incest, a sin punishable by castration and/or death." Nast's profound assessment of how race, gender, and power in the Oedipal drama played out psychically, spatially, and materially through various forms of colonization fails to fully account for black women's infantilization as "daughters" that not only bear the mark of incest, but endure it.

We must explain how this racialized oedipalization impacts black men, and how it relates to and impacts black women. More specifically, the hysteria around what was once called the "New Negro crime" (Giddings 1984, Chapter 1) of black male rape of white women must be seen as manifesting fundamental defense mechanisms, specifically projection and reaction formation; these defense mechanisms became more pronounced in the post–Civil War era because of the perceived threat to white male dominance and the need to reassert proprietary authority over previously subjugated bodies. As with all projections, individuals ascribe their own ideas, motives, and behaviors onto others (Mitchell and Black 1995, 27–29). Since white men affirmed their manhood by raping women, especially black women, they projected or assigned this motive onto black men as an expression of their quest for freedom. It also involves reaction formation, that is, a defense wherein "the ego obscures unacceptable hostile impulses by transforming them into their opposite" (26). "The angry person," for instance, "becomes overly nice, often insistently helpful, even suffocatingly kind . . . a clever cover for his nastiness" (26). As a reaction formation, the myth of the black male rapist and the attendant loathing of the rapacious black male brute and protection of white female purity are a reaction against or cover for the rapacious white desire for black bodies (male and female), and their perceived sexual power (Nast 2000; White 2001). To be sure, early black feminists "did not miss the irony in the contrast between the fiction of black men's molestation of white women and the very real rape suffered by black women. Sexual assaults on black women perpetrated by white men continued in the postbellum period as if slavery had not ended" (White 2001, 33). With the social contract embodied in slavery thrown into disarray, its remaking took shape through reassertions of dominance and control along a number of fronts—undermining political rights, economic exploitation, and cultural struggle—each of which was mutually constitutive and defined by sexual politics.

Our focus on lynching as a phenomenon that links racial oppression solely or primarily with harm to black men is limited, at best, and obscures the full impact of oppressive conditions on black women and communities. As I discussed in Chapter 2, black political thinkers and/or operatives often read black men as representative of black communities as a whole. This approach, Threadcraft (2016, 103) points out, parallels a more general focus on male embodiment in social contract theory and our ideas about the state. Under formulations that privilege male embodiment or only certain concerns associated with the public sphere, much that black women and communities experience is sidestepped (103). As she insists, we must secure "intimate justice" and, following Martha Nussbaum, seek a full range of "capabilities" for all (Threadcraft 2016, 142–47). I have highlighted black women's centrality to the social contract to abet this broader conception of justice.

As the foregoing discussion conveys, the centrality of black women as subjects, and especially their reproductive, sexual, and productive labors, to the social contract is reflected in the prerogative of access to black women's economic and sexual labor throughout the Civil War, Reconstruction, and Jim Crow segregation. Black women, who were still relegated to domestic work postslavery, continually strove to renegotiate more equitable labor conditions, with varying degrees of success (see, generally, Glymph 2008). In any case, however, rape and harassment remained ubiquitous realities in the lives and labors of black women.

This history of white male rape of black women and the role of race and gender in the social contract allows a clearer view of the race, gender, and class post-politics at work in cultural phenomena, like *The Help*. It gives a proper context for understanding the psychological defenses used regarding white male rape of black women, such as denial, disavowal, repression, and encryption into haunting (phantoms). That various psychological defenses are employed to sidestep, distort, or redefine this history reveals how white male rape of black women is part of the "unspeakable" (Morrison 2000; Rashkin 2008) of US history. In the next section, I explore the aforementioned defenses used to evade white male rape of black women.

The Help

For the purposes of this discussion, I focus attention on the ways in which the movie *The Help* presents a sanitized version of domestic labor as it relates to black women's vulnerability to sexual predation. To be sure, throughout the narrative we see glimpses of the impact of segregation on black domestic workers and their families, and how their labor of cleaning white homes and caring for white children enable a socialite circle of white females. Still, having to endure the humiliation of using separate bathrooms, a focal point of the film, was arguably not black domestics' most devastating problem.

Given the reality of black women's vulnerability to rape by white men, particularly in white homes where they labored as domestics, what are we to make of how this reality is elided in *The Help*? What is the ideological work achieved by the particular fantasy(ies) offered in this cultural representation of segregation? The movie version of *The Help*, like the novel upon which it is based, maps the layers of repression of the history of white male rape of black women present in society as a whole. We get nothing in this movie version that directly addresses the widespread threat of sexual assault black women in this profession experienced. The book version of *The Help*, although it renders a more complicated picture of the sexual politics of racial segregation, romanticizes white men's sexual assault of black women. The movie, in fact, focuses on a white female protagonist named Skeeter, who arguably serves as a white savior figure.

As a newly minted college graduate on her first job at the local newspaper in Mississippi, Skeeter (Emma Stone), the lead character in the film, is hired to write a cleaning column, secretly depending on a black domestic worker, Abilene (Viola Davis), for material. Skeeter soon plies her trade as a journalist by secretly recording the first-person accounts of black domestic workers, and then publishing them in a tell-all narrative that scandalizes the white, female, southern elite in whose houses they work. Simultaneously, the book putatively gives voice to black women's trials under segregation. Oddly, although she grew up in segregated Mississippi and the book and movie are set in the tumultuous period of the Civil Rights movement of the mid-twentieth century, Skeeter seems relatively clueless about the social, economic, and political codes regarding segregation. Consequently, she must immerse herself in the segregation laws in Mississippi to truly grasp the potential calamity that could befall anyone, especially blacks, challenging Mississippi's system of segregation.

Although initially reluctant to participate, Abilene, and then other maids, such as Millie Jackson (Octavia Spencer), a maid fired for using a "whites only" bathroom in the home in which she works, join in to tell their story. Skeeter and the black domestic workers produce a fictionalized account of the maids' stories that rocks Mississippi. In the end, Skeeter is offered a position with a major New York publishing company, while Abilene, and presumably the other maids, are left dealing with the fallout, but triumphant in heart and spirit for telling their Truth about the world in which they live.

In *The Help* (the movie) we see both the "doing and undoing" (McRobbie 2007) of feminism and antiracist politics foundational to post-feminist, post-racial fantasy in the early twenty-first century. *The Help* (the movie) ostensibly highlights Jim Crow segregation in one of the most powerful ways in which it operated. Black women's domestic labor has been materially and symbolically important for much of the nation's history, especially throughout the slavery, Reconstruction, and Jim Crow eras. The movie also touts arguably feminist principles of female independence from patriarchal systems, in the person of Skeeter,[5] a woman who is markedly different from her Mississippi friends in her appearance, attitudes, and priorities. She has red, curly hair, as opposed to tightly coiffed, blonde or brunette hair, dresses plainly compared to her cohort, and, though not totally uninterested in love connections, is more focused on her career as opposed to starting a family.

Skeeter's position as an outlier and rabble-rouser, in fact, is reinforced over and over throughout the film. Although we certainly learn about the maids as characters, much of the story turns on Skeeter's personality, her negotiation of the dicey racial and gender politics of her family and community, and her triumphant process of personal and professional self-actualization.

Skeeter as a character ironically undoes feminism and antiracism by suggesting that racism and sexism are bound by the geography and place of the US South, and can be overcome by knowledge. *The Help* (the movie) recognizes the reality of racism and sexism thematically, but only to suggest that they can be and arguably have been overcome through education and exposure of the truth. Although the film is titled *The Help*, it ultimately focuses on Skeeter. Abilene and the other domestic workers serve as an Africanist presence (Morrison 1993), that is, they are noble black characters that enable the self-actualization of whites. The domestic workers, ironically, are the "help" once again. Their labor or work in the film is produced in service to Skeeter's character in particular, absolving white guilt over racism more generally.

Others have likewise pointed out various limitations of the film. The Association of Black Women Historians, for instance, in a widely circulated "Open Letter to Fans of The Help," pointed out that the movie inaccurately portrayed black female domestic labor and black culture from the period. Noting that everything from the dialect to the scope of the story was lacking, they pointed out that the movie gave little attention to the constant sexual harassment and sexual assault to which black women were exposed as domestic laborers. Some raised questions about the usurpation of black women's voices, narratives, and experiences (see, e.g., Jordan-Zachery 2014). Scholars and other commentators will undoubtedly continue to explore diverse elements and the book upon which it is based.

Importantly, *Telling Memories*, the book that Stockett depended on for research, clearly demonstrates the reality of black women's vulnerability to rape and sexual harassment as domestic workers. The book, edited by Susan Tucker (1988), showcases narratives by black domestic workers and whites who hired black domestic workers as laborers. In this volume, we hear directly from domestic workers about their experiences— their struggles with rearing their own families as they worked to care for the families of others; the patterns of giving and receiving of gifts, clothes, or other items, and the intricate play of social relations and politics this entailed; the day-to-day negotiations of Jim Crow segregation, even as they labored in the most intimate spaces in white society; and, notably, the rape and harassment of black women by white men.

Tellingly, Tucker did not include rape or harassment as part of the questionnaire she developed for this study, even though she admittedly knew that this was part of what black women experienced (Tucker 1988, 19), a decision that is an example of white women's denial of white male rape of black women more generally. Tucker writes, "Though I had read of sexual exploitation of domestics in white homes—*Coming of Age in Mississippi* and *Soul Sister* come immediately to mind—I did not see this subject as something I should ask about, even as I designed the questionnaire. However, as I heard many references to mulatto women, I began to inquire further" (19). Questions about "mulatto women," however, revealed the deep suppression or rationalization of the knowledge of black women's sexual abuse. She explains:

> What I came to see was that white women, indeed, usually denied ever hearing of sexual exploitation of black domestics, either within the white home or by the men in the household. They denied it so completely that it was consistently a subject on which I got only a one- or two-sentence response that usually focused on men called "poor white trash." (19)

Tucker contends that this denial in part stemmed from white women's fear of rape, particularly by black men, and their perceived dependence on white men as allies or protectors (19). Perhaps in grappling with her own denial, Tucker stages a potential site of disruption of the silence about white male rape of black women in her book.

The very first narrative of the book *Telling Memories* centers on the life of Priscilla Butler, a black woman who was the product of rape and whose narrative focuses on the codes of silence and white male protectionism that was part and parcel of the workplaces that emerged in the shadows of slavery. Butler was born in 1909, a mere forty-four years after the abolition of slavery via the Thirteenth Amendment. Her mother worked for the Clinton family and was raped and impregnated by one of her employer's sons when she was herself a child. Butler explains: "My mother she was nothing but a child when I was born. I don't really know how old she was, because everything I have found out about her I've had to pick up—bits and pieces from what I heard and what my aunt told me" (Tucker 1988, 20). Her mother, who served as a nursemaid, indicated her wish that her own child never suckle other people's children, before her own, suggesting a distaste for the circumstances under which she labored (22).

Although she expressed doubt about the nature of her mother and father's relationship, her attitude toward her father ranges from tolerance to disgust and resentment, and she remains critical of the code of silence and denial that undergirds white men's exploitation of black women. Upon the death of her mother, Butler's father extended material care for Butler, to some degree, taking pains to disguise his identity. Specifically, he used his younger brother, Andrew, as a liaison in dealing with her and her family. In this way he was able to conceal his own identity. She claimed to harbor no ill will toward her father, but recognized that they were separated by a gulf of inequality (Tucker 1988, 22). She is not ambivalent. Butler relates: "So after that [her mother's death], I was raised with the best of everything. But I never did want anything to do with my daddy" (22). "My husband had to blow on me cold," she recounts, "to make me be nice to him" (22).

Butler's account further highlights that, although most whites were willfully ignorant of white male abuse of black women, the evidence of this was written in action and in flesh. Butler's father, like Strom Thurmond in a later generation (Mae Washington-Williams and Stadiem 2005), provided materially for the child who was the result of his sexual abuse. Butler observes, "Well, I don't know if it was rape or money or lust or affection or what that caused the mingling up. . . . My father felt something to keep up with me, but I don't know why he felt it—duty or guilt or what. I just don't know" (Tucker 1988, 24). Butler worked all of her life to find out details of her birth, but the silence surrounding such matters prevented her from knowing this. In any case, his actions, however contorted, gave further evidence of his interracial coupling.

Butler's circumstances raise a number of interesting questions about the nature of black women's sexual abuse, specifically in terms of discerning the nature of such relationships and making sense of the material support of children. For some, the possibility of romantic connections remains an open question. Nancy Valley, another domestic in *Telling Memories*, for instance, comments that her biological grandfather, a white man who owned her grandmother, had a child (whom he also owned) with her grandmother and "never did marry nobody else—nobody," suggesting that they were bonded emotionally, like husband and wife (Tucker 1988, 76). What do we make of material provision by a white male who fathered a child with black domestic workers? As Butler asked, "Duty or guilt or what [affection]?" (ibid., 24). Were there romantic connections that explain or were intermingled with miscegenation?

The answer, of course, lies in examining the power dynamics involved. Even though the peculiar institution was legally ended, the reconstitution of economic and social relationships remained profoundly grounded in the ideology and many of the practices of slavery. Butler's father was one of several white male family members who worked on the Clinton plantation, men who legally could enjoy unfettered sexual access to the black women they employed (Tucker 1988, 20). Other women were "mulatto," obvious products of sexual relations with white Clinton men, but the identity of these men was protected in a cloud of silence. As Butler amplifies, "That's just the way things had been. Everything is to protect the good name of the white men. But they didn't give a hat about the black women" (Tucker 1988, 21). Butler observes, "There was a lot of mulattoes on that plantation, but the womens wouldn't dare accuse those Clinton boys [of rape]" (22). Butler's observations relay the reality of black women's commonplace violation by white men during segregation. It is significant, in this context, to relay as well that Nancy Valley's father, mentioned above, whose own father was white, worked for black people and steered clear of whites; there was also little discussion of his father beyond his "attachment" to his mother (Tucker 1988, 75).

Some might think that white male rape of black women ended with slavery. It did not. During the Civil War and in the early postbellum period, black women continued to be subject to rape, harassment, and violence. In fact, although they sought relief from Union soldiers, Union soldiers often greeted blacks with violence, including rape (White 1999a, 164). Predictably, sympathizers of the Confederacy also used rape as one of its weapons of outrage and retaliation for their vanquishment. As esteemed historian Deborah Gray White relates, one woman, Rhoda Childs, for instance, was brutally raped by an ex-Confederate soldier, and beaten and further abused in a dispute over crops she and her husband were due; Childs elaborates: "'During the whipping one of the men had run his pistol into me, and said he had a great mind to pull the trigger'" (White 1999a, 174–75). As this example demonstrates, in the absence of slavery, when blacks were no longer property to be minimally protected for economic benefit, this violence arguably increased (174–75).

Again, Priscilla Butler, who was the product of rape under segregation, provides an account highlighting that sexual violation of black women during slavery remained a cornerstone of white-black social relations after slavery's demise. Butler reminds a white woman, one who expresses a distaste for interracial relationships—("[Priscalla,] I wouldn't want your [black] grandson to marry my [white] granddaughter" [Tucker 1988, 23])—that interracial sex, specifically between white men and black women, is nevertheless a basic reality. Priscilla Butler recounts,

> "There is a church there [in my hometown], one church there, that the white people go to, and you go over there, you going to find nothing but white people. . . . But when you walk in those [black] churches, you'll find black people, brown ones, tan ones, red ones." I [Priscilla Butler] said, "You keep on looking, you'll find them as white [looking] as you is." I said, "You know black man didn't do it." (Tucker 1988, 23–24)

Butler's observation points to the basic fact that, white male protectionism and willful ignorance notwithstanding, the evidence of white male rape of black women is, among other things, written in the flesh of the US population. The presence of blacks of different hues was a tangible reminder of the sexual exploitation. It is a profound irony that people worked so hard—and were allowed—to conceal what was, nevertheless, literally visible in plain sight. Consent to sex, moreover, presupposes that people have genuine choice. As MacKinnon (1989, 175) points out, "The law of rape presents consent as free exercise of sexual choice under conditions of equality of power without exposing the underlying structure of constraint and disparity." In a moral and legal environment that does not recognize black women's rape and an economic and social context that places black women and communities in a profound state of inequality and abasement, consent is not a true possibility, although the orchestration of such an illusion serves to deflect attention from abuse and blunt the trauma that such abasement entails. Hence, although Butler leaves room in the abstract for the "what" of her father's support being genuine affection, her attitude toward him reveals quite another assessment.

This material support Butler receives from her father can also be seen as part of the race and gender performativity constitutive of white heterosexual patriarchy. As a part of slavery, slave owners provided basic necessities for slaves. Likewise, employers of domestic workers postslavery provided them wages, and sometimes food and other items that allowed them to have only subsistence living, and not a living wage that would comfortably sustain their lives and advance their personal and family goals. As Tucker examines in an entire section of her book, moreover, gift giving was an important aspect of domestic worker–employer relations under segregation that was laden with symbolic meaning. The giving of gifts by white women, for instance, was not simply a means of charity or generosity, but a mechanism to assuage guilt and to further affirm the superiority of whites over their domestic workers. Likewise, the giving of gifts or material things by white male rapists underscores and affirms the identity of white men as patriarchs and provides not only a show of benevolence that belies the violence of their identity as rapists, but also affirms a superior, proprietary relationship relative to black women and their children.

That any of these domestic workers interviewed in *Telling Memories* discussed rape and sexual harassment or its ramifications for them and their families is remarkable given the "culture of dissemblance" (Hine 1989, 915–16) or silence surrounding rape, a silence enforced to protect white men and taken up by black communities to shield blacks from further harm. Tucker relays that, according to black domestics, black men resented their wives working in black homes; it undermined their male identity as providers and protectors (Tucker 1988, 152). One domestic worker shared, "My husband never wanted me to work in a home where the man was home. He knew that white men would try and brush up against me, maybe offer extra money, and this was an insult to him" (152). One domestic, Leila Parkerson, "saw firsthand how a white man could proposition a black domestic" (159). Another, Voncille Sherard explains that her white male employer "tried to force me in the bed . . . tell[ing] me how much more I could make if I would go to bed with him" (217). On another occasion, according to Sherard, a white Canadian man—a friend of the family for whom she worked as a domestic—exposed himself to her (217–18). Importantly, when she shared the latter scenario with her mother and grandmother, they seemed very familiar with this scenario and cautioned her against telling her father for fear of what might befall him, if he tried to address the harassment. Sherard explains, "I can remember their faces and the way they said, 'Please don't tell your daddy about this.' Their faces—it was like they'd heard this before" (218). The fear of retribution and a lack of justice for black female victims was, of course, a legitimate concern. Another domestic whose husband attempted to confront an employer who sexually harassed his wife, for instance, was fined twenty-five dollars and thrown in jail (Hunter 1997, 106).

The oral history relayed in *Telling Memories* echoes that of domestics in other historical studies. As historian Elizabeth Clark-Lewis (1994, 48) relays in *Living in, Living Out: African American Domestics in Washington, D.C., 1910–1940*, for instance, black women were advised not to be alone with white men or boys, or to flee if necessary, in order to avoid being raped. One laborer, Odessa Minnie Barnes relates, "Nobody was sent out before you was told to be careful of the white man or his sons. They'd tell you the stories of rape . . . hard too! No lies. You was to be told true, so you'd not get raped. Everyone warned you and told you 'be careful'" (48). Another worker, Ora Fisher explained that her father provided a razor blade to her as a weapon to be used if a white man tried to rape her while laboring as a domestic in a white family's home (48–49).

In addition to sharing warnings about the possibilities of rape, domestic workers also chose to do "days work," where they came for the day and returned home, as opposed to "living in," or staying in white families' homes. Historian Tera Hunter (1997, 106) explains: "The fear of sexual exploitation . . . discouraged women from choosing to live in. A black woman's body, in slavery and freedom, was treated as though it were not her own, nor even the conventional prerogative of her father or spouse." Some domestic workers opted to live with employers out of "convenience," but the majority avoided this (105–6). The persistent vulnerability of black women to rape, as Darlene Clark Hine (1989, 913–15) has persuasively argued, was likely a key factor in the Great Migration, the movement in the early part of the twentieth century of tens of thousands of blacks from the South to northern cities and to a lesser extent to points west, such as Texas and California.

Domestic workers, moreover, were often required to endure syphilis tests as a requirement for employment. Conventional medical thinking painted black people in general and black women in particular as sources of social taint, moral impropriety, and disease. In *Unprotected Labor: Household Workers, Politics, and Middle-Class Reform in New York, 1870–1940*, historian Vanessa May recounts that blacks were characterized as "'syphilis-soaked'" (May 2011, 130) and domestics, such as those in Newark, New Jersey, were often required to undergo syphilis tests, among others, even though the medical profession understood that this disease was sexually transmitted (129). In reality this fear of the communication of sexual disease and painting of black women as sexually loose had more to do with the proclivities of the men in whose homes they labored. May underscores, "Tellingly, few medical or cultural sources even hinted that white men might be the source of syphilis epidemics among domestic workers in white households" (130). In light of this historical reality, the movie version of *The Help*'s obsession with sanitation laws takes on a new meaning. It becomes a marker, again, of the repression of knowledge of white male rape of black women.

Given the reality of rape and harassment that plagued black women, and particularly the general substance and tenor of that history relayed in *Telling Memories*—again, a book drawn on by Stockett in writing *The Help*—one might anticipate that black domestics' experience of sexual abuse might be forthrightly addressed in the latter book. Sadly, this is not the case. Stockett takes pains to explain through Skeeter and other characters she fashions many of the difficulties blacks experienced dealing with public segregation—different seats in public accommodation, different access to food counters, different educational resources, among other things—and the patronizing, paternalistic behavior of whites toward domestics in white homes, but she does little to expose the intimate forms of terror visited upon black workers who were deemed "help." To the contrary, Stockett chooses to foreground a romanticized version of black female domestic workers' relationship with white men, via the fantasy of hidden romance between Constantine's mother, a black woman, and the white man who was Constantine's biological father.

Specifically, the main white female protagonist, Skeeter, has in Constantine, her family's domestic laborer, a second mother of sorts, one who helps a socially, physically awkward girl to feel positive about herself. To signify the closeness of the relationship Stockett tells the reader that when Skeeter is fourteen Constantine shares a secret with her: Constantine's father is white. This secret is revealed as they are working through a puzzle during a storm, the former perhaps symbolizing the scattered, unformed picture of racial politics and the latter, the storm, representing tumult that will soon engulf the country during the Civil Rights Movement. Constantine tells Skeeter that her father looks like Abraham Lincoln, the president known as the Great Emancipator, given his role in signing the Emancipation Proclamation, an obvious attempt by Stockett to conjure allusions to racial equanimity for Constantine's father. Constantine relays a loving relationship between her and her white father:

> Oh, my daddy looooved me. Always said I was his favorite. . . . He used to come over to the house ever Saturday afternoon, and one time, he give me a set a ten hair ribbons, ten different colors. Brought em over from Paris, made out a Japanese silk. I sat in his lap from the minute he got there until he had to leave and Mama'd play Bessie Smith on the Victrola he brung her and he and me'd sing: It's mighty strange, without a doubt[.] Nobody knows you when you're down and out[.] (Stockett 2009, 112–13)

Anticipating a storyline that will follow later in the book over difficulties Constantine will have with race, Constantine also relays a story of her father consoling her when she was having "hard feelings" (113). Although these are ostensibly nondescript ("One time I was boo-hooing over hard feelings, I reckon I had a list a things to be upset about, being poor, cold baths, rotten tooth, I don't know"), Skeeter gathers that there is a deeper meaning, that her father "apologized to her [Constantine] for," the hardship she faced because of race and a society that did not allow them to be an openly loving family (113).

Hence, although the black domestic workers in *Telling Memories* generally discuss the difficulties dealing with sexual predation when discussing black domestics' relationships with white men, Stockett affirms the white female denial of white male rape and harassment of black women, by crafting a fantasy of interracial romance, a rape-cum-love storyline that is a notable go-to strategy for discussing white male–black female sex. Skeeter gives no indication that she takes this story to be anything but a romance. In many ways, the fantasy of interracial romance that Constantine, Stockett's character, describes between her white father and black mother is the mirror opposite of the opening narrative of Priscilla Butler, the real-life daughter and domestic worker in *Telling Memories* whose description of her black mother and white father opens that book of oral history. Butler's domestic worker mother was raped and impregnated by her employer's son. Stockett enables the fantasy of interracial romance by leaving the reader no information about the nature of Constantine's mother and father's relationship. We know relatively little about Constantine's black mother, aside from the fact that she is tall. Since domestic labor is an employment option that black women participated in generationally, it is not a stretch to presume that her mother also was a domestic laborer—but this is something we cannot know. Also, where Butler's father only entered her life after her mother's death, and then only, at first, through his brother, Andrew, Constantine's father, a replica of Abraham Lincoln, comes to visit weekly. Where in *Telling Memories* Butler's feelings about her father range from disgust to boredom, in the book version of *The Help*, Constantine loves her father. This fantasy of interracial romance is borne out of a denial of white male rape and harassment of black women in general and as domestic laborers in particular. It typifies the "miscege-nation" Aimee Carrillo Rowe describes (and that I discuss in Chapter 2), where racial healing for the nation is signaled through white male–black female sex or romance.

Throughout most of the book version of *The Help*, Skeeter tries in vain to piece together what has happened to the family's longtime domestic worker, Constantine. Her mother brushes off her queries, and others are reluctant to speak of it. Eventually, after being pressed by a New York publisher to write about Constantine, a domestic worker writes out the narrative. Importantly, some of the narrative is relayed verbally. The bulk of it, however, is literally an "unspeakable thing, unspoken" (Morrison 2000), and is shared with Skeeter in written form, so that she can consume the reality of what happens in a mediated form of communication.

Skeeter learns that Constantine has a child who is so fair that she appears "white," and the difficulty and shame Constantine has dealing with this reality causes her to banish her daughter by giving her up to an orphanage in Chicago, Illinois. Having a child who looks phenotypically "white" (the child, Lulabelle, has a fair complexion and straight blonde hair) causes Constantine to experience a greater level of surveillance by whites. Stockett (2009, 572–73) writes, "White folks would stop her, ask her all suspicious what she doing toting round a white child. Policeman used to stop her on State Street, told her she need to get her uniform on." Black people also treated Constantine poorly, seeing her as "distrustful, like she done something wrong" (573). Neither relatives nor other community members would care for Lulabelle (572–73). Consequently, Constantine took her child to an orphanage for black children in Chicago, a decision she later regretted (572–74).

Although Lulabelle and Constantine try to reconnect years later, Lulabelle is banished once again, when Lulabelle's subversive racial play undermines Skeeter's mother's racist thinking. After Lulabelle gets Constantine's address from her adoptive parents and she writes Constantine, Lulabelle and her mother correspond, resulting in a planned reunion. But when Lulabelle arrives at Skeeter's mother's home, she happens upon a meeting of the Daughters of the American Revolution in progress, and Lulabelle quietly affronts the racial caste boundaries in place, mingling amid the women present, partaking of refreshments, and even signing up to be a member. Skeeter's mother, alarmed at the brazenness of Lulabelle passing as white, demands that Lulabelle leave and that she not return to her home, not even Constantine's quarters. She informs Lulabelle, as well, that her mother did not give her up because she was unable to care for her, but because she was ashamed of her. Thus, Lulabelle is banished once again because her light skin as an African-descended woman, and her violation of the raced and gendered social boundaries evidenced by mingling among white guests, troubles the social construction of racial segregation. Lulabelle and her mother, Constantine, both return to Chicago, where Constantine, described by Skeeter's mother as not fit for the foreign, cold environment, dies within a few weeks.

On the face of it, Stockett undoubtedly includes this narrative as a way to show the irony of racial constructedness[6]—and it certainly is not unique. It draws on similar themes from *Imitation of Life*, a famous film in which a sepia-toned black mother and her fair-skinned child confront the boundaries of a racial caste system (Kennedy 2017, 30–32). Aside from a putative assault on racist logic or play on popular themes about racism and black mammy figures in movies, however, the story also has a latent function of repressing a discussion of white male rape of black women and the shame this unspeakable secret unconsciously holds for white men and white women.

In her novel, Stockett creates a social environment that frames shame as a ubiquitous, defining element of the human condition. In doing so, she flattens the experience of shame alluded to in the case of Constantine's experiences with and treatment of Lulabelle. Skeeter, for instance, is ashamed of the elitism and racist and sexist views of her family, friends, and community. One black person, Minnie Jackson, is ashamed of her husband's abuse. The white woman who is from a working-class background is ashamed of her inability to have children. And, in the case of Constantine, as noted above, the specter of shame is raised in terms of her child, Lulabelle. Again, not only is she born out of wedlock and with a phenotype that raises questions of paternity, but Constantine gives her up for adoption as opposed to dealing with the putative difficulties of rearing a fair-skinned black child, a decision she comes to regret. In this free-floating environment of shame, there is little that distinguishes the defining contours of each person's "shame," and the travesty and white shame of white male rape of black women are never broached. She creates the type of "false equivalency" (Kennedy 2017, 34) that is a stock characteristic of "post discourses."

Moreover, setting this climactic revelation regarding Constantine and her daughter in this generalized environment of shame displaces the shame of white male rape of black women. Constantine becomes a vehicle through which the unspeakability of white male predation can be expressed. Skeeter's mother, who stands in for the racial and gender norms of the times, not only banishes Lulabelle because she dares to defy the carefully laid invisible lines of racial interaction, but also because her very existence is evidence that those lines are always already routinely transgressed by white men. This history and evidence are disavowed or repressed, but, in any case, demand an active defense to keep them from center stage.

This focus on Constantine's ostensibly shameful acts, of course, is made possible in no small part by the romanticized depiction and social amnesia regarding her father. Skeeter's mother, who made knowing about all of her employees' backgrounds and comings and goings her business, makes no mention of him. This man, moreover, an Abraham look-alike, appears as an understanding, engaged, loving father, who shares a mutually affectionate relationship with his daughter Constantine. For Stockett, the prototypical father is well loved by his daughters. Stockett writes of Mae Mobley, a white child featured in the book *The Help*, "all Baby Girl loves her daddy" (Stockett 2009, 687). One wonders under what circumstances this is always the case. Indeed, in order for little girls to love their fathers, they certainly cannot imagine them as rapists or sexual harassers. If little white girls who grow up into grown white women are to continue to love their fathers and by extension their brothers and other family members, it would be difficult for them to truly grapple with white male sexual predation or their role in maintaining a sexist, racist apartheid world order. Stockett's choices—to romanticize Constantine's relationship with her father, to ignore the reality of white male rape of black women, and to cast Constantine as afflicted with shame and unable to handle the reality of her personal family history of miscegenation represented in her daughter—conspire to repress historical and cultural memory of white male rape and harassment of black domestic workers.

As egregious as these layers of repression and displacement of shame in the book form of *The Help* are, they are amplified in the movie version of *The Help* with a suppression of even the storyline regarding Constantine's white father and fair-skinned black child. The movie retains the Constantine plotline, showing Skeeter's attachment to Constantine, Constantine's influence on Skeeter, and Skeeter's mother's avoidance of revealing what really happened to Constantine, but in a revised form. When the movie's version of the truth of what happened to Constantine is revealed, Lulabelle is not portrayed as fair-skinned, but a brown-skinned black woman, and her transgression of racial protocols in Skeeter's mother's home, while treated as problematic, loses its force and nuance with this altered storyline. In the movie version of *The Help*, moreover, Skeeter's mother is a somewhat reformed character in terms of her racial attitudes, even supporting Skeeter in resisting the threatening gestures of Hilly, one of the white women exposed in the book produced by Skeeter and the domestic workers in Jackson, Mississippi.

Tanya Ann Kennedy provides further clarity for Stockett's use of shame to avoid dealing with her own implication in the white racial politics in which she was reared. Kennedy (2017, 24–25) notes that Stockett began writing *The Help* the day after the attacks of September 11, 2001, thus signaling a desire for the comfort and "maternal nurturance" she received from the domestic worker, Demetrie, who helped raise her and a social context that she perceived as intact. Stockett (quoted in ibid., 28) writes, "'I feel a little ashamed to admit . . . it was not until I was 30 nearly 35 that I really began to question and think about for the first time in my life what Demetrie must have been thinking and feeling as she was taking care of our family.'" Although Stockett states that her intent is to give voice to black domestic workers, like the one she knew, she in fact gives voice to a white female perspective that is innocent of the political, economic, and social damage of racism. Setting the story in the decade before she came of age, Stockett positions readers to understand racism and blacks' experiences of it as a shame that is behind us. In this way, Kennedy (2017, 26–29) argues, Stockett's narrative serves as "temporal management" in which we revisit and refashion a past that serves our ideological needs in the present (in this case assuaging guilt for US racism and short-circuiting self-reflexivity about the political climate that facilitated 9/11). This desire to position racism as a thing of the past is a core feature of post-politics. It anesthetizes many to the ongoing reality of oppression and their own role in its perpetuation.

Significantly, despite *The Help* (the movie)'s defenses, the history of black female violation "haunts" this narrative.[7] Esther Rashkin (2008), drawing on the work of psychoanalysts Abraham and Torok (1994), observes that secrets can be repressed and transmitted unconsciously, and, therefore, come to "haunt" or cryptically remain in narratives. This is exactly what happens in the obsession throughout the book and movie with hygiene and cleanliness and defecation. Recall that Skeeter, the main character in *The Help*, learns of the segregation laws governing the state, and that her high-society friends are keen on passing sanitation laws. The use of white toilets is forbidden to black domestics, in fact.

This focus on hygiene parallels historical concern for and policing of black female domestics' sexual hygiene. Black domestics in New Jersey, as noted above, had to be tested for syphilis before being employed, as this was thought to run rampant among African American populations and was treated as if it were easily communicable, like a common cold, as opposed to being a sexually transmitted infection. The hysteria around black domestics' use of white bathrooms—like the hysteria around black women's supposed infection with syphilis—is a proxy for the sexual violation of black women that "infected" white domestic space. In this way, although the book and movie try to disavow or repress the history of white male rape of black women, it haunts both texts through the obsession with cleanliness. It gives special meaning as well to the use of feces placed in a chocolate pie to be consumed by a racist ringleader: what is consumed from "the space between" (Philip 1997, 94; McKittrick 2006, 46–52) black women's legs is not related to reproduction and life, but to annihilation or death.

Limitations on what can be translated to movies from their predecessor books will always occur. Less important than what explains the differences from novel to film, however, are the narrative implications and effects. What is the function of this movie's narratives and what does the redaction of significant historical facts from the book reveal? The foregoing analysis of *The Help* demonstrates defensive mechanisms at work, specifically how psychological defenses of disavowal and repression take shape, whatever the conscious motives or reasons people may have for making changes in novels that become movies or other shifts in narratives more generally. Figure 4.1 illustrates the transition from the defenses of denial, to disavowal, to repression evident in *Telling Memories*, and the book and then movie versions of *The Help*, respectively. Figure 4.2 depicts the "haunting" that is present, even amid the defenses invoked.

Moreover, pinpointing the disavowal and repression in the book and movie versions of *The Help*, respectively, is important not only in examining how these psychological defenses operate but why they matter. Tracing these defense mechanisms provides occasion to review the political function of black women's sexual abuse in its connection to US civic membership and political development. In this context

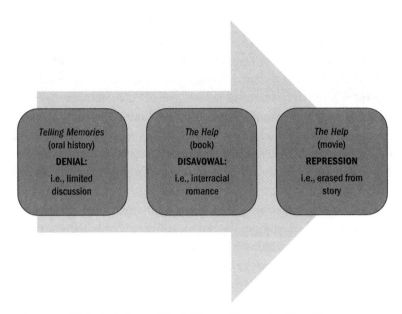

Figure 4.1. White Male Rape of Black Women/Domestics: Transition in Defenses

we can better explain the insinuation of this history in the primary, stereotypical symbols of black womanhood—the mammy and the Jezebel—and their current mutations, and the influence of these symbols in culture, law, politics, and other domains. Reviewing the political function of black women's sexual abuse helps us to understand how melodramatic frames of victors and villains are generally not applied to black women as rape victims, particularly as it relates to white male rapists; why the prevalence and lack of convictions for black female rape, regardless of the race of the perpetrators, is not seen as part of a black political agenda or US social crises; and how the repression and disavowal of black female rape is institutionally driven. The next chapter discusses the MeToo movement and details, among other things, how the alleged rape of a black immigrant housekeeper by an important global white male figure is a practical example or case study of how the unspeakable secret of black women's abuse and its attendant signification of black women as paradigmatically unworthy plays out in the institutional context of the law.

Of course, some might say that the spate of movies including depictions of black female rape by white men in recent years cuts against the notion that this is somehow repressed. We have seen, for instance, a plethora of new movies documenting the "history" of racial oppression, or otherwise focused on themes related to slavery or Jim Crow, which usually involve or include white male rape of black women. *The Butler* (Daniels 2013) includes in its opening scenes a white overseer sharecropper having his way with a black female worker (played by Mariah Carey). *Twelve Years a Slave* (McQueen 2013) depicts several instances of sexual abuse of black women by white men, with one particularly vicious scene. Quentin Tarantino, in his penchant for revenge films and fetishization of black masculinity, produced *Django Unchained* (Tarantino 2013), a spaghetti Western remake of the classic *Django*, in which a black male husband seeks to reclaim his wife who has been abducted by a brutal slave master. And, of course, Nate Parker's 2016 movie *Birth of a Nation* (Parker 2016) inserted an example of white male rape of a black woman, which black men avenged.

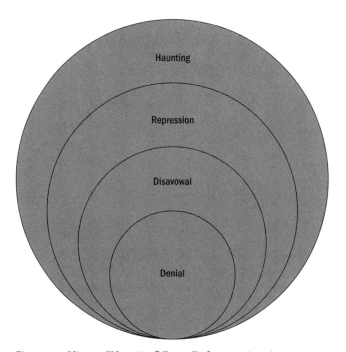

Figure 4.2. History "Haunting" Every Defense against Awareness

Notably, in each case, these inclusions of black female rape by white men affirm familiar storylines in popular culture that displace black women's subjectivity, construct fantasies of disavowal, or show black women to be traitors. In *The Butler*, Mariah Carey's character is twice victimized—first by the rape and then by the misdirection of its meaning. The rape of Carey's character is relevant to the story not in and of itself, but because it highlights the inability of the black male character who plays her husband to protect her. Similarly, in *Django Unchained*, rape serves as a metaphor or sign of black male patriarchal insufficiency. Django's, Nat Turner's, and others' revenge of white male rape of black women assuages black male woundedness through its narrative of vindication and revenge. These narratives are nothing new. As others, such as Sarah Projansky (2001, especially Chapter 5) have argued, in post-feminist narratives involving black women and rape, the focus is often on male characters.

Twelve Years a Slave is distinct in its focus on the brutality of slavery. But what does it tell us about black women? More specifically, what does it tell us about rape? The main black female character in the show, Patsy, is a fully dominated female. She works harder than men on the plantation, is raped by her master, and is degraded along with the other slaves in myriad ways. The rape scene focusing on this character shows an inert Patsy being acted upon by her white slave master. We see her pleading but not fighting back. During the scene his pleasure and omnipotence or seeming omnipotence provide the visual focus. Elsewhere in the film, rape serves to highlight the vulnerability of black male slaves and the complicity of black women with the slave system. In an opening scene, for instance, a black woman is carted off on a slave ship with other captured slaves with her black male counterparts looking on. In a conversation with Alfre Woodward's character, the audience learns that Woodward's character has been "wed" to her white plantation owner, and although she tells of a coming time of reckoning because of the unrighteousness, brutality, and injustice of slavery, she suggests to Patsy that Patsy's owner's affections might provide her an equally diminished life of service or abuse as in her own case.

What all of these movies have in common is a deferral of acknowledging the brutality of forced and coerced rape, substituting instead a narrative of black male woundedness or inserting a less problematic fantasy. The latter especially serves as a form of disavowal, where, as noted earlier, unwanted realities are evaded not by total repression but by substitution of a less offensive or palatable viewpoint. With *Django Unchained*, despite the rape, the black male protagonist is seen as growing stronger because, able to exact revenge on his owner, he can be the rightful patriarch. With *Twelve Years a Slave*, black women are either depicted as desiring, if not coveting, sexual abuse by white men in exchange for less brutal enslavement, as with Woodward's character, or black women are depicted as so debased and overcome by enslavement that they are the ultimate Other. What is conveniently discounted is black women's resistance. Black women are surely especially oppressed based on race, gender, and other grounds, but to not include a holistic picture, which includes their efforts at resistance (Davies 2014), fails to capture their humanity, as does, ironically, its opposite, that is, an overemphasis on romanticized heroic representations. Such movies as *The Butler* and *Twelve Years a Slave* are particularly troubling in that they claim to be "based on a true story," and thus are taken as fact as opposed to a fictionalized representation of what writers and directors take as truth.

Conclusion

In this chapter I have advanced several arguments. First and foremost, I have examined the repression of the history of black women's sexual abuse by white men as it relates to post-politics and melodrama. In keeping with other chapters, I have shown how melodrama and post-politics can usefully shed new light on common issues in the study of gender and race and ethnic politics. Hence, I have explored what this repression of white male rape of black women means for political theory and US-based American political development; I have done this by examining the implications of this repressed history for understanding theories of social contract. Although the classic understanding of the private-public dichotomy maps one dimension of white male–white female relating, black women's subjectivity exposes a relational dynamic in which race, class, and gender are mutually constitutive constructs within the context of the social contract. More specifically, if white women's bodies are identified specifically with the private sphere, it is as the formal, legally recognized lady of the house. Black women, particularly when they function as domestic workers, are considered as being "like one of the family" (Collins 2006, Chapter 1) and serve as stand-ins for a repressed dimension of Western thinking. As the "'other' of the 'other'" (Wallace 1990, 53), they signify the forgotten, the dispossessed—bodies that can be placed in the home, in the field, and bear the mark of being abject or utterly traversed. Black women are the limen between the public and the private. When we acknowledge that domestic spaces are places of labor, we see that there is no true split between the public and private (A. D. Davis 2004).

Although some people argue that white men choosing to enter into and develop romantic relationships with black women in the context of slavery, Reconstruction, or Jim Crow complicates our understanding of racial relationships and power and gender, this is highly contestable. The notion that people can enter into loving relationships assumes a level of agency that is simply not possible in the racialized dynamics under slavery and segregation. In any event, white men are generally positioned as choosing the terms upon which they relate to black women. Moreover, no single trend regarding white males relating toward black women undermines the weight of what is normative; in its exceptionality, it proves the rule.

White male rape of black women and the repression of this history have profound implications for understandings of politics. Acknowledging this history rewrites our interpretation of the social contract. Moreover, it highlights the centrality of black women to US-based American political development, and the operation of gender, race, and class dynamics. Among other things, it also disrupts a simplistic notion of white feminism as enlightened or progressive in terms of racial politics, as the figure of Skeeter in *The Help* represents.

Jane Flax (2010) underscores the United States' failure to mourn its history of slavery and race/gender oppression. As Freud noted, when grief is not allowed to run its natural course, it leads to a sort of melancholia. This melancholia makes one sick and weighs down one's heart, undermining psychological and physical well-being. A true mourning is the only way to expunge it. Although I do agree with the general idea of melancholia as it relates to the evasion of the impact of slavery and its aftermath, I underscore a slightly different understanding of mourning.

As Harold Bush Jr. (2007, 36) has argued, grief is something that never ends, and it is not true that "time heals all wounds." As he notes, in some cases, grief can become more debilitating as time goes on (37). The work of mourning then is not an end in itself, but an ongoing process.

Key to this mourning is the "speaking" of what have heretofore been "unspeakable things unspoken" (Morrison 2000). According to Rashkin (2008, 20), the speaking enables the ability to overcome the trauma, not in terms of "forgetting" it or "moving on" in a way that suggests a disconnection from the experience, but in a way that "signifies rather that the subject has surmounted an obstacle to being and can now reengage in the (still challenging) process of going-on-being." In contrast to melancholia, what mourning through speaking enables is an eyes-wide-open approach that enables a healing process, but with an understanding of our human frailty and a watchfulness to those habits, structures, and critical cultural shifts that may damage it once again.

Resisting melodramatic, post-feminist, post–Civil Rights narratives through speaking about the role of white male rape of black women becomes an imperative on multiple levels. Antisexist, antiracist activists especially should underscore this history. Often in our accounts of race and rape, in our classes or our texts, we are sure to mention the myth of the black male rapist, which we should. But this is at best an incomplete treatment and, at worst, a subtle and unintentional means of burying the racist reality of white male rape of black women and its historical significance to US-based American political development and its contemporary effects. The history of the reality of white male rapists of black women should be taught alongside and in its connection with the myth of the black male rapist. Women's rights organizations and Civil Rights organizations should themselves revisit this history as a means of informing their political practice, at least if they intend to respond to the needs of those black women who are arguably part of the constituencies they claim to represent.

The next and final chapter examines melodrama and post-politics in terms of the MeToo movement. We see how the repression of racialized, sexual violence, particularly as experienced by black women, serves as a bellwether for the larger society, and how the MeToo movement embodies the return of the repressed and disavowed sexual predation commonplace in society.

5

MeToo?

Black Women, Melodrama, and Sexual Harassment

You know, I'm automatically attracted to beautiful—I just start kissing them. It's like a magnet. Just kiss. I don't even wait. And when you're a star, they let you do it. You can do anything. . . . Grab 'em by the p****. You can do anything.
—Donald Trump (Bullock 2016)

For most of the trial, the man who nurtured his father-figure image faced the greatest challenge of his life without the presence of his family to lend support. In the front row reserved for Cosby's supporters, there were often empty seats.
—Roig-Franzia (2018)

In 2017, *Time* magazine chose the MeToo resistance as its Person of the Year. Key figures associated with the heightened exposure of sexual harassment—farm worker Isabel Pascual, lobbyist Adama Iwu, veteran Hollywood actress Ashley Judd, Uber engineer Susan Fowler, and pop singer Taylor Swift—were featured on the cover, along with a partial image of an anonymous individual. Dubbed "the silence breakers" (Zacharek, Dockterman, and Edwards 2017), each of these individuals, along with many others, in some fashion resisted and exposed sexual harassment in their respective careers in ways that spurred further exposure of harassment and activism against it. As *Time*'s editor in chief Edward Felsenthal (2017, 32) observed on the choice for Person of the Year, "The galvanizing actions of the women on our cover . . .—along with those of hundreds of others, and of many men as well, have unleashed one of the highest-velocity shifts in our culture since the 1960s."

Although recent years have seen exposure of sexual violence and harassment in the Catholic Church (Carroll et al. 2002a; 2002b);

educational institutions, such as Penn State (Rohan 2012); and even an Atlanta megachurch (McKinley and Brown 2010; Kenneally 2011), among other settings, the public outing of Harvey Weinstein served as a tipping point in national attention to sexual harassment. Ashley Judd and others discussed the predatory behavior of Weinstein in the pages of the *New York Times* and the *New Yorker*. Alyssa Milano used the #MeToo hashtag on Twitter, asking for others to chime in regarding their experiences, and the response was overwhelming. Social media, such as Facebook, but especially Twitter, amplified and ignited concern regarding the Harvey Weinstein sexual abuse scandal in particular and sexual abuse more generally. *Time* reported, "The hashtag #MeToo has now been used millions of times in at least 85 countries" (Felsenthal 2017, 32). With almost dizzying speed, in subsequent months the public witnessed a cascade of mostly women, but also some men, revealing the ways in which they have been abused particularly in work settings. The list of those publicly accused of harassment include, but is not limited to, Hollywood notables such as Kevin Spacey and Louis C.K.; news figures such as Matt Lauer and Tavis Smiley; and politicians such as Al Franken.

The election of Donald Trump as president set the stage for this eruption of attention. During the 2016 presidential campaign, the public heard, via a leaked audio recording, Trump in his own words describing the ways in which he sexually assaulted women, as one of the epigraphic quotations recounts; boldly noting how he liked to "move on" women without invitation or consent and even "grab 'em by the p****" (Bullock 2016), the explicit evidence of Trump's predatory behavior initially seemed to threaten his presidency. Trump sidestepped a destructive end to his campaign, however, through cunning maneuvers. During one of his final debates with Democratic presidential candidate Hillary Clinton, he showcased women who had allegedly been harassed or who had affairs with Bill Clinton. Media framing, produced by his surrogates and supporters, labeled and dismissed Trump's words "as locker room" talk.

Subsequently, in response to Trump's election, women's marches were staged in the nation's capital, in every state, and even in other countries. Although not without controversy surrounding their aims, tactics, and relative lack of diversity along a number of fronts, the marches, which featured some protestors donning pink "p**** hats," registered general discontent with Trump's presidency, drawing crowds and attention that eclipsed the president's inauguration occurring on the same day.

Although the current mobilization against sexual harassment is the result of many sources, Trump's election is undoubtedly a precipitating event. With a sitting president arguably serving as "predator in chief," some were moved to action by this fact. Susan Fowler, a whistle-blower formerly employed with Uber, relates, "'I remember feeling powerless . . . like even the government wasn't looking out for us'" (Felsenthal 2017, 33). Ashwini Tambe conveys a similar perspective. Riffing off of psychiatrist Frantz Fanon's notion of horizontal violence, Tambe suggests that we are witnessing "horizontal action" (Vedantam 2018). Just as the racially oppressed, unable to attack their oppressors, may instead direct their anger toward those around them (hence, Fanon's characterization of horizontal violence), individuals in response to Trump take "horizontal action" to respond to "those perpetrators close at hand" (Vedantam 2018). Tambe observes, "I think the election of Donald Trump has served as a trigger, and it has provoked a great deal of fury and impatience because he represents, for many people, the ultimate unpunished predator" (Vedantam 2018). The horizontal action enacted in the MeToo campaign has galvanized a great deal of support and facilitated exposure and censure among the broader public. This nascent leg of the latest movement against sexual harassment is still unfolding, but *Time*'s choice of the MeToo movement is undoubtedly a worthy one to mark the important shift in attention and action in this moment.

Noticeably absent from the cover marking this historic era, however, was Tarana Burke, the progenitor of the MeToo framework, a limitation commentators were swift to mention. Tarana Burke founded a group, Just Be Inc., to support sexual assault and harassment survivors ("'Me Too' Creator Tarana Burke" 2017). As part of her work, she initiated a MeToo campaign as a means of fostering connection among survivors and countering the shame and loneliness often associated with their experiences. As commentators noted, although Burke appeared within the pages of the issue, this omission of Burke from the cover embodied a serious kind of whitewashing, one that mirrored the general whiteness of the victims and the sidelining of harassment faced by black women and other women of color, as well as their contributions to the movement against sexual violence and harassment in the workplace (see, e.g., Estrada 2017; Murray 2017).

In this chapter, I build on the work of Chapter 4, which talked about the various defenses used to evade the reality of white male rape of black women. More specifically, I deepen our exploration of liminality by showing how race, gender, and class operate to sideline black people in discussions of sexual harassment. Liminality, as you recall, tracks with melodrama's production of pure victims and pure villains, where social and political issues are individualized and read into personal relations in domestic or private space. In the case of sexual harassment, the power of melodrama works to thwart justice for victims, framing concerns as individual, personal issues rather than institutional practices, focusing attention instead on the relative virtue and virtuelessness of those involved. But what does liminality mean for black communities? Or how does liminality operate regarding black communities and sexual harassment? How does liminality, which situates individuals betwixt and between social positions, operate in the context of sexual harassment and rape?

I argue that black people are generally denied the space of "victim" in the melodramas that appertain to rape and sexual harassment. Black women, because they are defined as abject others, particularly in relationship to white women, are unrapable in most contexts. As I relate in Chapter 4, a range of defenses are activated to deny white male rape of black women, which has ongoing implications, including that black women are arguably more vulnerable to rape by all perpetrators. Indeed, although white rape victims are demeaned and attacked in the context of rape, particularly in trials, white women in general at least have access to being considered valued and protected. This explains in part why the default face of the MeToo movement has been that of elite white women. The figure of the black matriarch—in all her various iterations—frustrates efforts to see black women as subjects of harm. Rape then is not seen as a consensus issue (Cohen 1999, Chapter 1) in black politics, and black women are not the default of the "rape victim" category.

I examine two case studies that highlight how black women are not seen as representative victims imagined in US society at large or that emerge from black cultural pathology melodrama. The first case study I examine looks to the extraordinary situation of Dominique Strauss-Kahn's rape of Nafissatou Diallo, a black immigrant domestic worker in

New York. We view how Diallo is a liminal subject: the initial public and prosecutorial support of Diallo gave way to denigration of her. The case allows us to see the complicating factors of not only race, but class and immigration status, where some immigrants are deemed good and acceptable and others are placed beyond the embrace of social acceptance and protection. This case also highlights the transnational business masculinity (Connell 2012) that can trade on sexual access, including rape.

In the second case study, I examine business masculinity regarding a domestic figure, Bill Cosby. With Cosby, we are able to examine the ways in which the powerful can groom, harass, and rape others systematically. At one level, this bears similarity to Weinstein and others who are similarly situated as power brokers within particular industries and workplaces. But more than that, with Cosby, we come full circle in seeing how the Moynihan-inspired black cultural pathology melodrama serves as a key post-feminist, post-racial frame for understanding culture and politics. Cosby played a prototypical father figure—not only a super minority, but also a symbolic father on screen, as I discuss more later in the chapter. As I explain in Chapter 2, black symbolic fathers, among other things, are seen as representing an idealized patriarch who serves as a stand-in for the black community. I show how, as a black symbolic father, Cosby's private predation is yet consistent with an interpretation of manhood that enacts ultimate control, including control of others' careers and bodies. This second case study thus enables us to see both the way in which harassment and assault play into pernicious forms of business masculinity and how the melodramas spawned by black cultural pathology melodrama play a specific role in black cultural and political discourse.

As a road map, I develop my argument in three movements. First, I highlight key moments in the history of black women's opposition to harassment and rape—from slavery to early harassment cases and, of course, the Clarence Thomas Supreme Court hearings. Second, I explore the two aforementioned case studies focusing on International Monetary Fund chief Dominique Strauss-Kahn's alleged rape of a black immigrant domestic worker, Nafissatou Diallo, and Bill Cosby's decades-long predation. The former usefully highlights transnational business masculinity (Connell 2012) and the unique challenges of black immigrants relating to rape. As I discuss at length later, the latter shows how Cosby-as-symbolic-father addresses his own wounded masculinity through "père-version" (Wright 2013), that is, self-authoring—or self-fathering. Like others, I see black women as canaries in the coal mines regarding the fight against sexual harassment, and find in these case studies poignant examples of exactly how power operates through melodramatic framing to undermine justice for victims. Third, I offer sadomasochism as an analytic that can help us to understand the operation of harassment and rape in workplaces and suggest that whistle-blowers and their experiences can aid our comprehension of how power operates to constrain and further traumatize rape victims. I argue, among other things, that access to people's bodies is a prerogative of white supremacist, masculinist culture—not an anomaly, but a feature that is shaped by and constitutes an ongoing legacy of the peculiar institution.

Black Women and the History of Sexual Harassment

In *Southern History across the Colorline*, Nell Painter (2002, Chapter 1) underscores the need to take a "fully loaded cost accounting" of slavery's impact. She contends that we have never adequately assessed the enduring effects in the United States of the peculiar institution on cultural norms, psychology, and institutions, not just in black communities, but also for the nation as a whole. Legal scholar Adrienne Davis (2004, 468 [emphasis in original]) echoes similar sentiments in her work on slavery, explaining, "Despite its historical specificity, the plantation offers a paradigm case of sexual harassment, domestic violence, rape, and incest as on a continuum of *sexual* violences. . . . [And] despite our desire [as feminists] to preserve sex as the realm of the positive, part of labeling slavery a sexual economy is to remind us that we can't always conveniently segregate private, intimate relations from market, work relations, or sexual harassment from other forms of violence against women." In this work, and especially in the case studies I explore below, I see the production of transnational business masculinity and a patriarchal priority of sexual access in workplaces as bearing the imprint of slavery.

Relatedly, although many people associate the fight against sexual harassment and feminism more generally with white women, it is important to recover and highlight the active role that black women have played resisting what we have come to know as workplace sexual harassment. Black women, as liminal subjects, are defined in the context of sexual harassment as abject figures, Others who are deemed the opposite of virtuous womanhood. We can push back against the erasure of black women as survivors of harassment and rape by focusing in on their experiences. As I demonstrate throughout this chapter, centering black women's experiences not only makes their role as black political women visible, it shows black women as classic canaries in the coal mine. Their experiences and responses often prefigure more visible, later examples.

As indicated above, for instance, Adrienne Davis shows that we can think of plantations as workplaces and examine the sexual harassment that occurred there. Davis explains the nature of slavery as a sexual political economy, that is, a means of exploitation that, for black women, extracted "productive, reproductive, and sexual labor" (Davis 2004, 457). Davis also highlights the ways in which black women's resistance to their exploitation and abuse in the context of slavery represents some of the earliest resistance to sexual harassment. She argues that understanding black women in particular and black communities in general and their resistance to slavery helps us to rethink several critical debates. She contends that understanding sexual harassment and resistance against it in the context of slavery "puts the sex back in sexual harassment" (468), underscoring that although power is a critical analytic, the reasons for and function of harassment are manifold, and it does not escape this particular element. Again, importantly, understanding plantations as workplaces where sexual harassment occurred and underscoring black people's resistance to their exploitation in this regard help us to explode the mythology that feminism is a "white woman's thing," disrupting the common time line associating the origins of feminist activism in the United States with Seneca Falls.

Even after the end of slavery, we find black women resisting sexual assault in the workplace. As recounted in Chapter 4, one reason that black women shifted to doing day work as opposed to living with employers after Emancipation was to escape or mitigate the harassment they experienced in domestic work. Families educated young women about the possibilities of abuse and in some cases furnished them with weapons. These and other forms of resistance continued throughout the Jim Crow era as well. When the mid-twentieth century witnessed political upheaval and revolutionary impulses because of social movements, black women participated and, indeed, often led politically (see, e.g., Robnett 1997). In this context, black women figured critically in the fight to establish sexual harassment law and served as plaintiffs in several of the foundational cases for using Title VII of the Civil Rights Act as a basis for sexual harassment litigation.

In her important work *The Women's Movement against Sexual Harassment*, lawyer and scholar Carrie N. Baker (2008) recounts the decades-long struggle to alter public consciousness and establish a legal basis for fighting sexual harassment. Baker's work is notable for several reasons. She outlines the long history of harassment, including in the context of US slavery, as well as significant efforts at resistance prior to the social movements of the mid-twentieth century (1–3), but shows how different milestones in sexual harassment law were achieved by a wide array of activist lawyers, feminist and civil rights networks, and a diverse group of women, including not only white or other professional women, but also black women and other women of color and working-class women in traditionally male-dominated trades (3–4). Her work lends valuable insight into the development of the movement against sexual harassment over time along several, interrelated theatres of contention—public discourse, political organizations, the legal system, public policy, and workplaces. She disabuses readers of the notion that the fight against sexual harassment and feminism more generally are the purview of mainly white middle-class women. As many know, there are two main types of sexual harassment: one based on quid pro quo discrimination, where workers are forced or pressured to submit to sexual conduct in exchange for employment or promotion, and the other based on hostile work environment claims. Although black women played a role in several sectors of the movement, including developing hostile workplace claims, they had a particularly prominent role in the earliest civil rights litigation (see, generally, Baker 2008).

Specifically, of the six cases that formed the bedrock of precedent for claims under Title VII of the Civil Rights Act, three featured black women as plaintiffs (Baker 2008, 15). In each case, workplace superiors (two of whom were black and one of whom was white) made sexual advances that were rebuffed, and the women met with adverse employment actions as a result. Paulette Barnes, for instance, the plaintiff in *Barnes v. Train*, was twenty-eight years old when her boss, Norris

Snyder, continually attempted to press a personal relationship upon her, "suggesting that he would promote her if she had a sexual affair with him" (16). Snyder used several reprisals in retaliation, eventually eliminating her position and demoting her (16). Diane Williams (*Williams v. Saxbe*), an administrative worker with the Justice Department's Community Relations Service, was subjected to greater scrutiny and unfairly evaluated and fired after she resisted advances from her married, black male supervisor, Harvey Brinson. Brinson was notorious for "dating" subordinates and reportedly meted out better work opportunities to those who succumbed to his predation (16). Kimberly Taufer, Margaret Miller's white male supervisor at Bank of America, terminated her after she rejected his quid pro quo offer. Taufer arguably stalked Miller by boldly showing up at her home carrying wine and sharing, "'I've never felt this way about a black chick before' and that he would get her 'off the machines' if she would cooperate with him sexually" (16–17).

These three women were working-class women and, thus, especially vulnerable economically. Moreover, it is more than ironic that two of these women worked for institutions that were supposed to advance justice and the public good. What are the social messages conveyed when those charged with protection are among the targeted perpetrators of injustice? Still, significantly, for Barnes and Williams, their exposure to civil rights policy and law proved to bolster their awareness and framing of their circumstances as discrimination under Title VII. Moreover, their cases, along with the others, marked an important shift in the public and legal community's conception of workplace violations based on gender. Instead of seeing these as individualistic or "personal" matters, the public and courts were pushed to comprehend sexual harassment as a systematic, institutionalized form of objectifying women and restricting and controlling their economic opportunities and conditions of employment. And as Baker (2008) astutely observed, the foundational cases, "filed between 1971 and 1975" (15) preceded the popularization of the term "sexual harassment" (25).

Given the foregoing, it is necessary to understand that in 1991, when Anita Hill testified about Clarence Thomas's sexual harassment during his confirmation hearings for his appointment to the US Supreme Court, she followed in a tradition of black women exposing sexual harassment and bringing it center stage for public debate. Few who were alive at the time can forget the riveting public display during the hearings surrounding Clarence Thomas's nomination. Widely televised, the hearings featured salacious details regarding allegations of sexual harassment perpetrated by Thomas against Hill while he directed the Equal Employment Opportunity Commission (EEOC), the agency designated to oversee antidiscrimination enforcement. Commentators (see generally authors in Morrison 1992) before and after emphasized a range of issues, from the lack of gender diversity in the Senate, to the compromising and deleterious effects of black conservatism, to how and the extent to which sexism is relevant to black politics.

The hearings highlighted black women as liminal subjects in several ways. Although, as Pearl Cleage (1993) has pointed out, it is problematic to ignore Anita Hill's conservatism or shape her into a black feminist shero (75–80), her treatment during the hearings, by the broader public, and in black communities is diagnostic of the limitations of politics as it concerns black women.

In some ways, Anita Hill served as a sacrificial lamb for feminism. She was compelled to share her story of victimization at the hands of Thomas under heavy scrutiny. (Other alleged victims did not testify.) The hearings facilitated a broader discussion of sexual harassment in public life for a time and were used to promote electoral campaigns for women. The year after the hearings was often dubbed the Year of the Woman, given the spike in women running for public office. Mired in liberal notions of representational politics, the NAACP found itself immobilized. How could an organization that promoted black representation fight against a black nominee (Bickel 1992)? This exposed the enduring connection between black identity and black political interests, and a refusal to fully confront the reality of black conservatism. It also exposed or highlighted how sexism is seen as a "cross-cutting," as opposed to "consensus," issue in black politics (Cohen 1999, 13–16), the effect of which, in this instance, was to set Anita Hill and her claims of harassment at cross-purposes with the interests of black people as a whole. The relative denial of sexual harassment and treatment of Hill in black communities prompted black scholars and activists to publish a full-page ad in the *New York Times*, in fact, powerfully titled "African American Women in Defense of Ourselves" (White 1999b, 15–16). If liminal subjects are at times betwixt and between social positions, Hill, who arguably served as a model of middle-class respectability and achievement, was, in this moment, treated as abject and placed outside of the US national and black communities.

The hearings are also important as a case study in the operation of political melodrama in black and US politics. Thomas and his handlers mobilized historical framings and associations with racial trauma to enact a racial melodrama that identified Thomas with symbolic racial harm. Grindstaff wants to recuperate melodrama as a feminist genre (Grindstaff 1994, 53), a project in which, in the case of this book, I am not invested. Nevertheless, she powerfully relays how the introduction of sexual harassment as a consideration in the hearings shifted a public political process to a private melodrama. She states, "Thomas's efforts to be colorless and invisible within the white male power structure—to be just another Supreme Court Justice—were thwarted when Hill stepped forward and fixed the nation's gaze upon him. His sudden visibility as a sexual harasser left him one alternative: the emergency exit marked 'race'" (Grindstaff 1994, 54). The message sent by his confirmation was that sexual harassment was an insignificant matter in the realm of political and legal concern.

The next section focuses on a contemporary case of sexual harassment that prefigures many elements of the transnational business masculinity represented by Trump and the experiences of black women often ignored in mainstream discussions of the MeToo movement. It highlights as well the melodramatic framing of immigrants as good (deserving of legal protection and public support) and sinister (potentially criminals or loafers posing threats of potential corruption to the nation).

Case Studies

Fall of the House of Kahn

In 2011, a domestic laborer, Nafissatou Diallo, leveled rape charges against Dominique Strauss-Kahn, the former head of the International Monetary Fund (IMF). In the Strauss-Kahn incident, his alleged rape of an African immigrant in the United States drew the whole world's attention. Before this scandal, Strauss-Kahn enjoyed notoriety as an international power broker. A well-known economist, he was head of the IMF, one of the most visible and powerful global financial institutions. He was, moreover, a favored potential political contender for an upcoming election for the French presidency, predicted to unseat then sitting president Nicolas Sarkozy. Following Diallo's police report, however, police stopped a plane scheduled to depart for France, removing Strauss-Kahn, and placing him in jail, a story that made for dazzling headlines and biting news commentary about the popular figure.

In the opening weeks of the trial coverage, the hotel maid who brought charges against Dominique Strauss-Kahn (DSK) was portrayed as a "good immigrant" and, thus, a worthy victim. News stories, such as the one written by Mosi Secret that appeared in the *New York Times* (*NYT*) on May 15, 2011, noted details that emphasized her youth and immigration status, which suggests vulnerability, as well as her hard-working nature. The *NYT* quoted one neighbor commenting on the alleged victim and her daughter, for instance, who stated, "'They're good people. . . . Every time I see her I'm happy because we're both from Africa. She's never given a problem for nobody. Never noisy. Everything nice'" (Secret 2011). Another story, in the *NYT* on May 16, a day later, cited "the alleged victim's older brother," indicating that "his sister was tired and in pain"; he elaborated: "'She's a wonderful, hard-working woman, that's why she's in pain'" (Eligon 2011). Meanwhile, descriptions of DSK were correspondingly framed as the exact opposite. Described as a testosterone-filled, "aging lothario" (Celona 2011), DSK's prior sexual conduct was highlighted. A previous affair that he had with a "subordinate" at the IMF was cited (Baker and Erlanger 2011), as was his ostensibly notorious womanizing, with one alleged victim, a reporter from France, supposedly describing DSK as a "'rutting chimpanzee'" (Italiano 2011).

This sympathetic rendering of the victim of this case changed, however, in June. One set of meetings in particular, which occurred on June 8 and June 9, proved to be the turning point. There Diallo met with the district attorney's (DA) office to follow up for trial preparation, without the aid of her personal attorney, Thompson. Prior to the meeting Diallo told Thompson that her claim to having been raped by Guinean militants was false. She indicated that the story she provided to back up her request for asylum was totally fabricated, a story provided to her by an immigration counselor to ensure her passage to the United States. Before leaving for a business trip, Thompson relayed this to the prosecutors. This disclosure set a negative tone for the meeting with Diallo. During her time with prosecutors, Diallo, without the benefit of her attorney's presence, was riddled with questions, in what was now an arguably hostile setting (Solomon 2012, 81–88). She was also found to have provided inaccurate information about her income in order to gain low-income housing, and carried someone else's child on her taxes to lower her tax burden (84–85). Thompson eventually insisted the prosecutors' interrogation end until he could be present, but the tide turned in terms of the DA's office support for the case. The following weeks were marked by mistrust and negativity between prosecutors and Thompson and his client.

In the midst of this downturn, prosecutors leaked distorted information regarding Diallo that would prove consequential in the media narratives and public support for Diallo. On July 1, 2011, the *NYT* broke a story about a conversation she purportedly had with her fiancé, who was in prison, where, according to one source, "'She says words to the effect of, 'Don't worry, this guy has a lot of money. I know what I'm doing'" (Dwyer and Wilson 2011). This seemed to foreground a voracious appetite for money and buoyed speculation that DSK was being set up. As I discuss below, the facts were different from what was relayed in this story. Nevertheless, once this story broke, the damage was done. After this point, where prior news stories had initially described her as a victim, they now painted her as a lying, scheming, opportunistic ne'er-do-well, who cavorted with criminals. Some stories focused on the aforementioned contradiction of earlier claims of rape. Other stories focused on inconsistencies (see, e.g., Dwyer and Wilson 2011). The DA's office moved to alter DSK's bail July 1, 2011 (Solomon 2012, 105), and eventually to dismiss the case (120).

To the public, this case may have seemed rightly to come to an end. A closer examination, however, suggests that, in the end, the administration of her criminal case led to various levels of revictimization: by the media, by a cultural context unwilling to comprehend structural issues tied to her identity as a working-class immigrant, by prosecutors concerned about losing a high-profile case, and even, at one level, her own lawyer, who, though diligent in some dimensions, provided an opening for her case to crack by not performing due diligence in accompanying his client in her fateful June meetings with the DA.

The media provided a layer of injustice in this case by allowing the feeding frenzy surrounding this high-profile case to make them cut corners in their fact-checking and trading on melodramatic narratives of pure victims and villains. The media, of course, has always been interested in sensational events and cases involving high-profile individuals. Given the international notoriety of DSK and his presidential ambitions in France, this was especially so. But given the advent of televised court hearings, media missteps in high-profile cases have particularly deleterious repercussions. Indeed, as other commentators have noted, the O. J. Simpson (OJ) trial in particular marked a turn in legal TV coverage. Cable News Network (CNN), now a worldwide provider of news, was essentially the house that OJ built, gaining its increase in market share from this trial (Lipsitz 1997). With the OJ criminal trial, we also saw an uptick in courtroom hearing commentators and an explosion of televised court hearing viewing, on Court TV and similar outlets, at arguably unprecedented levels by the broader public from the comfort of their homes. With the ability to watch television trials, hear round-the-clock commentary, and now additional outlets for discussion on social media, there are what I would term new communities of assessment. But, ironically, although there is increased legal exposure that has enabled new communities of assessment, there is not necessarily corresponding legal literacy. And the public trial in some instances more heavily influences whether or not something gets tried in a court of law, how it is framed, and how juries might respond.

In this DSK affair, the misstep of the *NYT* in particular proved to be especially damaging. It chose to break a story about the conversation that suggested that the alleged victim cavorted with criminals, but, more than that, was centered on Diallo seeking financial gain, hardly the stance that many would expect from a supposed victim. As previously noted, the *NYT* wrongly stated that a day after the attack Diallo spoke to Amara Tarawally, a male friend who was imprisoned (Solomon 2012, 76). Furthermore, as Solomon (106) notes, news organizations, such as the *NYT*, typically back up quotes from at least two sources when information is anonymously provided, but neglected to do so in this instance. The language that was quoted came from what the *NYT* knew was a mere summary or "digest" of two separate conversations (106). Moreover, the *NYT* apparently neglected to contact either Diallo or Tarawally for their perspectives on what had been discussed (254–55). Furthermore, subsequent evaluation of the conversation, which was spoken in Fulani, revealed that her statements were misinterpreted. The conversation, which happened two days after the attack, not the day after as the *NYT* erroneously reported, showed Tarawally raising the issue of potential financial gain, with Diallo deflecting, indicating such matters were her lawyer's domain (76). This latter, accurate interpretation is a far cry from what the *NYT* presented. Given the reputation of the paper, however, the damage to this woman and her case was already done. The DA's office made no effort to correct this mischaracterization of Diallo (189–90).

The administration of justice was also hampered in this case by the inability of the legal system and the broader culture to comprehend the structural challenges—what Crenshaw (1991) refers to as structural intersectionality—facing black female immigrants. Neither the prosecutors, the media, nor the general public were able to understand the complex choices that women have to make in negotiating the often-difficult terrain of their native home countries and that of the United States. Diallo used a story provided by a person specializing in immigration assistance in order to ensure her application would be accepted, provided false information on her taxes and applications to secure a better financial outcome and living situation, and worked with members of the immigrant community to get ahead, including some who were apparently involved in criminal activity. The choices that Diallo made were not only incomprehensible to the prosecution, but also provided sure evidence for lack of credibility in general. But the ethical nature of those choices becomes at least arguably clear when you consider the very difficult challenges she confronted and the negotiations that she had to make on a day-to-day basis to acquire and sustain basic life resources for her family.

That Diallo made such choices is arguably more suggestive of the fraught nature of the cultural, economic, and politico-legal environment in which immigrants currently operate, as opposed to her character. Therí A. Pickens's discussion of Anne DuCille's take on intimacy and how this parallels disability is instructive here. Pickens (2012) writes, "Anne DuCille once said . . . that her lack of intimacy was not just her problem, but also ours. Her logic was that a lack of intimate relationships between people speaks volumes about the social environments that deprive people of those relationships." For Pickens, duCille's framing suits disability access. "Black Studies has done too much work on institutional racism," she asserts, "to sit silent while institutional ableism relies on racist rhetorics to run amuck" (Pickens 2012). Similarly, Diallo's choices are "not just her problem, but also ours." We have to ask hard questions about the ways in which our immigration system fails to support the broadest conception of social justice, to provide equitable treatment, and to provide safety nets and sufficient resources to facilitate the well-being of immigrants.

In any event, the choices and the background of any witness as it relates to questions of veracity in character, while important to consider in a case, are issues to be brought before a jury, as a jury considers the weight of the evidence, circumstantial or otherwise, and the believability of witnesses. The choices that this person made do not, for some, throw her credibility into question, mean that DSK did not rape her, or that the rape could not be proven to the satisfaction of a jury. In short, she should have had her day in court.

Although the media and the DA's office hampered the administration of justice, even the victim's own attorney fell short despite his best efforts to keep her case before the public. Early on in his representation of Diallo, her attorney, Thompson, decided to take a trip to attend a Second Circuit Judicial Conference, in lieu of accompanying his new client to a meeting with the DA's office (Solomon 2012, 81–82). Thompson acknowledged that it was his gravest misstep in his handling of the criminal case (83). As previously noted, Diallo disclosed to her attorney that she recounted a false story of political repression and gang rape to the DA's office, one that she had been coached to use to gain asylum; Thompson promptly relayed this disclosure to the DA's office (81–82). The conference he decided to attend in lieu of accompanying Diallo would arguably be beneficial for his career. In his absence, prosecutors spent time over two days, June 8–9, 2011, interrogating Diallo in ways that now reflected their view that she was not a victim but rather an untrustworthy woman. In fact, at one point, after speaking with someone from the prosecutor's office, Thompson requested the questioning be stopped (86–87). During the interviewing, Diallo asked prosecutors to "Please stop yelling at me" (83), and her daughter, who was present in the vicinity, overheard the tenor of the exchange and saw her mother "kicked out" of an interrogation room (87). Unfortunately, the DA's office would, from then on, descend into a trail of avoidance and mishandling that would end in dismissal of the case.

Thompson continued in his representation of Diallo, valiantly squaring off with the DA's office and working consistently to focus attention and public debate on the issue of Diallo's charges of victimization at the hands of DSK. The evidence and arguments he had to work with were substantial. As Solomon notes (2012, 175), the accounts of those who encountered Diallo immediately after the alleged assault were incredibly powerful, as "each had recounted Diallo's story in almost identical fashion." This is important because the testimony of "outcry witnesses," that is, those who encounter victims in the immediate wake of an alleged crime, is taken to be most reliable (37–38). Second, the physical evidence solidly linked DSK to the victim. There was semen found on the top of her uniform, indicating the truth of her claim that oral sex had occurred. Also, his skin cells were found on her pantyhose, suggesting that he did indeed attempt to remove her pantyhose or touch her in her crotch, as she described. Third, DSK's defense floated theories supporting their side of the case that are either dubious, inconsistent with the evidence, or conveniently ignore the impact of trauma on victims. For instance, the idea that the alleged victim walked into a room, and, when faced with a naked DSK with penis erect, instantly desired him is far from a rock-solid defense, as is the idea that the hotel maid who wore two pairs of pantyhose and was seen gagging in hotel footage after the incident spitting his semen out was likely always already open to prostitution with rich hotel clients. This view is an example of the psychological defense of disavowal, discussed in Chapter 4, where counternarratives are developed to displace a more troubling truth. The fact that she went back into the room in which she claims to have been savagely raped and then exiting can be easily understood as the kind of action a trauma victim in shock would perform, attempting to complete her job she so desperately needed as a single mother, but being too disoriented to do so, as opposed to a trip back to see if she had been left an expected payment for services rendered, as the defense suggested.

The story that someone would have to believe to suggest that this was some kind of consensual relationship is at best a stretch. Alan

Dershowitz, who originally supported the dismissal of the case, changed his mind when he got hold of additional facts concerning how the discrepancies could be explained (Solomon 2012, 227), utilizing the DSK affair as a case study in one of his courses at Harvard in which he provided a mock closing for the case (234–39). Dershowitz is a familiar participant in the new communities of assessment we have seen in the post-OJ era. To say the least, his incorrect judgment, based on limited information, is the kind of cautionary tale we should take heed of when weighing early analyses of high-profile legal cases.

In short, notwithstanding whatever issues were raised in the press, as one investigator said, the bottom line is that this is something that should have been seen by a jury. "In the end, her lies about her past complicate the case but don't necessarily gut it" (Solomon 2012, 251). The weight of the stereotypes associated with black female sexuality in particular, especially given the history of white male exploitation of domestic workers, militated against this case getting the kind of attention it deserved. The melodramatic framing of the case left us only with split representations in which to imagine Diallo. Diallo was shaped first as a pure victim and then as a pure villain; she was a good immigrant who garnered sympathy, and then, a thief, liar, and money-hungry swindler—the epitome of national contamination. Because of the kind of repressed or disavowed history of sexual assault of black women, her status as an immigrant, and the melodramatic racial, sexual, and class dynamics at work, she did not have her day in court.

Although it is tempting to view this case as a situation between one man and one woman, the larger implications are worth considering. DSK represents a type of pernicious, transnational business masculinity. Connell (2012, 94) describes this new "transnational business masculinity" as one that is grounded in neoliberal politics and priorities and "is the masculinity associated with those who control its dominant institutions: the business executives who operate in global markets, and the political executives who interact (and in many contexts, merge) with them." This transnational business masculinity, moreover, incorporates sexual access and objectification of women's bodies. Connell (2012, 94) explains, "Transnational business masculinity differs from traditional bourgeois masculinity by its increasingly libertarian sexuality, with a growing tendency to commodify relations with women. Hotels catering to businessmen in most parts of the world now routinely offer pornographic videos, and in some parts of the world, there is a well-developed prostitution industry catering for international businessmen." Dominique Strauss-Kahn was arguably the epitome of this type of transnational business masculinity, although Donald Trump now contends for this dubious distinction. Trump is infamously associated, as his epigraphic quote at the beginning of this chapter reminds us, with a rapacious masculinity that sees women as objects to be plundered for his own use and that demonstrates his privileged status along several fronts.

In the case of Dominique Strauss-Kahn, he was the "political executive" over the IMF, a chief international regulatory financial body, and so inhabited the prestige and power of the political operative and business elite. Again, at the time of his arrest he was poised to contend, some think successfully, for the French presidency. His extramarital affairs and sexual harassment, as well as his predilection for orgies and prostitutes (Lichfield 2015), the latter of which came to light in the press subsequent to the US rape case's dismissal, are examples of the "libertarian sexuality" Connell describes. And while I do agree that there are in some cases novel ways in which technology and industries are being advanced to cater to transnational business elites today, transnational business masculinity is less a departure from traditional bourgeois masculinity, as Connell suggests, than it is a slicker, transnational version that highlights the commodification of women's bodies and sexual access as a defining prerogative of dominant masculine norms.

The DSK case highlights the sexual predation that defines dominant masculinities in general, and the greater expanse of control and access to women's bodies available to transnational business elites. This, in fact, is exactly what the MeToo movement exposes. The DSK case exemplifies as well the fact that poor women, particularly poor women of color and especially black diasporan women, are often the targets of transnational business elites' sexual predations (Fanon 2008). This same culture of access particularly to women of color is something that informs this case.

Furthermore, Diallo's social location as a black woman and status as an immigrant represent important intersections with transnational politics. As an immigrant and particularly as an African immigrant, the harm visited upon her was illegible within US mainstream politics and arguably even within black politics. In this instance, the alleged rape of this woman did not register as a community violation. The commentary about the case as a whole did not evoke outrage from mainstream Civil Rights organizations, and the kind of support that she did receive came from coworkers who were situated in unions or women of color who were writing on their blogs or in other outlets. This, again, highlights that issues concerning black women in general and particularly in this case black immigrant women are not understood as "consensus issues" supported by a cross-section of the black community, but "cross cutting" issues that point to and represent fissures within black politics (Cohen 1999, see especially Chapter 1). Diallo's immigrant status is also significant because it highlights how the notion of blackness and what constitutes "African American" is shifting. Demographic data on the United States tell us that there have been increasing numbers of African immigrants and black immigrants from the Caribbean and elsewhere in the African Diaspora, so much so that our understanding of blackness and who can claim the term "blackness" or "African American" is unsettled (Greer 2013; Smith 2014). An expansive pan-African or transnational idea of black politics and surely black feminist politics has to account now for the difference African Diasporan identity makes and the difference ethnicity among blacks makes as well.

The next section focuses on the second case study, centering on Bill Cosby. We move from looking at transnational business masculinity and rape to more directly examining how the black cultural pathology melodrama framed both Cosby's public and private personae and actions. We see how blacks as liminal subjects—framed as idealized super minorities, and in Cosby's case a symbolic black father—and as abject others, drove Cosby's père-version (Wright 2013), or destructive self-fathering.

Bill Cosby, Fatherhood, and Perversion

Much has been written about the "Cosby Moment" (see especially Gray 1995) in US culture. *The Cosby Show*, which featured an upper-middle-class black family, dealing with the day-to-day problems associated with domesticity, appealed to a broad set of audiences and is seen as a watershed moment in black televisual representation, one that self-consciously opposed stereotypical images found in prior shows, such as *Amos 'N' Andy* and *Good Times*, among others. Because of the show's success, its namesake, comedian Bill Cosby, enjoyed a special place in the pantheon of black cultural icons and influencers. Even prior to the show, in fact, Cosby was immensely popular. He was well known for, among other things, his television and movie appearances. His doctorate in education and Fat Albert cartoon, along with clean, family-focused comedy he developed later in his career, paved the way for *The Cosby Show*. Neither criticisms of the show for its failure to take on social and political issues or showcase diversity within black communities nor Cosby's public speeches deriding the poor (discussed more later) substantively damaged his overall popularity. The storm of controversy surrounding revived allegations that Cosby raped women, over several decades, changed that reality forever.

Cosby's exposure came after comedian Hannibal Burress discussed Cosby's rape allegations during an October 2014 comedy show in Philadelphia, Cosby's hometown. During the comedy routine, Burress chided Cosby for his views on the black poor (Matthews 2014). Cosby's perspective on the state of black America was made (in)famous on May 17, 2004, when he gave a keynote speech (discussed further shortly) at a celebration hosted by the National Association for the Advancement of Colored People (NAACP) commemorating the fiftieth anniversary of the historic *Brown v. Board of Education* decision. The Supreme Court case, which invalidated *Plessy v. Ferguson*'s "separate but equal" doctrine, provided a legal basis to fight legalized segregation, beginning in education. In the speech Cosby recounted key elements of the black cultural pathology paradigm or melodrama (Alexander-Floyd 2007). As noted in previous chapters, within the confines of the black cultural pathology melodrama, black people are held responsible for a host of problems that assail their communities, including, but not limited to: poverty, drug use, and high rates of incarceration. Cosby, at times to audience applause, recounted well-rehearsed ideas associated with this black cultural pathology melodrama, naming a lack of proper parenting and parent absenteeism as sources of disorder in poor communities.

For Cosby, reflecting on the anniversary of *Brown* meant acknowledging that white people or the state were not responsible for black communities' problems, but blacks themselves were. Likening the situation of blacks to a boxing match, he suggests that, like a defeated boxer, black people are down and out, not because of what the victor has done, but because of what the loser has failed to do. Bereft of the self-respect common in prior generations, Cosby claimed, poor blacks do not consider how their actions will reflect on their parents. Cosby (2004) noted, for instance, the following:

> But these people—the ones up here in the balcony—fought so hard. Looking at the incarcerated, these are not political criminals. These are people going around stealing Coca-Cola. People getting shot in the back of the head over a piece of pound cake! Then we all run out and are outraged: "The cops shouldn't have shot him." What the hell was he doing with the pound cake in his hand? I wanted a piece of pound cake just as bad as anybody else. And I looked at it and I had no money. And something called parenting said if you get caught with it you're going to embarrass your mother. Not, "You're going to get your butt kicked." No. "You're going to embarrass your mother." "You're going to embarrass your family."

Cosby, at times objectifying poor black people by referring to them as "it," chided them for not speaking properly, dressing properly, or having the proper moral commitments. Although the speech sparked some controversy in the weeks and months following its delivery, the ideas conveyed were nothing new, and some, like Kweisi Mfume, then executive director of the NAACP, offered tempered support. Mfume, who hugged Cosby after he delivered the address, did not want to let other actors off the hook, but essentially agreed with the substance of what Cosby conveyed (Harris 2004). Cosby went on to expound on his ideas in other fora, most notably a *New York Times* bestseller titled *Come On People: On the Path from Victims to Victors*, written with well-known black psychologist Alvin Poussaint (Cosby and Poussaint 2007). Notably Poussaint was also the psychologist who consulted on *The Cosby Show*.

So it was the black cultural pathology melodrama that Cosby made famous in his "Pound Cake" speech that provided the basis for Hannibal's comedy routine in 2014, a routine that he fittingly performed in Cosby's hometown of Philadelphia. Stating Cosby was the "smuggest old man," he noted, among other things, the hypocrisy of Cosby criticizing young black men for being irresponsible by not pulling their pants up, while Cosby was charged with rape. Burress (quoted in Matthews 2014) states,

He [Cosby] gets on TV [and says] "pull your pants up Black people, I was on TV in the '80s! I can talk down to you cause I had a successful sitcom." Yeah, but you rape women, Bill Cosby, so . . . I don't know what I'm doing by telling you [the audience]. I guess I want to just at least, make it weird for you to watch *Cosby Show* reruns. Dude's image is, for the most part, a public Teflon image. I've done this bit on stage and people don't believe me, people think I'm making it up. I'm like, "Bill Cosby has a lot of rape allegations," and they go, "No, you do!" No! They call me Captain Kick-Em-Out. That sh** is upsetting. If you didn't know about it, trust me, if you leave here, Google "Bill Cosby rape," that sh** has more results than "Hannibal Burress."

Clips with Burress's joke about Cosby subsequently proliferated through social media, bringing heightened attention to earlier allegations of Cosby's misconduct. Social commentators also weighed in. Roxane Gay (2014) noted, "Rapists make us less uncomfortable than rape victims. . . . If we don't doubt them, we do not have to doubt ourselves. That's why the charm of Cliff Huxtable—a fictional character [made famous by Bill Cosby]—is more important than the words of so many women." Brittney Cooper, writing for Crunk Feminist Collective, noted the irony that Cosby's rapacious personality was only taken seriously when criticized by Hannibal Burress, a man (Cooper 2014). She lambasted Cosby, criticizing his hypocrisy and drawing out the implications of his private misdeeds for his public persona as a father figure on the *Cosby Show* and as a popular advocate of black respectability. "And since Bill Cosby is a rapist," she explains, "his avatar Cliff Huxtable is a representational terrorist, holding us hostage to a black family that never was" (Cooper 2014). Cooper (2014) insists that Cosby's fall spells (or should spell) the death of the models of masculinity and femininity that Cliff and Clair Huxtable, respectively, represent (Ibid.). Similarly, Lauretta Charleton (2014) recounted the many instances the world looked away from Cosby's misdeeds, pointing out that, even before Hannibal's skit regarding Cosby went viral, Tom Socca noted the rape allegations against Cosby.

During this season of renewed focus on Cosby, specific attention was drawn to a suit involving Cosby in 2005. In this suit, Andrea Constand, a former University of Pennsylvania basketball staff member, claimed that Cosby drugged her and assaulted her. There were seventeen other women, who remained anonymous, who reported similar misconduct. The DA did not pursue the allegations at the time. In the wake of the media storm following Burress's comedy show, the case regained renewed attention. Eventually, as I discuss, a new DA decided to pursue the case.

Adding to the media storm, former alleged victims Barbara Bowman and Tamara Green shared op-eds via the *Washington Post* and *Entertainment Tonight*, respectively. Bowman observed that Cosby, who purported to want to mentor her as a teenager and aspiring actress, raped her repeatedly:

> In one case, I blacked out after having dinner and one glass of wine at his New York City brownstone, where he had offered to mentor me and discuss the entertainment industry. When I came to, I was in my panties and a man's t-shirt, and Cosby was looming over me. I'm certain now that he drugged and raped me. But as a teenager, I tried to convince myself I had imagined it. (Bowman 2014)

Bowman's stated reaction ("I tried to convince myself I had imagined it") is an example of the psychological defense of denial. It is a reflection, as well, of the sadomasochistic dynamics that, on her account, pervaded her relationship with Cosby, a point to which I return later. Bowman expresses disappointment that attention was only belatedly being given to the claims by her and others of Cosby's predation (Bowman 2014). In her op-ed, Tamara Green, among other things, responded to criticism from Whoopi Goldberg about Green not doing a rape kit after the rape she claimed occurred in the 1970s. Green (2014) states, "It's fair to say, 'I wasn't there, and I don't know.' It is not fair to say, 'Well, isn't doing a rape kit normal when you're raped?' Normal? What's normal about being in hand-to hand combat for your life?" These women recounted the outlines of a basic sadomasochistic pattern Cosby exhibited: a woman who was an associate of some kind—either in the entertainment industry or hoping to break into it, or a possible mentee of Cosby's or someone with whom he worked—found themselves offered a pill, to "relax" as in the case of Patricia Leary Steuer, for a headache as with Cindra Ladd (Kim, Littlefield, and Etehad 2018), or, like actress Joan Tarshis (Wells 2014), provided a drink by Cosby ostensibly laced with Quaaludes or some other chemical. Women reported waking up during or after being raped by Cosby. Most did not pursue legal recourse or public censure against the well-known, well-regarded, and well-to-do public figure.

Cosby faced several immediate consequences because of the renewed exposure regarding rape allegations. TV Land stopped airing *The Cosby Show* (Kim, Littlefield, and Etehad 2018). A Netflix comedy special eponymously titled *Bill Cosby 77* was held off (Regan 2014). Two late-night talk show appearances, including *Late Night with David Letterman*, were cancelled (V. Gay 2014). Stand-up dates were dropped (Kim, Littlefield, and Etehad 2018). Amid this swarm of activity, Cosby refused to comment himself, but had his attorney, John P. Schmitt, indicate that "his client would not dignify 'decade-old, discredited' claims of sexual abuse with a response" (Elber 2014).

Because most of the cases or incidents raised were so old, they fell outside of most statutes of limitations, that is, the legal time limits in which someone can file suit. The DA, Kevin R. Steele, was able to move forward in the prosecution of Constand's case, however, just prior to the end of the statute of limitations for the crime Cosby allegedly committed. After six days in the courtroom and as many days of deliberation, the resulting 2017 courtroom saga ended in a mistrial (Bowley, Pérez-Peña, and Hurdle 2017). The jurors, "composed of six white men, four white women, one black woman and one black man," were unable to come to a unanimous decision—even after over fifty solid hours of deliberation (Bowley, Pérez-Peña, and Hurdle 2017). The 2018 retrial yielded a different outcome.

The 2018 trial resulted in a unanimous decision of guilty on "three counts of sexual assault" (Roig-Franzia 2018). On the 2014 evening in question, Cosby, according to Constand, gave her "three round blue pills," to calm her nerves—pills he referred to as "'your friends'" (Roig-Franzia 2018). Constand was there to speak to Cosby about her plan to leave her position at Temple. Although Cosby had supposedly made advances toward her on two prior occasions, Constand testified that she had rebuffed them and that Cosby "got" that she was uninterested. For Constand, Cosby, a well-known Temple alum and trustee, served as a mentor; the pills incapacitated Constand, impairing her speech and leaving her immobilized, as Cosby penetrated her digitally and used her hand on his penis to masturbate. According to Constand, the next day she was "shocked and confused." Before she left, she walked to the kitchen where Cosby reportedly told her, "There's a muffin and a tea on the table" (Stewart and Dillon 2018).

As is typical, the prosecution and defense provided diametrically opposed theories and themes. The prosecution, for instance, framed Cosby as an icon who had a hidden life of abuse of those, like Constand, who trusted his fatherly persona (Bowley and Hurdle 2018). The defense suggested that Constand was a money-grubbing woman set on making money off of a vulnerable target. In the opening, for instance, Cosby's attorney Thomas Mesereau Jr. remarked, "You are going to be asking yourself during this trial, 'What does she want from Bill Cosby?' And you already know the answer: 'Money, money and lots more money'" (Bowley and Hurdle 2018). The adversarial position arguably operates through melodrama, at least in terms of a focus on victors and villains. In this light, as I discuss below, melodrama is arguably important to most rape and sexual harassment trials, but it takes on special resonance in the context of contemporary black culture in general and Bill Cosby's role in black culture in particular.

Bill Cosby's inner circle, specifically his press team and wife, Camille Cosby, spun melodramatic narratives in the days following the guilty verdict that drew on familiar gendered and raced codes, such as lynching and the black male under threat. Cosby's publicists, Ebonee Benson and Andrew Wyatt, offered a full-throated defense of Cosby and rebuke of the prosecution on *Good Morning America* (ABC News 2018). Both suggested that Cosby fell prey to a calculated "agenda" to target and falsely accuse Cosby (ABC News 2018). In the interview, Benson insisted,

> Again, we're talking about accusations that have not been followed up with any evidence besides what our defense attorneys did. There was evidence completely, blatantly, selectively, overlooked by the commonwealth in this situation, again, women who knew who this man was, they had an agenda, they sought their agenda, and then years later, come with accusations because they woke up and saw someone on TV, again, of course they would feel that way, of course they would feel that they want him to spend his life in jail, because that's been the agenda they set out for from the beginning. (ABC News 2018)

In this same interview Benson also references the Emmett Till case, as an example of a case where a man was falsely accused and convicted based on a white woman's lie. Anyone with a passing knowledge of Civil Rights history will recall that Till, a fourteen-year-old from New York visiting relatives in the South, was tortured and brutally murdered for allegedly whistling at a white female. Publicity about the killing spread nationally. The framing of the accusations against Till highlighted the myth of the black male rapist (Davis 1981) and the ways in which white society polices black bodies, particularly black male bodies, as ubiquitous threats to white womanhood (i.e., white sexual purity). The white men were not held guilty at trial and bragged about the killing, in print, a short time after it was over. The Emmitt Till murder became a touchstone and symbol of racial injustice during the Civil Rights movement and beyond. Attention was drawn to the case again in 2017 when Carolyn Bryant Donham, the white woman who accused Till of whistling at her, admitted that it was a lie (Pérez-Peña 2017). Thus, in drawing this analogy between Cosby and Till, Benson directly framed Cosby as an innocent black male being targeted because of racial animus by a group of people set to bring him harm on the word of a lying woman. It recalls, as well, as discussed in earlier chapters, the way that black men are often seen as representatives of the race.

Benson's counterpart, Andrew Wyatt, further developed the theory that Cosby was falsely accused and targeted based on race by likening the outcome of the trial to a public lynching. In the interview, Wyatt opined,

> And George [Stephanopoulos], this became a public lynching. What they did, what Gloria Allred [an attorney representing several of Cosby's accusers] was able to do, she took a salt and pepper shaker, she shaked out a lot of salt, and sprinkled in a little black pepper, and the south came east, and that's what we saw. (ABC News 2018)

This frame of Cosby's trial constituting a public lynching translated into the sentencing phase of the case as well. Shortly after his sentencing, many on social media circulated a cartoon showing Cosby hanging from a tree marked "US (WHITE) JUSTICE" juxtaposed against a list of notable accused white rapists or harassers (such as Harvey Weinstein, Roman Polanski, Donald Trump, and Woody Allen) who, at the time, had not undergone trials. The bottom of the cartoon showed a large crowd of mostly white men and women, but also ostensibly black figures as well. One historian, Darryl Scott (2018), appropriately stated,

> This [cartoon representation] does a disservice to our ancestors, women, and history. Those who were lynched were considered victims because they did not have their right to a legal trial. They were murdered by people lacking the authority to try them and take their lives. Bill Cosby had a trial and he is still alive.

The apparent emphasis on perceived differential reckoning for rape and harassment based on race, provides a distorted, race-first analysis. It is distorted because it offers a simplistic mono-focal analysis suggesting racial disparity is the most important consideration, even in the case of holding sexual abusers accountable. It is as if, as others have also observed, that some folks want black men to have an equal opportunity to abuse women with abandon. In this framing, black men strive to enter (to riff off of Angela Davis) a "deformed equality" where they can be "equal oppress[ors]" (Davis 2000, 88). It is also a distortion because many black men were lynched, as we know, because of the myth of black male rapaciousness. Cosby as a lynching figure is an outlier, at best: he is actually a convicted rapist.

Whether these themes resonated with many African Americans or others is debatable. It is important to consider, however, why, of all of the competing frames and theories a publicity team could devise, they would gravitate toward these in particular. As Hazel Carby (1987) and others have observed, lynching stands as the ultimate symbol of racial oppression, one that, despite the fact of black women and children's lynchings, remains associated with black men (Simien 2011). It embeds black men as primary targets of racial oppression. As mentioned earlier in this chapter, the term "public lynching," ironically, was exactly what Clarence Thomas used to describe his recounting of charges of sexual harassment by Anita Hill during the Senate hearings to confirm his nomination to the Supreme Court.

Notably, in her public statement, published May 3, 2018, on Facebook, Camille Cosby relayed similar themes. Beginning her piece with a reference to the US Constitution and the historic exclusion of various groups, Cosby characterized her husband, Bill Cosby, "an American citizen," as beleaguered and maligned. For Camille Cosby, the jury had made up its mind prior to the trial. She (Cosby 2018) expounded, "The overall media, with their frenzied, relentless demonization of him and unquestioning acceptance of accusers' allegations without any attendant proof, have superseded the Fifth and Fourteenth Amendments, which guarantee due process and equal protection, and thereby eliminated the possibility of a fair trial and unbiased jury." Like his publicists, she also brought up Emmitt Till, as well as a more recent case, one involving Daryl Hunt, a man unjustly incarcerated for allegedly raping a white woman, who was eventually exonerated based on DNA evidence. Camille Cosby also pointed to a host of reactions to the allegations against Cosby that were highlighted in the wake of Hannibal's 2014 viral comedy routine, from cancelled or pulled shows to withdrawals of honorary degrees. Given the public renouncements of Cosby and his career prior to the trial, she doubted if the jury could be unbiased and called for an investigation of the prosecutor in the case, whom she deemed unfair and acting with ill intent. The problem, she averred, was not Cosby's but the country's, for Cosby, she asserted, received "mob justice, not real justice" (Cosby 2018).

Outside of Cosby's inner circle, another register of lament about the guilty verdict tied into a theme, foreshadowed by Brittney Cooper (2014), that emerged in the wake of the media storm following Hannibal's viral comedy show, namely, the demise of Cosby as a prototypical father figure embodied in Cliff Huxtable, the character he made famous in the landmark *Cosby Show*. Errin Whack (2018), in her reporting on the trial for the Associated Press, captured it best:

> It is difficult to overstate the pride, admiration and sense of ownership many black Americans felt watching Bill Cosby at the height of his career in the 1980s and '90s. . . . All of which explains why the comedian's downfall Thursday [at his second criminal trial] was met with particular pain, disappointment and conflicted feelings in the black community. For many black people, news of Cosby's sexual-assault conviction was hard to hear, even for fans who believed his accusers.

This sentiment echoed previous comments from those heartbroken over the loss of Cosby as an idealized father figure. For Rachel Swarns (2016), Cosby was "the funny man who felt like family," appearing each week as a testament to the black people in her family and community who rarely were acknowledged on screen, she wrote in the *New York Times*. Swarns (2016), who stopped watching the Cosby show, held out hope that she would be able "to reconcile [her] conflicted emotions, to separate the character from his maker;" "For now," she explains, "I am still grieving." Wesley Morris (2018), also writing for the *New York Times*, opined, "If Judge Steven T. O'Neill sent Mr. Cosby away for the rest of his life, that sentence couldn't undo what he's convicted of having done to Andrea Constand, his accuser in two trials. It also can't undo what he once did for me, which was to make me believe in myself. This is foundational, elemental, cellular stuff. There is no surgical procedure to rid me of it. Anyway, I don't want to lose that belief, just the man who ennobled me to possess it in the first place. Maybe we're all compartmentalizing." Morris captures well the reality of Bill Cosby–cum–Cliff Huxtable as prototype and the identification it could generate. In psychoanalytic terms, identification has been defined in different ways; generally speaking, however, it connotes an affinity for characteristics of another that one wants to model (see, e.g., Freud 1989, 335–41; Laplanche and Pontalis 1988, 205–7). Cliff Huxtable and his family, thus, provided a model of a respectable, middle class family. In the calculation of social representation, they exhibited values and behavior that cast them as good and virtuous, and that were in contradistinction to the polar opposite against which good, respectable blacks are set: the black underclass.

Morris (2018) continued, "'Just like us' was the dream of the show, right? 'Best behavior' blackness. That's one way to think about it, the cynical, uncharitable, myopic way, the way you'd think about it if you wanted to psychologize Bill Cosby as Cliff Huxtable." No. It's not "cynical," "uncharitable," or "myopic"—just accurate. The "Just like us" theme of the show for which Cosby became famous was always a counterpoint to the "Come on, people" black cultural pathology melodrama for which Cosby is infamous. The theory and operation of liminality I have explored throughout the book, in fact, helps us to make sense of Cosby's penchant for moralizing. The Pound Cake speech (discussed earlier in this chapter) in which he railed against the black poor, rehearsing well-worn stereotypes and images about the black underclass, articulates the unspoken, but arguably implicit message of the *Cosby Show*. The stable, middle-class black family idealized on the show was always the antidote prescribed by many scholars, pundits, and politicians throughout the *Cosby Show's* heyday.

Interestingly, like Obama (see Chapter 2), Cosby's personal relationship (or lack thereof) with his biological father may account for his moralizing stance toward poor blacks. In his biography of Cosby, *Cosby: His Life and Times*, Mark Whitaker (2014) relays the difficult relationship Bill Cosby Jr. had with his father, Bill Cosby Sr. The senior Cosby was an alcoholic who physically abused his wife (28). He joined the navy when Bill Cosby Jr. was young. According to Whitaker, "[Cosby Sr.] returned only for brief leaves and short periods between tours, during which he sired two more sons but otherwise spent most of his nights drinking in local saloons" (31). Bill Cosby Jr.'s family, always struggling financially, lived in the projects, his family's poverty a source of "shame" for the young Cosby (40). Although Cosby decries a more general failure in parenting today than in the days of his youth, his own upbringing was not a picture of a more idyllic past. Like President Obama, when Cosby complains in speeches or books about the failure of parenting in black communities, whether he acknowledges it or not, he is arguably speaking in light of personal experience, specifically with his father. Significantly, as I discuss below, we can see even his serial rape of women as a perverse attempt to install himself as the powerful father figure he never had. In this way, sadly, Cosby's fatherly TV image is not a contrast to his real-life rapaciousness; both are representative of Cosby as a symbolic father who can emerge from black cultural pathology thinking. It is a stark example of the dangers of liminality represented in black cultural pathology discourses that wrongly focus on supposed black degeneracy and family breakdown as a cause for black oppression.

The next section takes us further into understanding how liminality operates in the context of black communities and rape. More specifically, I elaborate on what the two case studies about rape and harassment in the workplace discussed earlier can tell us about how power operates in a sadomasochistic register. I theorize, as well, how shining a light on rape and harassment places one in the same situation as whistle-blowers, placing oneself outside of the bounds of community. This threat to community expulsion amplifies, in the case of black people in particular, the denigration and marginalization threatened by occupying the abject end of the liminal subjects binary.

Sexual Harassment and Sadomasochism in the Workplace

As previously noted, in order to do a "fully loaded cost accounting" of slavery (Painter 2002, Chapter 1) as a paradigmatic case in terms of workplaces, we have to show how forms of sadomasochistic control operate in US workplaces and industries. Taken together, the two case studies featuring Dominique Strauss-Kahn and Bill Cosby further highlight the legacy of slavery through the persistence of sadomasochistic power in the workplace. The Cosby case along with others helps us understand how workplace policies and employment laws meant to fight sexual harassment are undermined. I draw on Lynn Chancer's classic work, *Sadomasochism in Everyday Life: The Dynamics of Power and Powerlessness* (1992), to illuminate its operation in contemporary workplaces where sexual harassment is concerned.

In this book, Chancer expands our understanding of sadomasochism beyond the sexual frontier to encompass a range of social and political relationships. Four elements comprise the "sadomasochistic dynamic," namely: (1) "excessive attachment" or dependency of the sadist and masochist; (2) relations that are sedimented such that they are "repetitive and ritualistic"; (3) a developing, "dynamic" mode of relating that can potentially reverse positionalities; and most importantly (4) significant fallout for the masochist for resisting the sadist's position or power (1992, 3–6). Chancer advances several important "caveats," including that there is a difference, for her, between the social sadomasochism she describes and the consensual sexual relationship in which people relate sadomasochistically, although she does see some general connection between the two (2). She does not equate every relationship where there is hierarchy or a power differential with the social sadomasochism she investigates (2). She also draws a distinction between "limits and conditions"—limits being necessary and common and productive for social operations (e.g., a teacher providing guidelines for a student) and conditions based on coercion and problematic outcomes (e.g., a teacher ridiculing or punishing a student who asks questions about material) (5–6).

In the workplace, capitalism provides the defining contours of daily interactions and is deeply sadomasochistic in its operation. Indeed, as Chancer observes, each element of sadomasochism—in this case, specifically, dependence between capitalists and workers, ritualized modes of relating, an at least theoretical potential for reversibility of positionalities, and the ability of capitalists to enact punishment and degradation upon workers—is present in the context of the US capitalist workplace as sadomasochism (1992, 93–104). The third element, potential for reversibility of positions, is particularly evident in those workplaces, which are bureaucratized, as even bosses or managers may be "submissive" to higher-ups, but "sadists" to those whom they supervise (98–99). For those who may find this characterization of capitalist workplaces an overreach or unfounded, Chancer's comparison of organized crime as an extreme example of a day-to-day reality of US workplaces is instructive. She writes,

> Like sadomasochism, US capitalism is based on a conditional form of social psychology that brings severe repercussions—the potential loss of livelihood, itself symbolic of the ability to live—should it be questioned too independently. An excessive form of dependence, or social symbiosis, is thereby created. I would remind the reader of the earlier comparison between capitalism and organized crime. Just as associating sadomasochism with its more blatant sexual/violent manifestations masks its wider presence in social interactions, so organized crime may be only the tip of a work-related iceberg. It is not difficult to see the structure of organized crime as sadomasochistic, yet this seemingly deviant instance may be only a highly dramatized manifestation of the vague threats that underlie work relationships and of the fear that pervades them on a more ongoing and less visible basis. (122)

Although the parallels between sadomasochism and capitalism are generally present, they are undoubtedly heightened in this moment of advancing economic insecurity—what some have called precarity (e.g., Schram 2015). The rise of transient forms of labor, loss of pensions and other job benefits that anchored previous generations, and the ongoing attack on unions all make for a ratcheting up of the sadomasochism of work under US capitalism.

Against this backdrop of sadomasochism in the workplace, sexual harassment's sadomasochistic nature comes into greater relief. The two legally recognized forms of sexual harassment, quid pro quo sexual harassment and hostile work environment sexual harassment, capture generalized and more direct elements of a culture of harassment in the workplace. As previously noted, with quid pro quo sexual harassment, an employer or other employee directly coerces a worker to perform sex in order to gain, maintain, or impact the nature of employment. With hostile workplace harassment, speech or conduct of a sexual nature is offensive or harmful to someone in the work environment and impairs their ability to execute their work responsibilities. Both forms of sexual harassment are deeply reflective of the sadomasochism in everyday life Chancer describes.

Although it is tempting to think of rape as a separate offense unrelated to harassment, it is important to note that the same set of acts or circumstances can give rise to multiple legal claims or political analyses. Recall that the actual legal claims under which Cosby was found guilty were aggravated indecent assault. However, rape should be seen, as Adrienne Davis (2004) points out, as part of a continuum of acts constituting sexual harassment. In this light, Cosby's trial and the DSK affair provide us textbook cases of sadomasochism in the workplace as represented by sexual harassment, and, in different ways, highlight black women as liminal subjects. Strauss-Kahn saw it as his prerogative to rape women, in the case of Diallo—a black woman who, as an abject liminal subject of the US state, did not occupy a position of virtuous womanhood, and whose working-class, immigrant status deepened her experience of abjection. Furthermore, although other cases, such as the Barnes case discussed earlier, involve direct pressure or coercion, Cosby utilized trickery and false representations. He lulled women into thinking he was a helpful, fatherly mentor. Tamara Green and others were invited to be his mentees in their search for career success. Constand, the plaintiff in Cosby's trial, saw Cosby as someone on her job who could serve as a mentor. Whatever the initial context, Cosby gave his female victims drugs, thus nullifying their consent. Although some might see an unconscious victim as lacking the interaction typically associated with masochism, an unconscious victim represents the most dominated object of sadistic aims. It is a process through which people are "abjected" (Tyler 2013). Cosby abjected or made of Constand and the others he drugged the ultimate masochists: completely out of control. In such instances, Cosby positioned himself as supremely sadistic—a master. His positioning on the side of the virtuous, respectable continuum of black liminality—as America's dad—gave him cover for his rapacious ends. Moreover, as I discuss shortly, his penchant for rape can be seen as a means of enacting a perverse malignant patriarchy or symbolic fatherhood.

Some might take issue with the use of sadomasochism to understand sexual harassment, or see in sadomasochism a different set of useful possibilities.[1] One scholar and Lacanian psychoanalyst, Colin Wright, for instance, suggests that sadomasochism be seen as a form of perversion—that is, in fact, père-version. For Wright, sadomasochism should be seen not as a contract between individuals, but a relation of individuals, sadist and masochist, to a "third element"—the signifier. Wright (2013) suggests, in fact, that sadomasochism depends on a failed or unrealizable patriarchal standard and, thus, opens up "an ethical orientation—with ethics being understood . . . as an unyielding fidelity to the singularity of a desire." With père-version we find desire pursued outside a "pre-existing place in a contemporary symbolic order devoid of fathers that can stand on their own two feet" (Wright 2013). I quote Wright (2013) at length to do justice to his claims:

> Père-version locates the need for the stabilizing function of law not in the imposed structure of the Name of the Father, in, that is, the overwhelming being of a primordial father who sadistically enjoys all and to whom we must masochistically subject ourselves. On the contrary, père-version locates the relation to a father (not the father) in the singular and ethical invention of the particular speaking subject who finds a way of knotting some form of consistency that works for them, and only them, as Lacan explored in James Joyce's sinthome. If Joyce's absurd ambition as an artist was to master creation enough to become his own father, this may have been a compensation for the fallibility of his drunken,

profligate father, yet we have Portrait of the Artist and Ulysses to show for it. This is still an ethical relation to the law, but one very far from the dutiful and ultimately masochistic adherence to a list of pre-existing, sadistic commandments.

With Joyce, his seemingly delusional ambition harms no one but himself, and leaves us all—the literary world, at least—enriched. But what if this self-authoring—self-fathering—is destructive?

Defiance of the existing symbolic order, I would suggest, is not the best or at least only standard of evaluation in thinking through ethics, as the Cosby case study demonstrates. Cosby's devotion to a singular desire—his destructive self-authoring—provides a cautionary tale. We need an understanding of sadomasochism that can account for Cosby's sadomasochistic père-version and fully appreciate its operation outside of the relating of individuals in supposedly consensual situations. Sadomasochism as an analytic of power, finally, must account for the ubiquity of sadomasochism and its operation on several levels of scale.

Could it be that sadomasochism is a means of installing, maintaining, and policing patriarchal formations, including in the workplace? Is it possible that, in the aftermath of mid-twentieth century feminist unruliness and social and political change on a number of fronts, sadomasochism remains a critical means of resisting substantive equality? For black communities in particular, can the focus on a perceived crisis in patriarchal family formations, father absence, and wounded masculinity lead, in some cases, to perverse consequences?

I contend that the Cosby affair, in particular, serves as a template for the types of exposure that have become commonplace during the MeToo resistance. In fact, some have seen his second criminal trial involving Andrea Constand as the first legal litmus test of the MeToo era (see, e.g., Williams 2018). To be sure, we can see in the case of Cosby, as we can with Weinstein and others, the long-term consolidation of patriarchal power within industries. The public debate came to focus on exposing those assaulting others. Melodramatic framings that focused on the perceived shortcomings of victims began to give way to a focus on alleged perpetrators and calls to action, once accusers exhibited critical mass. In this light, it is interesting to consider how the DSK case would have turned out differently if it were transpiring now. It is worth noting that the same Manhattan DA, Cyrus Vance Jr., who passed on prosecuting DSK and once decided not to pursue Weinstein when he had the opportunity, chose to move forward in the prosecution of Weinstein, securing a conviction in 2020 on two counts, "rape" and "committing a sexual criminal act" (Nawaz 2020). Vance does not regret not prosecuting in 2015, maintaining that the decision was based on sound evaluation, given the entirety of the evidence they had at that time, including an audiotape of Weinstein making certain admissions (Nawaz 2020). Nevertheless, Vance did allow that the social climate is different now, stating, "The way the public in a jury receives this evidence at a trial is different. We have seen in the last several years in our sex crime prosecutions that there is, I think, a greater awareness by jurors and those who are evaluating evidence that victims of sexual assault, survivors don't always react in the same or predictable way. . . . So, I think there has both been a public shift in understanding [regarding sexual assault] and other significant differences between now and 2015" (Nawaz 2020). Would that greater awareness extend to black victims such as Nafissatou Diallo, or other immigrant women with complicated histories and difficult circumstances in which they try to survive?

To be sure, despite recent wins in high-profile cases, such as those involving Cosby and Weinstein, and the counter-hegemonic discourse on rape expressing support for survivors, the contest for public opinion is far from settled, suggesting that activists for "intimate justice" (Threadcraft 2016) will remain in a protracted battle. In the fall of 2018, the United States found itself in the midst of another historic controversy involving yet another Supreme Court nominee, Brett Kavanaugh, who has been accused of sexual predation. Among the many arguments raised in his defense, including the preposterous notion that he was a virgin in high school and, therefore, could not have attempted rape, were age-old questions about why the accuser, Dr. Christine Blasey Ford, did not come forward. Those who wonder why victims wait to report harms with which they are afflicted or choose not to report altogether are naïve about the stakes involved for individuals who buck institutional power and the prognosis for their success. Time will tell how the MeToo movement evolves. In support of the effort to strike while the iron is hot, we should embrace sadomasochism as a critical analytic and understand the plight of victims as that of whistle-blowers.

In fact, it is helpful to think of women and other victims of sexual harassment and the sadistic control to which they are subjected in the same vein as that suffered by whistle-blowers, because it helps to explain how they are positioned socially and in terms of power within institutions. Although many think of whistle-blowers as romantic or heroic figures, the reality they experience is a far cry from these associations. Whistle-blowers, whose claims of exposure often fall on particular actors, are seen as stepping outside of and threatening institutions, not protecting or salvaging them (Alford 2001). The reprisals they face are similar to those experienced by sexual harassment victims. Instead of working to uphold general principles or values, especially when they are threatened or violated, many prioritize their individual well-being and commitment to those they see as positioned to protect or promote their careers. Similarly, sexual violence victims know well the potential dangers of speech, even though that speech may be a means to effect change for themselves or others (Alcoff and Gray-Rosendale 2018, 180–81). It is noteworthy that much of the power of MeToo claims of sexual abuse comes from the fact that more than one, and often many, accounts are brought to light concerning alleged serial rapists or harassers. Within institutions and their attendant industries, most stand alone. Furthermore, how do we empower victims of abuse to come forward when they are making a singular claim of harassment, not backed up by numbers of other claimants? Whistle-blowing gives us a way to further understand and, thus, counteract the plight of those harmed by sadomasochistic work dynamics in general and those manifesting as sexual harassment in particular.

As political theorist C. Fred Alford explains in his provocatively titled meditation on the twentieth anniversary of Foucault's *Discipline and Punish*, "What Would It Matter If Everything Foucault Said about Prison Were Wrong?: *Discipline and Punish* after Twenty Years" (Alford 2000), disciplinary power may not capture the full scope of how power operates. Alford notes that Foucault based his understanding of prisons on literature about Bentham-type panopticons that were not widely used and do not necessarily define common prison systems in the United

States. Through his study of the US penal system, he finds that something other than surveillance is often at work (125–31). As he explains, prisons are "nonopticons" (128–31), where prisoners are kept out of sight. The architecture of nonopticon prisons, with their focus on controlling entering and exiting and the mere counting of bodies—leads to a failure to see, and thus recognize, the personhood of prisoners at all (128–31).

Elsewhere Alford (2001) further observes that, in the case of whistleblowers, feudal power becomes a much better framework for comprehending what is at work. He explains, "The organization is more feudal than we know. Power is decentralized, and power is personal, located in the figure of the boss" (101). It is not, according to Alford, that surveillance and disciplinary power are unimportant. They are. But, just as subjects found themselves governed by and beholden to particular feudal lords, the average worker pays much more attention to what their supervisors or senior powerbrokers expect than they do general principles of justice or the public good (103). "To say that the whistleblower experiences his or her world as feudal is to point out that this is how power looks from the bottom up" (102). For most, the focus on maintaining employment, advancing one's economic and social position, and avoiding conflict takes precedence over all else, even more so in an era of economic precarity. Coming to grips with the sadomasochistic, feudal nature of US workplaces is critical to advancing the fight against sexual harassment.

Conclusion

The MeToo movement has brought critical attention and action to fighting sexual harassment, including rape in the workplace. In the midst of this renewed agitation, black women and their harm and resistance to it cannot be sidelined. This chapter has underscored the important role black women have played historically in resisting their experience of harassment in workplaces, including in the context of slavery. The case studies examined here illustrate how black women and their experiences can provide guidance to understanding harassment or rape more within the broader society as well. With Strauss-Kahn we see an example of transnational business masculinity that was a notable forerunner in public discourse to Trump as US head of state or his compatriot

Jeffrey Epstein. We saw, too, how black women, who are not generally viewed as victims, can be easily villainized, with immigrants like Diallo experiencing special vulnerabilities. With Cosby, we saw an example of père-version used to assuage wounded masculinity and the many ways in which Cosby's life was informed by and affirmed black cultural pathology melodrama. In both, we are reminded of the importance of sadomasochism as an analytic of power, and the jeopardy that targets of harassment face—a special jeopardy that makes them subject to feudal power, even as in the case of whistle-blowers.

Conclusion

Turbulent Futures: Post-Politics as an Analytic

In this Conclusion, I would like to offer a metaphor that is helpful in understanding both the form and substance of this book, *Re-Imagining Black Women*, and gestures towards the legacy I hope it obtains. The metaphor is taken from the physics of flow. In the physics of flow, substances like liquid or air are either laminar or turbulent (Bernard and Wallace 2002; Davidson 2015). In laminar flow with fluids, for instance, typically at slow volume or speed and high viscosity, we see a layered, relatively consistent stream of motion. In contrast, with turbulent flow, liquid streams in a multidirectional, dynamic fashion. The movement does not appear as seamless and can seem disruptive. Peter Davidson (2015, viii) explains, "Turbulence is all around us. The air flowing in and out of our lungs is turbulent. . . . Turbulence controls the drag on cars, . . . and it dictates the weather. . . . The liquid core of the earth is turbulent." Although I would not suggest that the political world is susceptible to the same modes of investigation as the natural world, the metaphor of flow is helpful in capturing the dynamism and ubiquity of phenomena discussed in this book.

First the form. In this work I have forged a methodology that is post-positivist and turbulent. The interpretivist tradition from which I hail emphasizes social constructedness and perspectival frameworks. I have spent much of my time as a scholar studying political narratives, in theory, policy, and social movements, and their framing function, that is, the way they guide, justify, and incite or forestall behavior. I am also an interdisciplinarian, and by definition I take this to mean at least two things, namely: commitments to the integration of disciplinary insights and to allowing the questions we want answered to guide our research (Lattuca 2001). Interdisciplinary work typically ushers in a challenge to our disciplinary expectations of knowledge production and what I like to call the "Nixon questions" of epistemology: What can we know and how can we know it? Although my work is anchored and seeks to integrate scholarship in women's and gender studies and political science, the questions I have tried to answer about shifting and competing frames for understanding racism, sexism, and class inequality have drawn me into media studies and, especially, psychoanalysis.

To be sure, other researchers might well turn to producing survey data or qualitative interviews to assess post-politics, but I explicitly use narrative analysis in ways that join cultural studies and political approaches. I assess discourse formation along a number of sites—cartoons, media stories, movies, TV shows, and political discourse. In doing so, I critically analyze cultural and political texts in ways that are not only top down, but bottom up. I am able to capture the construction of frames in ways that not only highlight the role of electoral or state actors, but also a range of individuals and communities in everyday contexts.

I noted in the Introduction that those wedded to disciplines or specific discourse communities may experience uncomfortability with the mix of concepts and literatures from different fields, the questions asked, and the means used to answer them. The grounding in dominant disciplinary norms, in particular, can effect laminar flow, a predictable, consistent stream of knowledge production and expectations. The post-positivist, interpretive, interdisciplinary approach can produce turbulent flows of information, concepts, queries, insights, and transformations.

The turbulent methodology is especially apt because it captures the turbulent nature of culture and politics. Although I examine post-politics and melodrama as a throughline for the book, themes and issues—such as black cultural pathology, domestic labor, assault, and male woundedness, among others—are not neatly contained in a laminar flow, but surface and resurface throughout different chapters, at times with very different expressions, or the same element in a different context. I explored the nature of liminality, melodrama, and post-politics, organically over time, seeking to gain clarity and demonstrate how post-politics and the melodrama that is its handmaiden can give us deeper understanding of this current political era. So, although the general progression of people, events, and questions are laid out more or less chronologically, the past is never past, as Faulkner reminds us, and questions and themes flow dynamically within and across time periods and chapters.

Now, for substance. The multidirectional, dynamic mode of turbulent knowledge production maps the turbulence of post-politics substantively as well. Predictably, since the election of Donald Trump, a self-styled nationalist (Forgey 2018), we have seen a rise in white nationalist rhetoric, protest, and attacks (see, e.g., Farley 2019; Sonmez and Parker 2019), with the Southern Poverty Law Center reporting an "all-time high" of 1,020 "active hate groups" in the United States (Beirich 2019, 13). The violent protests in Virginia a year after Trump's election are but one notable example. As many recall, white nationalists in Charlottesville violently reacted to protestors advocating for the removal of a statue of Confederate General Robert E. Lee (Shear and Haberman 2017). One nationalist protestor actually drove a car into a crowd of people, killing one woman, Heather Heyer. Although he originally condemned the violence, days later at a press conference Trump averred, "'I think there is blame on both sides. . . . You had a group on one side that was bad. You had a group on the other side that was also very violent. Nobody wants to say that. I'll say it right now'" (Shear and Haberman 2017). The false equivalence the president drew between groups of protestors by stating there are good people on both sides and his general failure to condemn violence perpetrated by those with racist views has given a green light to his most violent supporters. Whatever their actual influence on hate groups (Beirich 2019), Trump's ban on immigration from countries with large Muslim populations and his characterization of migrants hoping to seek asylum as a villainous, criminal horde of invaders also fit within his nationalist politics. Children and families have been separated and kept at our borders in squalid conditions. We have also seen historic marches, most notably the Women's Marches held all over the country on his inauguration day, in response to his presidency (Donovan, Sherman, and Rentz 2017), and held each year thereafter. There is a renewed effort to counteract attempts to erode reproductive freedom, as well. Given the divisive nature of the Trump presidency and the ensuing response, it might seem that the time of post-feminism or post-racial politics has come and gone—that we are, in fact, well past that now.

But, part of what I have argued in *Re-Imagining Black Women* is that we need to have a broader understanding of post-politics, one that centers black women as subjects. Much attention has been given to forms of post-politics that focus on liberal notions of formal equality or that suggest that progressive politics and social movements are no longer necessary (see, e.g., McRobbie 2007). I examine this manifestation of post-politics as well. I have also argued, however, that there is a need for an expanded view of post-politics. Sarah Projansky (2001), for instance, in her typology of post-feminism, includes not only the "doing and undoing" of feminism, in McRobbie's terms, but direct backlash and a push for traditionalism, among other things. Although the liberal equality version of post-politics may be popular it has circulated simultaneously with a range of other post-politics narrative frames.

The nationalism of Trump, for instance, is an extension of white nationalism that has been prominent, particularly among conservative forces in this country, for some time. Political scientists have been particularly keen to point out the nature of white nationalism at the close of the twentieth century and the dawn of the twenty-first. In *The New White Nationalism in America: Its Challenge to Integration*, Carol Swain (2002), for instance, warns of growing white nationalist sentiments, particularly in online environments, in response to black and minority advancement. She counsels that there is a need to engage such perspectives in order to quell their potentially negative outcomes. In his groundbreaking work, *White Nationalism, Black Interests: Conservative Public Policy and the Black Community*, Ronald Walters (2003) traced the expression of white nationalism through a range of public policies, including public education, for instance, where he examines the resegregation of US schools. In my own work, *Gender, Race, and Nationalism in Contemporary Black Politics* (Alexander-Floyd 2007), I examine the mutually constitutive nature of black and white nationalisms. The white nationalism I examine is aligned with the state, that is, through party politics and the operation of government. These various, interrelated forms of nationalism, blatant white supremacy, and conservative party politics have developed alongside of liberal equality frameworks. Together, they are among a range of post-political fantasies that resist social justice aims, either through arguing that we essentially have enough equality and do not need further political change or to hearken back to a time before the interruption of social movement activity into the putative bliss of foregone eras.

Review of Key Arguments

The case studies in this book signal the need for attentiveness to turbulence in our understanding of politics. Melodrama as a genre tries to force experience into a laminar model of easy choices, the polarities of ideal citizen subjects versus abject figures, the deserving and underserving, the virtuous and the villainous. How do we disrupt this simplistic, ubiquitous framing device? Each chapter has tried to expose the operation of melodrama and liminality, and to do so using an often overlooked or disavowed aspect of politics.

Chapter 1 examined black conservatism, and the splitting or liminality framing the representation and reception of Condoleezza Rice. We do not attend to conservatism in black politics in the measure we should, given its prevalence ideologically and the growing number of black conservatives on the national stage politically. The protest model that is identified with black literature (Tate 1998), I argued, holds true for political analysis as well. We can find in black conservatism critical examples of the key conundrums and questions regarding race in the United States. The post-political fantasy of integrationism seems chimerical in the case of Condoleezza Rice. She is beloved by conservatives and held out as a model of integrationism. She occupies the position of the idealized, citizen subject. She is known as "Condi" in a melodrama of closeness that positions her as "close" to Bush and his family and to, by extension, conservatives and their vision of the United States. Still, even in this capacity, she is deemed to be "like one of the family," positioned in the tradition of "the help" within domestic understandings of racial relationships. Her relegation to the domestic relation of "the help" is also significant because Rice and the disruptive potential she holds as a high-powered, intelligent, singular political figure is constrained and diminished by coming under the paternal order of the Bush family. Simultaneously, she is dogged by a melodrama of closeness—"Condilicious"—grounded in a range of stereotypes of black women. She is reviled as a "space invader" (Puwar 2004) or intruder into a national and international political arena, and those even on the left tap into race and gender registers of representation in their critique.

Knowing about turbulence can help us comprehend political figures, like Rice, and the broader political questions her public life invokes. In liberal or formal notions of equality that focus on the breaking of barriers and descriptive representation as an end in itself, there is an assumption of organized, layered flow. Layers of assumptions fall upon each other as in a laminar flow of political effect: representation always equals progress, or, at least, more often than not it will tend toward progressive outcomes. The political field is often much more turbulent in terms of the forces of substantive representation, ideology, and outcomes. What are we to make of the fact that a black woman breaks a particular occupational and political barrier, if her doing so is occasioned by her support of empire, her modeling of prototypical representations of blackness that fly in the face of true equality and recognition of one's humanity? We can recognize that black women are produced as liminal subjects at a macropolitical level and that this reality impacts the public reception of figures like Rice, on the one hand, and, on the other, critique her function in support of empire and war. The danger of identification or symbolism, when it proceeds uncritically, is to assume that one's experience of racism, sexism, or other forms of oppression jives with only certain political commitments or ideology. Whatever Rice confronts in terms of racism and sexism, for instance, she still hails from a middle-class background, pursues the goals of political conservatism, and aids and abets integrationist frames that undermine social justice politics.

Although he is not a Republican, President Barack Obama provided another example of melodrama and the production of blacks as liminal subjects. We can see, too, how an assessment of President Obama can benefit from an appreciation of turbulence. Chapter 2 examined gender, another underexplored aspect of black electoral politics. Specifically, in lieu of asking about deracialization as a dominant frame in electoral politics, I looked at gender as it impacted Barack Obama's personal narratives, electoral strategies, and governance. In exploring his initial historic presidential run I demonstrate how, instead of being a deracialized candidate, Obama was an ideal post-racial, post-feminist candidate. I look to the Moynihan Report as a dominant urtext for post-politics and show how many of the ideas we associate with post-politics, from a focus on self-regulation and a turn away from the state and liminality, were all embodied in the report and forecasted this emphasis in the broader society. I assess a range of ideas, such as wounded masculinity, a focus on family breakdown and its reconstitution, and interracial relationships as a means of symbolizing racial unity, what Rowe (2007) refers to as "miscege-nation." These ideas were prevalent in popular culture, as I demonstrate by looking at *Grey's Anatomy* and *Crash*, two defining cultural sites of this historical era. I show how these ideas were also part and parcel of the breakthrough Obama 2008 campaign. In doing so, I highlight the mutually constitutive nature of culture and politics, something I hope foments greater attention across disciplines that tend to emphasize one or the other, but not their interaction. I also look at Obama as a super minority figure who occupies the respectability end of polarities of black liminality, and as a black symbolic father, a figure who stands in as a representative for the black community as a whole, a position he arguably wrested from Jesse Jackson.

I also discuss the operation of Obama as a black symbolic father, particularly in terms of black cultural pathology melodrama. He serves as a point of identification and idealization and black manhood; a replacement figure for absent black fathers; and an enforcer of patriarchal norms. This black symbolic fatherhood explains the "authoritarian" (Ndubuizu 2014) posture he adopts toward black audiences at home and abroad. It also accounts for his signature program with which he closed his presidency, his My Brother's Keeper (MBK) initiative. A direct result of black cultural pathology thinking, this initiative builds on black male crisis ideology that has been popular for decades across the political spectrum (Legette 1999; Alexander-Floyd 2007). I raise questions about the utility of advocating for an "us too" approach to inserting women into the ideological field of this initiative, something that Obama, importantly, did not allow. I argued that the White House Summit on Women and Girls of Color upheld a complementary or reformist model that, along with MBK, was essentially undemocratic in character and supportive of respectability politics. It was a compromise strategy that exposed the limits some saw in critiquing head-on an ideologically bankrupt initiative that was, nevertheless, supported by a symbolically important president who was under siege and enjoyed strong backing among blacks. Ideally, accountability and opposition, when necessary, would have been hallmarks of black politics, in this context. This posture would require an embrace of political turbulence, including and not limited to the ability to critique politicians like President Obama and freely exercise criticism and debate where they and their policy choices or inaction are concerned. Again, the Obama case study demonstrates how the politics of identification and popularity can conspire to prevent robust democratic engagement.

Chapter 3 turned to an examination of melodrama and liminality in terms of wounded masculinity and popular culture. I assessed the work of Tyler Perry, the most prolific black filmmaker of this era, and how his work fits within post-politics. In contrast to the work of Spike Lee, another successful black filmmaker, which focuses on exposing racism, albeit with limitations concerning gender and class politics, Tyler Perry's work focuses on self-rehabilitation and a return to traditionalism. I dissect his first film, *Diary of a Mad Black Woman*, because it provides a template or fantasmatic for the rest of his work. This movie bears resemblance to other post-feminist narratives that feature stories of return and self-regulation. Like other post-feminist narratives, it focuses on self-examination. Perry's movie, in fact, is a black version of *Bridget Jones's Diary*, an iconic post-feminist story. It differs, however, given the focus on black cultural pathology melodrama and wounded masculinity. In fact, I question the function of Tyler Perry's racialized gender cross-dressing that trades on a composite of stereotypes or symbols of black womanhood, such as the mammy/matriarch, Sapphire, and Jezebel. I argue that, while the film provides messaging for black women that critiques their choices for partners, among other things, it is very much a story *for* black men and *of* one black man: Tyler Perry.

The movie villainizes middle-class black characters who distance themselves from the black community and forsake patriarchal family values, and reinstalls patriarchal authority, in part, by usurping the power and position of women. The main character, Helen, is rehabilitated in terms of her black femininity and reconnected with her family. As she sheds her wayward middle-class elitism and embraces home, she is rewarded with a love interest who is a working-class man. Perry reinstalls patriarchal authority in two ways, however. Through Madea, he occupies the strength and authority associated with the matriarch, commandeering it to preach guidance about appropriate gender roles and community formation. Just as blackface minstrelsy or racial cross-dressing entailed an appropriation of the stereotypical qualities associated with minstrel figures, so, too, does Perry's racialized gender cross-dressing facilitate a means to fantasize the reclamation of power, position, and authority associated with black matriarchs. Through Helen, Perry is able to exact revenge for the abuse he experienced as a child and assuage his wounded masculinity. Helen, like Madea, is also a composite character. Using Freud's ideas about dreamwork, specifically condensation and displacement, and the concept of multivocality via free association, I illustrate exactly how Perry, through the character of Helen, forgives Charles, the patriarchal stand-in for his abusive father, but not before doing unto others exactly what has been done unto him. True to melodramatic form, larger social problems are evaded or reduced to micro-level concerns of the family and villains become victims and vice versa, in a cycle of relating in which traditional family values are restored.

Chapters 4 and 5 consider melodrama, liminality, and sexual assault and rape, other repressed and disavowed aspects of black and US history and politics. Chapter 4 focuses on the repression and disavowal of white male rape of black women. It recounts a brief history of white male predation toward black women during the slavery, Reconstruction, and segregation eras. The return of the repressed is a common theme from Freud's work, and this reality is certainly borne out in terms of this history. This chapter counters this "enforced forgetfulness" (Spillers et. al. 2007) by not only recounting this history but also by explaining its importance to US social contract theory and nation-building. We can rewrite what we understand about US-based American political development when we consider this history. Black women are central to definitions of home. Black women are a defining counterpoint to white femininity, and their abuse shores up white masculine and feminine identity. Black communities in general serve as a constitutive outside analytically and legally in terms of nationhood. Paradoxically, however, the public-private split in spheres, a hallmark of the white sexual contract, does not obtain for black people who are segregated educationally, socially, and in other ways, but who labor in private spaces as well.

I focus on the history of white male rape of black women because of its centrality to nation formation and the social contract, on the one hand, and its repression and reassertion on the other. The "return of the repressed" also manifests in another iconic example, namely, *The Help* (Stockett 2009). I look to three sites to explore these issues, specifically the book and movie versions of *The Help* and the oral histories upon which the book was based. The laminar view of the book focuses on the young white female character, Skeeter, who seems out of step with the racial codes of her southern hometown. Skeeter returns home and searches for a beloved mammy she had growing up, Constantine. Meanwhile we see her negotiating attempts to wed her to the racial and gender norms that are her birthright. Skeeter writes a tell-all book based on domestic workers she interviews called *The Help*. Skeeter is a virtuous savior figure in the end who rides the good fortune generated by this book to a career in New York, leaving behind domestic workers who participated in the book to deal with the aftermath. She symbolizes a new feminist, post-racial future, and literally and figuratively leaves old racial and gender regimes behind her.

The turbulence of *The Help* is captured, however, by unpacking the history of white male rape of black women embedded in this story. In assessing this history in relation to *The Help*, I begin by tracing how the history of black women's violation in domestic spaces is relayed in *Telling Memories*, a book based on oral histories of black domestic workers and the white women in whose homes they labored. Although discussed, albeit in limited fashion, white women generally deny white male rape of black women. I then showcase how the book version of *The Help* disavows this history by presenting a romantic relationship between a black domestic worker and a white male. Finally, I examine the movie version of *The Help*, where the history of white male rape of black women is erased or repressed completely. I also discuss how a large plot element, namely a domestic worker's abandonment of her child because she is too fair and appears white, is elided in the movie. Moreover, Constantine's daughter, in the book version, racially passes at a whites-only meeting at her mother's employer's home. As a result Constantine and her daughter are thrown out. In the movie version, Constantine's daughter does not have fair skin and this element of the plot is effaced. I contend, however, that even in the case of the movie's repression of the history of white male rape of black women, this history haunts the movie or reasserts itself through the movie's obsession or trope concerning sanitation, hygiene (in bathrooms), and fecal matter. I aver that, amid this repression and disavowal, this history will continue to haunt and trouble our present and futures, until we mourn or account for the history of white male rape of black women.

The final chapter takes a turbulent view of melodrama and liminality in terms of the MeToo movement. Melodrama translates social and political problems into individual concerns, is pathos driven, and features clear victims and victors. In legal melodramas involving sexual harassment and rape, there is a concerted effort to deny the space of victimhood to those who are harassed or assaulted. Although this is a problem, particularly for women, antiblack racism adds a different dimension. Black people in general and black women in particular are not regarded as victims. They are seen as abject others and, thus, unrapable in most cases. Ironically, this is true, even given black women's disproportionate experience of harassment and violence relative to others and the fact that they have been some of the earliest and leading resisters to harassment and assault. I highlight the role of Tarana Burke in founding the MeToo movement. Moreover, I push against the "enforced forgetfulness" (Spillers et al. 2007) regarding black women's contributions to fighting harassment and rape by noting key moments of that history, including resistance under slavery, the work of black female plaintiffs in some of the earliest Title VII cases that formed the legal basis for fighting sexual harassment, and the controversy surrounding the Clarence Thomas hearings, which served as a flashpoint for igniting conversation around the issue.

I then turn to two case studies that reveal related but distinct issues regarding black communities and harassment and rape. The first case study features former International Monetary Fund chief Dominique Strauss-Kahn's rape of Nafissatou Diallo, an immigrant and hotel domestic worker in New York. It shows how Diallo is first framed as a pure victim, and then as an unworthy one, as the weight of stereotypes and assumptions attached to black women as sexual subjects and the realities she faces as an immigrant bear down on public conscience. I also pinpoint Strauss-Kahn as a prime example of the international business masculinity that neoliberalism has spawned, where powerful men who traverse the international political and business world continue to see the violation of women, especially women of color, as their prerogative. It is unsurprising that Kahn's transnational business masculinity (Connell 2012), which was not legally censured in the United States when the victim was black, is on full display with Donald Trump as president of the United States. In the second case study I focus on celebrity comedian Bill Cosby. Black cultural pathology melodrama is important to Cosby in terms of his career and serial predation. Although some see his idealized father figure epitomized in the figure of Cliff Huxtable on the *Cosby Show* at odds with the reality of Cosby as a rapist and harasser, I show how they are connected. Cosby represented himself as a model of respectable citizenship and a benign patriarch. Cosby offers himself as a model for abject black others. This is most especially evident in the ways in which he has infamously railed against the black poor, rehearsing well-worn stereotypes about black family breakdown, irresponsibility, and immorality among poor blacks. Just as Barack Obama castigates blacks for their lack of priorities and offers himself as an idealized father figure as a politician, Cosby serves as a black symbolic father in popular culture. Unsurprisingly, he, his wife, and other supporters marshal tropes of black male endangerment, such as lynching, to frame his 2018 conviction on assault charges.

Contributing to a "fully loaded cost accounting" of slavery (Painter 2002), I end by illustrating how sadomasochism is a necessary and powerful analytic in understanding harassment and assault in workplaces. Drawing on Lynn Chancer (1992)'s classic *Sadomasochism in Everyday Life*, I explain how sadomasochism operates in workplaces as it relates to harassment and assault, using the case studies of Strauss-Kahn and Cosby as illustrations. Furthermore, in the case of Cosby, I account for his own wounded masculinity and father abandonment, as a driver of his attachment to black cultural pathology melodrama and penchant for rape. I maintain that we can see his sadomasochistic predation as a form of "père-version," or a form of destructive self-authoring or self-fathering. I suggest that victims of harassment and rape are similar to whistle-blowers, and that understanding how power operates in their lives can help understand the journey of harassment and rape victims.

Turbulent Futures 2.0

In *Re-Imagining Black Women*, I analyze issues and questions spanning almost two decades—the opening decades of the twenty-first century. I have labored to demonstrate the importance of melodrama as a political genre in understanding US and black politics, focusing in particular on the production of blacks in general and black women in particular as liminal subjects caught betwixt and between polar positions of respectable super minorities and abject figures. As the foregoing suggests, attending to the oft-neglected aspects of political life, such as black conservatism and the urtext of integrationism, gender and black cultural pathology melodrama and electoral politics, wounded masculinity and the use of fantasy to reassert traditional patriarchy in popular culture, and the repressed and disavowed histories of white male rape of black women and the impact of sadomasochism in workplace rape and harassment, explodes laminar or unitary models of political analysis. The lessons from these case studies bear continued relevance today and the future.

As noted above, post-politics (or post-feminist, post–Civil Rights, and postleftist politics) is best seen as a repertoire of frames and fantasies that challenge the outcomes of the social movements of the mid-twentieth century. Even amid the fascistic elements of the current political context, when there are brazen attacks against and attempts to roll back reproductive freedom, anti-immigrant fervor, a reckless retreat from ethical norms in domestic and foreign policy, among many other actions, we see liberal notions of equality and representation at work as well. We also find many reeling from the virulent, renewed conservatism represented by Trump's presidency, and searching to understand or reframe the expectations ushered in for many by changes in society and politics, post-1965 in general, and with the presidency of Barack Obama in particular.

I contend that the proliferation of certain forms of liberal post-feminist melodramas accounts for the unqualified, or at least immoderate, hope that we were in a post-racial, post–Civil Rights future, a future beyond the need for broad-scale social activism, talk of revolution, or attention to the reproduction of conservative ideology and the encroachment of neoliberalism into every aspect of our society. If, as political scientist Andra Gillespie (2019, 194) suggests, "After the mainstream media declared America 'post-racial' in the wake of Barack Obama's election in 2008, few would have predicted that five to six years later, the high-profile murders of unarmed blacks . . . would birth a social movement [i.e., Black Lives Matter]," it is in no small part due to the success of post-racial, post-feminist ideology in overtaking public and political imagination, including among academics. There have always been those, for instance, critical of Barack Obama's politics, including when he was operating in state government (see, e.g., Reed 1996). There have always been some who saw the election of Obama as not a new beginning of racial harmony, but rather a means of neoliberal race and gender management that suited Wall Street and elite interests, particularly in an increasingly demographically diverse country (see, e.g., Reed 2008; Street 2009; 2010; Alexander-Floyd 2012b; Harris 2012). The emergence of Black Lives Matter or other political resistance in this era is less a sign of "empowerment" vis-à-vis the election of Obama, and more of an indication of the dissatisfaction stemming from unrealized expectations. A focus on deracialization, "situational" (e.g., Franklin 2010), "quasi-" (Gillespie 2019, 196) or otherwise might have to give way to or at least account for post–Civil Rights, post-feminist ideology as discursive and political formations.

Significantly, many of the forms of post-politics discussed in *Re-Imagining Black Women* continue to abound, more than midway through President Trump's (hopefully last, put potentially first) four years. Senator Kamala Harris, an early contender for the Democratic Party's presidential nomination, provides a case in point. Space does not permit me to elaborate all the ways her persona and campaign reflect post-feminist, post–Civil Rights ideology, but a few examples, drawn from her memoir *The Truths We Hold: An American Journey* (Harris 2019) and political career and reception, will suffice. First, Senator Harris fashions herself as a symbol of respectability. Her origin story emphasizes that her parents are immigrants, her mother from India, her dad from Jamaica (4). She ties herself to the Civil Rights movement as part of her legacy as well, trumpeting her parents' activism when they were in college (5, 7–9). She also affirms her support for civil rights and shores up her racial identification and street cred by claiming she is an Oakland native, deeply embedded in the black community, immersed in communal involvement at Rainbow Center, a local center grounded in black history, culture, and civic participation (16–19). Although she spent at least six of her formative years in Canada, she downplays this fact, spending barely two pages on this time in her life (19–20). Hers is also a parable of progress. Kamala, set on being a prosecutor since law school, goes on to be a prosecutor, then district attorney, attorney general for the state of California, and finally a US senator. She claims to be "a prosecutor in my own image," bearing all of the weight of her unique experiences, from her mom, community, and alma mater, Howard University (26). She would use the office of prosecutor, moreover, to make policy (36). One way that she has done this is through incarcerating the parents of truant children (Redden 2019). In this way, she disciplines putatively wayward parents. It is the kind of paternalistic, public shaming of black, largely poor women, that has been commonplace because of the black cultural pathology melodrama. This background of paternalism and public shaming are likely a critical factor, among others, explaining her lack of support during and eventual withdrawal from the Democratic Party primaries.

Kamala Harris finds company with other political figures in continued support of black cultural pathology melodrama. Former President Barack and former First Lady Michelle Obama, for instance, have positioned themselves as models of respectability, a counterpoint to and antidote to abject blackness. In this vein, Barack Obama continues to pursue his My Brother's Keeper (MBK) initiative. In February 2019, the Obama Foundation (2019) hosted a town hall on an MBK Rising! tour, featuring a conversation between Barack Obama and Stephen ("Steph") Curry, star basketball player with the Golden State Warriors. While there he continued to promote ideas grounded in black cultural pathology melodrama. In characteristic fashion, he presented ambivalent viewpoints, noting, when asked how black women could support black men, that black women have their own set of challenges, but also that men need to be understood. He states that, unlike women, men do not have the same opportunities to discuss their "vulnerabilities, challenges, doubts, lack of confidence, etc." Young black women need to "support" black men he intones, yet advocates young black women "having high expectations and demanding accountability from young men" (Obama Foundation 2019).

Further, noting that he was quoting his wife, Michelle, he stated that "moms sometimes, they'll raise their girls, but they'll mother [spoil] their boys," adding that "they will overcompensate for the challenges that are out there by saying 'oh, honey that's okay,' even though sometimes it's not. And, I think sometimes our young women allow young men to get away with stuff that they probably should not" (Obama Foundation 2019). This claim—"That mothers raise their daughters, but spoil their sons"—places blame for perceived problems in black communities on black families, as opposed to structural sources of poverty and oppression—on men for being failed patriarchs, and on women for raising them as such. The claim is also noteworthy, because, although not original, it was the calling card of black nationalist Jawanza Kunjufu when, beginning in the 1980s, he trafficked his series of slender books, *Countering the Conspiracy to Destroy Black Boys* (Kunjufu 1985; 1986; 1990). As I have discussed elsewhere (Alexander-Floyd 2007), Kunjufu, along with Louis Farrakhan, leader of the Nation of Islam, were among some of the most visible proponents of black cultural pathology thinking in the closing decades of the twentieth century. Less visible, but still ubiquitous, were conservative Christians and community leaders who espoused similar views.

Finally, emphasizing the importance of lifting up respectable examples of manhood, Obama decried "overcompensation" through affirming malignant ideas about manhood. Obama (Obama Foundation 2019) explains,

> And what we want to do is to create a space in which young men of color and young men generally don't have to feel as if for me to be respected and admired in my community, I've got to act a certain way. A lot of the violence and pain that we suffer in our communities arises out of young men who nobody's said to them what it means to be respected. And so they're looking around and, well, I guess being respected means I might shoot you or I can make you back down or I can disrespect you and there's nothing you can do about it. And, that is a self-defeating model for being a man. So, we have to constantly lift up examples of, examples of successful men who don't take that approach. . . . If you are really confident about your financial situation you probably are not gon' be wearin' an eight pound chain around your neck, because you know, oh I got bank. I don't have to show you how much I got. I feel good. If you are very confident about your sexuality, you don't have to have eight women around you twerkin'. I mean, why are you all like—You seem stressed that you gotta be acting that way. 'Cause, I've got one woman who I'm very happy with so—and she's a strong woman. So I think part of the

challenge we have is that oftentimes racism historically in this society sends a message that you are less than and weak, we feel that we have to overcompensate certain stereotypical ways we men have to act.

These ideas, which were met with applause and affirmation, rehearse the black liminality in which blacks are often framed and that stem from the black cultural pathology melodrama discussed throughout this book. Embedded in Obama's language is an image of abject black male others who are violent, irresponsible, and operating from a dysfunctional model of manhood juxtaposed with respectable models of manhood, represented by people like Obama and Steph Curry. The reality of black visibility in occupations once foreclosed because of racial barriers and social mobility for some African Americans amid the reality of growing and deepening poverty and ongoing racial and other forms of discrimination is naturalized on one level, as it is seen as a function of misplaced choices and unproductive responses to historical conditions of oppression. The fact Obama can promote black cultural pathology melodrama thinking even in the midst of affirmed and resurgent racism and economic exploitation by monied classes in the Trump presidency is not remarkable. It affirms, unfortunately, a central thesis of this book, which is that post-politics in all of its manifestations is best seen as a repertoire of fantasies, frames, and ideological calling cards that oppose social justice, whether it be through direct backlash, appropriation of terms, ironic use of stereotypes, a call for traditionalism, or a suggestion that fighting for progressive social change is no longer necessary. It is not unsurprising to see calls for renewed activism and the circulation of these ideas drawn from black cultural pathology melodrama that suggest that success can be gained through personal rehabilitation, responsibility, and respectability. They are part of the ongoing contest of ideas and speak to the ongoing force and range of post-politics thinking and commitments.

Fortunately, this effort to promote Obama's My Brother's Keeper initiative did not proceed without critical commentary. In one welcome response, Derecka Purnell (2019) lambasts Obama's efforts, stating, "Mr. Obama's comments reinforced toxic masculinity and they didn't really give us an alternative. In the town hall, there was no black feminism, nothing that recognized the ordinary humanity of black girls and women; they were either on a pedestal or on the floor." The need for direct resistance to Obama's My Brother's Keeper initiative is as urgent as ever.

Relatedly, for her part, Michelle Obama has continued to endear herself to many, and in ways that ultimately uphold the neoliberal post-politics to which Barack Obama ascribes. Her blockbuster book, *Becoming* (Obama 2018), has garnered record sales. The success of the book was bolstered by slick advertising, strategic involvement of influencers in key areas, and a nationwide tour that boasted some hefty prices for admission. Despite its overwhelming commercial success and positive reception by most critics, Michelle Obama's *Becoming* contributes to the respectability politics that has hampered black and US politics. As Keeanga-Yamahtta Taylor (2019) explains, Michelle Obama's *Becoming* affirms individualist striving as a means to personal success. "*Becoming*," she observes, "normalizes power and the status quo while sending the message that the rest of us only need to find our place in the existing social hierarchy to be happy" (Taylor 2019). As in Barack Obama's Philadelphia compromise speech (see Chapter 2), Michelle Obama situates racism as something that is largely a thing of the past, with vestiges that can be dismissed with the proper attitude. Together, I contend, they represent "Brand Obama," a dynamic duo that self-commodifies their personalities in line with the dictates of neoliberal post-politics fantasies.

Another example, stemming from the controversy concerning singer R. Kelly, provides a spark of hope. Since his breakout hit, "I Don't See Nothing Wrong With a Little Bump and Grind," in the early 1990s, R. Kelly has been a mainstay in R&B music. Early in his career, however, people raised questions about his relationship with the late singer Aliyah. Kelly, who wrote the song "Age Ain't Nothing but a Number" for Aliyah, secretly married her when she was underage. Rumors about Kelly's penchant for underage girls always circulated, and there was even the release of a hard-core porn videotape Kelly made featuring himself and a fourteen-year-old girl, where he was seen directing her to simulate prostitution, urinating on her, and performing sexual acts with this child (Hampton 2019; Salam 2019). Although Kelly was eventually tried, he was found not guilty (Hampton 2019). Throughout much of his career, however, Kelly's reputation for child sexual abuse did not tarnish his reputation and support among most of his fans and others within and without black communities, and certainly not in the music business. Fortunately, in the spring of 2019, a six-episode documentary titled *Surviving R. Kelly* (Hampton 2019) shifted public sentiment in some corridors. In the documentary, Kelly, himself a victim of sexual abuse by a neighborhood boy and female babysitter, systematically grooms and psychologically and sexually coerces young girls. He is aided and abetted by his coterie of staff and supporters, who actively assist with or turn a blind eye to his predation. Kelly's abuse is fully consistent with the coercive control model well-known for those who address intimate-partner violence (Stark 2007). Like Cosby, Kelly grooms and cultivates targets in no small part by promising them opportunities in the music industry, thus constituting his actions as rape and sexual harassment. Like Cosby, he enacts a form of père-version (Wright 2013) in which he attempts to assuage his wounded masculinity by trying to self-author or self-father himself. As illustrated in the documentary, he even forces his victims to refer to him as "daddy" (Hampton 2019). In 2017, when word got out about his sex cult, he lost major revenue from concert ticket sales ("R. Kelly Come & Get 'Em!" 2017). After the airing of the documentary, new charges were brought against Kelly in Chicago (Carissimo 2019).

Kelly's controversy is important not only because it is yet another contemporary example of the operation of post-politics, particularly with the denial of père-version at play, but also because it highlights the ongoing interplay of politics and social change. Social movement scholars emphasize various models for social change, including, notably, frame alignment (see, e.g., Snow et al. 1986), resource mobilization (see, e.g., Springer 2005), and opportunity structures (see, e.g., McAdam 1999). Organized political activism against sexual harassment and rape has been ongoing since the mid-1960s. A confluence of factors account for the response to the *Surviving R. Kelly* documentary, including the proliferation of commentary on social media; renewed resistance and, as Ashwini Tambe explains, "horizontal action" (Vedantam 2018) spawned by Trump's presidency; and committed laborers, such as Tarana Burke, Aisha Shahidah Simmons, producer of *No!*, a documentary film on rape in black communities (Simmons 2006), and Scheherazade Tillet, cofounder of A Long Walk Home, among many others. Salamishah and Scheherazade Tillet have suggested that the attention and reaction to

Surviving R. Kelly marks a turn in the MeToo movement, one that— finally—centers black women (Tillet and Tillet 2019). One surely hopes this is the case, although it is difficult to overstate the entrenched resistance to attending to pernicious sexual politics in the United States, including among black communities.

To be sure, as I have argued throughout *Re-Imagining Black Women*, centering black women in discussions of post-politics is long overdue. My analysis suggests several, but does not exhaust the full range of, necessary interventions for scholars and activists. The uptick in political celebrity, represented not only by Trump but in a different vein the Obamas, provides an urgent area in which to explore neoliberalism and post-politics. Following Dyer, Renée Cramer observes that celebrities affirm social norms either by representing idealized values or, ironically, their transgression; in this way, "[S]tars serve to reinforce the status quo, and in particular to reinforce particular values that are considered 'under threat'" (Cramer 2016, 14). Obama and Cosby, as detailed in Chapter 2 and Chapter 5, respectively, through their own forms of celebrity, affirmed patriarchal notions of family under the guise of black cultural pathology melodrama. The liminal status of black women must also continue to be examined in studies of black women in national and cultural politics, and counteracted through political activism by groups and individuals. Narrative analysis that examines melodrama as a political genre and the production of liminality can be a powerful intellectual tool that can complement important, traditional modes of analysis and theorizing. The insights that post-politics as an analytic generate can inform the priorities and agendas of political organizations and community groups as they work to undermine the dominant controlling images that continue to affront and assail black women and their communities. In *Re-Imagining Black Women* I convincingly demonstrate that, by looking at what is neglected and repressed, we can better assess the tensions and driving forces of culture and politics. The protocols of race (Tate 1998) and gender often operate, in politics and academia, with an assumption of laminar flow. These protocols must give way to a black feminist frame of reference that can apprehend the turbulence present in black and US life and politics.

Coda

Post-Politics in the Era of COVID-19

As I finalize this book, the world is caught in the grips of a pandemic. The novel coronavirus disease of 2019 (COVID-19) that is presumed to have begun its journey in the city of Wuhan, China, has now spread to every continent. As I write, the United States now has the largest numbers of any country of those infected with COVID-19 ("Coronavirus in the U.S." 2020). Importantly, with the lack of systematic, broad-scale testing, even those figures likely represent an undercount. The disease has taken lives, sent the economy into a tailspin, and changed day-to-day life as many undertake mitigation through social (physical) distancing. How is this crisis a function, in many ways, of the politics that gives rise to the production of liminal subjects? How has political melodrama shaped the narratives and outcomes of the response to this modern-day crisis? What does it suggest about the way forward in the midst of turbulent political futures?

In a very real way, this crisis is a prime example of the horrors of neoliberalism and its concomitant spread of global capitalism. As I explain in the Introduction, for decades, there has been an effort to shift concern for the public good to that of personal responsibility as a means of addressing social problems. As I have discussed throughout this book, the production of citizens as liminal subjects and the proliferation of melodramatic frames to justify it have been a key means of facilitating this shift. In tandem with this, the federal government in particular has been commandeered to support financial markets, facilitate the spread of global capitalism, and maximize corporate profits. It is a bitter irony that the push for transnational markets, travel, and influence, for some under the guise of bringing people closer together culturally and fostering cooperation, has facilitated the spread of a modern-day plague that has taken and altered so many lives and largely placed people within and across countries in competition for vital resources.

This neoliberal project has borne much bitter fruit, including, among other things, a public health infrastructure that is seriously lacking. For instance, although New York governor Andrew Cuomo has been, for many, a leading light in this crisis and applauded for his handling of COVID-19, his prior actions helped to leave New York in a vulnerable position in the first place. As Akash Mehta (2020) points out in her piece, aptly titled "Even in a Pandemic, Andrew Cuomo Is Not Your Friend," "Decades of cuts to New York's heath care services, many of them championed by Cuomo, have contributed to the present crisis." Moreover, amid this historic challenge, Cuomo is seeking to cover a budget shortfall, not by taxing the rich, but by cutting Medicaid, thus leaving the poor even more vulnerable amid the COVID-19 pandemic (Mehta 2020).

In addition to an underfunded and underdeveloped public health infrastructure, neoliberalism is evident in the handling of the economic downturn. In an election season, where people openly wondered where money would come for some of the progressive policies advanced by Democrats, such as Bernie Sanders, there has been no hesitation in shelling out trillions of dollars to shore up Wall Street (Urie 2020). Wiping out student loan debt to the tune of over a trillion dollars would be a boon to the economy, for instance, likely increasing home purchases and, according to Moody's vice president William Foster, raising the real gross domestic product in the United States "by $86 billion to $108 billion per year" (Arnold 2020). Medicare For All, championed by Vermont senator Bernie Sanders and contender during the 2020 Democratic primaries, would have a powerful effect on the economy as a whole (see, e.g., Archer 2020). If it were present in this crisis, in fact, undocumented immigrants and poor people would not be denied the lifesaving care they need, afraid to seek medical attention for fear of imprisonment or deportation or of acquiring medical debt they cannot pay, respectively. The initial relief package passed by the federal government had generous bailouts for corporations with some, but minimal, oversight or strings attached. In contrast, the average person received a meager $1,200, and that full amount only if they made $75,000 or less, are not undocumented workers (Narea 2020) or do not owe child support (Still, Long, and Uhrmacher 2020). The response to COVID-19 by other nations, such as Canada, which is providing $2,000 a month for up to four months, to all who experience COVID-19-related income loss (Department of Finance Canada 2020), highlight the debased austerity of US capitalism under neoliberalism.

Unsurprisingly, neoliberalism is also seen in the narratives used to avoid accountability. President Trump went from ignoring to downplaying the threat of COVID-19 to reluctantly addressing it in fits and starts (Krugman 2020). In the process, he abjected Asians, blaming the Chinese for COVID-19 and describing it as the "Wuhan" or "Chinese virus" or "Kung Flu" (Reny and Barreto 2020). As a result, Asians in the United States have been targets of hate crimes and public ridicule. Russell Jeung, a San Francisco State University professor tracking anti-Asian discrimination due to COVID-19, records that at least one hundred incidents a day are being reported (Inskeep 2020). This discrimination and harassment are verbal and physical, and disproportionately impacting Asian women (Inskeep 2020). Jeung flags Trump's "us-versus-them binary" as a key driver of COVID-19 discrimination. This binary is an example of the production of liminal subjects endemic to capitalism, especially under neoliberalism. Furthermore, it amplifies the concern for contracting the virus among those who already hold "xenophob[ic]" attitudes (Reny and Barreto 2020).

Trump also avoided accountability for the virus by recklessly suggesting that US workers should be back full force by Resurrection (Easter) Sunday or mid-April 2020 (Krugman 2020). Trump backed off those claims, but not without much effort by Dr. Anthony Fauci, the nation's chief immunologist and head of the United States National Institute of Allergy and Infectious Diseases, and his team. Trump's approach, nevertheless, demonstrates the depraved priorities of the US nation-state. It also showcases the ridiculous ends to which the Republican base and Republican politicians will follow this president (Krugman 2020). Politicians such as Texas lieutenant governor Dan Patrick suggested that the elderly, who are seen as especially vulnerable to the virus, would not mind dying to get the economy back on track. Patrick stated, "Let's get back to work. Let's get back to living. Let's be smart about it. . . . And those of us who are 70 plus, we'll take care of ourselves. But don't sacrifice the country" (Ecke 2020). More pointedly, conservative diehard Glenn Beck announced, "'I would rather die'" (Mulraney and Lenthang 2020) than allow the economy to plunge into the proverbial abyss. Such absurd positions cut against the recommendations of medical experts and scientists in order to place profits before people.

The production of liminal subjects and focus on political melodrama are the handmaidens of neoliberalism, and this has been one of the main arguments guiding this book. As the foregoing attests, although my work focuses on black politics it provides insights that are relevant for this moment and beyond. This global crisis is an indication of things to come. The devastation of the environment, encroachment of agribusiness, underfunding of public infrastructure, and deterioration of social and material support for the public good have weakened governments' capacity for sustaining conditions for our survival. This recent COVID-19 pandemic reveals the ravages of neoliberalism; it is not its cause. As one social media post stated, "Capitalism is the disease; the virus is just a symptom." If this is the case, then what is the solution, including, but also exceeding, a response to COVID-19?

We need to revolt against neoliberal, transnational capitalism and its production of liminal subjects, where some are seen as upright and worthy civic members, while others are deemed abject outsiders. Public welfare cannot be achieved through self-governing subjects, guided by rationality, self-development, and norms of respectability. Public welfare is the responsibility of the state. As Imogen Tyler reminds us, "What the conceptual frame of abjection reveals is that neither the subject nor the nation-state is a solid or unitary entity, but rather an assemblage of practices. The borders of the subject and the state are continually being made and undone" (Tyler 2013, 46). We must remake these borders of state and subjects to support the common good. The revolts that have begun to emerge against COVID-19 provide a critical example. Schoolteachers and other workers have threatened sickouts in order to shut down school systems (see, e.g., Shapiro 2020). Gig workers, especially the shoppers and other often minimum-wage employees risking their lives to provide basic needs, such as food and medicine, to those in quarantine, are particularly vulnerable economically and to this virus, given their employment. Still, they have courageously organized to push back against the behemoths of industry, such as mega-billionaire Jeff Bezos's Amazon, and gig economy companies, such as grocery delivery giant Instacart, in order to fight for safer working conditions, hazard pay, and sick leave (see, e.g., Russ 2020). These efforts have emerged in a historical context in which US labor, beleaguered by conservative governments and hostile litigation, has nevertheless pushed back against the encroachment of neoliberal capitalism through renewed and expanded organizing and strike capacity (Press 2018). In the words of Dr. Martin Luther King Jr. ([1968] 1986, 279), "Something is happening in our world." It is far from certain, and as it does we see through a glass darkly. We can just as easily continue to fall in lockstep with the authoritarian proclivities of the likes of Donald Trump, with his strongman bluster with which so many personally identify. We can redouble our efforts to protect ourselves and our families, competing with others in a zero-sum game with life-or-death consequences. Or, as Cedric Johnson asks in his powerful meditation on the neoliberal politics that caused the Katrina catastrophe in New Orleans, "Might we surmount our various ecological and social challenges through collective action and democratic planning?" (Johnson 2011, xii). Our choices lay before us. Unquestionably, it is only through our bold action to rewrite the course of history that we can secure a future that can withstand the turbulence around and before us, to unravel the pull of liminality and usher in a new day.

ACKNOWLEDGMENTS

It took several villages to raise this book.

I would first like to thank my colleagues at Rutgers, some of whom have moved on to other pastures, but many of whom supported me in ways that were vital to completion of this book. A special thanks to Susan Carroll, Cynthia Daniels, Leela Fernandes, Marisa Fuentes, Mary Hawkesworth, Jane Junn, Mona Lena Krook, Rick Lau, Beth Leech, Lisa Miller, Kira Sanbonmatsu, and Deborah Gray White. Our Women's, Gender, and Sexuality Studies senior department administrator, Monique Gregory, ensured that I had the proper resources and assistance, and Suzy Kiefer, our former WGSS administrative assistant; Colleen Lord, our current WGSS administrative assistant; and Feronda Orders, our WGSS program coordinator, offered administrative support and encouragement as well. Rick Lau, my political science department chair; William Field, our political science undergrad director; Wendy Silverman, our department administrator; Jennifer Watkins, our undergraduate program coordinator, and the rest of the political science staff have been simply great! They make working in political science a pleasure.

Rutgers has top-notch libraries. I am especially grateful to our women's studies librarian, Kayo Denda, and the fabulous library staff at Douglass Library, especially Andres Martinez, Chiaki Mills, and Raymond Butler.

I was fortunate to be able to present my work in several venues. The manuscript benefited from critical contributions from discussants and interlocutors at annual meetings of the American Political Science Association, the Association for the Psychoanalysis of Culture & Society, the Cultural Studies Association, the National Conference of Black Political Scientists, the National Women's Studies Association, and the Southern Political Science Association. A special thanks to Wendy Smooth, whose feedback on the Rice chapter, especially, helped me to think about the contributions of the work to political science; and Melanye Price who read early versions of my Rice and Obama chapters, as a discussant.

For three years (2011–2014), the Washington Center for Psychoanalysis's Psychoanalysis for Scholars Program provided fertile ground for my thinking about psychoanalysis and black politics. Kevin Popp's generosity and tutelage were indispensable. His leadership of the program provided an intellectually stimulating environment for myself and the other participants. I thank Kevin, along with the other participants, particularly William Mark Habeeb, Juan José Fernadez Ansola, and Richard Seldin, for their fellowship, intellectual engagement, and commentary on my work. Patricia Gherovici welcomed me into the Philadelphia Lacan Study Group, for which I am extremely grateful. She is brilliant, kind, and patient. If anyone can teach Lacan to any- and everyone, she can. Always worth the trip. I am particularly indebted as well to the vibrant and welcoming community of the Association for the Psychoanalysis of Culture and Society. They welcomed me to their executive board, and I presented every chapter of this work at one of their annual meetings and benefited from questions and dialogue about my work. I am especially grateful for input and support from Lynn Layton, Marilyn Charles, Jane Hassinger, and Michelle Stephens. I am also indebted to Olivia Lewis-Chang, for sharing her perspectives on psychoanalysis, as well as many good folks at the William Alanson White Institute for Psychiatry, Psychoanalysis, and Psychology, most especially Philip Blumberg and Elizabeth Hegeman, who both encouraged me during the final stages of completing this book, and Seth Aaronson, who made it possible for me to complete this journey, while embarking on a new one.

I presented this work at several universities. Thanks to Linda Alcoff for inviting me to present my work at Syracuse University; Keisha Lindsay at University of Wisconsin, Madison for inviting me to present my work; Cynthia Blair, Cedric Johnson, Sekile Nzinga-Johnson, and the faculty of African American Studies at the University of Illinois, Chicago, who hosted me at their university; Beth Posner Ginsberg at the University of Connecticut who invited me to speak; and Renée Cramer at Drake University who invited me to keynote a lovely conference on contemporary celebrity culture at her university.

While at Rutgers, I participated in two yearlong seminars that helped to germinate the first and final chapters in this work. Dorothy Hodgson, the director of the 2007–2008 institute for research on women, and the participants, especially Temma Kaplan and Edgar Rivera-Cologne, offered critical engagement on my framing concept of liminality in general and the political significance of Rice in particular. The Rutgers Center for Historical Analysis Black Bodies (2017–2018) seminar afforded me time to meditate and develop my ideas on the MeToo phenomenon. A special thanks to the seminar directors, Marisa Fuentes and Bayo Holsey, as well as Kim Butler, Quiyana Butler, Kali Gross, Shannon Eaves, Edward Ramsamy, Savannah Shange, Deborah Gray White, and the other participants.

Students in my courses at Virginia Tech and Rutgers were an inspiration to me. I am especially grateful to my Black Women in the US; Sex, Race, and Videotape; and Black Feminist Theory students, who were valuable interlocutors as I tried out my ideas.

Several friends and colleagues read and commented on various chapters. Renée Cramer gave me tremendous and detailed feedback on Chapter 4. Albert Samuels provided critical insights on Chapter 1 in its final stages. Gordon Govens provided extensive edits and commentary on the sample chapters I sent out for review, as well as Chapter 2. Laura Gillman, my colleague at Virginia Tech and dear friend, has assessed almost the entire book, from the beginning of the project. She is a tough critic, who holds no punches. I hope that the final project does justice to their efforts.

I cannot express enough gratitude for my writing and accountability tribes. The Scrappy Scribblers online group provided daily support and accountability. Most of us started off as strangers or acquaintances and have become friends. We have checked in daily, worked through thorny work and personal issues, read books together, formulated writing challenges, and otherwise lifted each other up. Beth Posner Ginsberg, Maisha Shabazz Akbar, and I also laughed and hollered, complained, strategized, and held each other up during weekly phone check-ins for several seasons. Renée Cramer, Taneisha Means, and I coauthored a piece. Beth and Renée gave me opportunities to share my work at the University of Connecticut and Drake, respectively. Others, like Valeria N. Sinclair-Chapman and Byron D'Andra Orey, offered encouragement and emotional support. All of us Scrappy Scribblers held space for each other. Fall 2017 I had the good fortune to participate in a semester-long

National Center for Faculty Development and Diversity program. I met interesting scholars through this program, namely Joseph O. Jewell, Lily Khadjavi, and Rie Suziki. We continued to offer support to one another even after the program, and it was a great encouragement and accountability system. Two other writing groups anchored much of my actual writing time. The biweekly 8 AM Princeton Meetup group provided a write-on-site community. Thanks to everyone and especially to Maryann Eberle for her faithfulness and warm disposition. Allison, Nicole, and the rest of the crew, your presence and encouragement at The Grind coffee shop made all the difference. Shalonda Kelly, Sylvia Mendez-Morse, and I met virtually three days a week to write on many projects. I am grateful to have both Shalonda and Sylvia in my life.

Unbeknownst to me, my life would be greatly enriched by the people I met at a one-week publication camp at Easton's Nook in summer 2017. I spent a week working, laughing, dancing, walking, and sharing with some of the best people. Riana Elyse Anderson, Matthew J. Graziano, Courtney McCluney, Noelany Pelc, and the late Jeannine Skinner: I love and miss you all. Jacquie Mattis and Nadine Mattis, I do not have adequate words to express my appreciation for your love, kindness, and direction. Knowing you makes New Jersey feel like home. I have met so many people that I love to connect with at the Nook. The both of you have built an amazing community and place for work and refuge, and for that I am truly grateful. This book would not have been finished without you.

I am grateful to *Politics and Gender* and the *National Political Science Review*, having published earlier versions of some of the material that appears herein in two articles, "Framing Condi(licious): Condoleezza Rice and the Storyline of Closeness in US National Community Formation" (vol. 4 [2008]: 427–49) and "But I Voted for Obama: Melodrama and Post–Civil Rights, Postfeminist Ideology in *Grey's Anatomy*, *Crash*, and Barack Obama's 2008 Presidential Campaign" (vol. 13 [2012]: 23–39), respectively.

Ilene Kalish, Executive Editor, Social Sciences, for NYU has been an excellent editor. She sought me out at a conference, and we had the best discussions about my work and the field. I am grateful for someone who gets my project and who has guided me through this process. I have had an amazing experience with her, as well as Sonia Tsuruoka, Assistant Editor, Social Sciences, and the entire team at NYU Press.

My church families have provided much needed support and guidance while writing this book; I especially thank Jacqueline Tina Flowers, Darrell L. Armstrong, and Lillian G. Moore, pastors at Time of Celebration Ministries Church in Houston, Texas; Shiloh Baptist Church in Trenton, New Jersey; and Macedonia Baptist Church in Newtown, Pennsylvania, respectively.

My friends, both far and wide, have encouraged me in various ways, given me a hard time when needed, and provided plenty of good times. I especially thank Shanna Batten, Rhonda Cormier, Caryl McFarlane, Laura Gillman, Candace Hurst, Tamara Jackson, Leela Fernandes, April Few, Cedric Johnson, Shalonda Kelly, Marcia LoBrano, Jacqueline Mattis, Nadine Mattis, Elizabeth Mitchell, Touré Reed, Paula Marie Seniors, Ingrid Reneau Walls, and Tiffany Willoughby-Herard.

My family has been a sustaining force in my life. We have been through so much together in the time that I have produced this work, including the transition of my paternal uncle, Donald ("Aldox") Lee Alexander; my sister-in-law, Yvette Marie Alexander; and my second oldest sister, Kathy Ann Alexander Holmes. All of them valiantly fought cancer. This book is dedicated to their memory.

We have also survived the 2016 historic flooding in Louisiana, among many other trials. My parents, Theresa and George Alexander Sr., have continued to teach us much about life and what is truly important. Dena A. Nabers, Kathy A. Holmes (deceased), Danny Alexander, Connie J. Garrett, George Alexander Jr., Nedra M. Alexander, and April L. Greenhouse, I am so grateful to have had such good womb-mates and friends on this journey. You all inspire me. My sweet honey bunnies, aka my nieces and nephews (Ashleigh, George, Ernie, Shaya, Markeisha, Danielle, Kamryn, Tamron, Marley, Julian, Reese, and Derick) and great-niece and -nephews (Ariyah, Kindell, and Kainen), I adore you, and I hope that whatever I do in life makes yours better and this world a better place to be.

Most of all, I thank God, the Ancient of Days, who is my rock and my salvation and my very present help in times of trouble.

NOTES

INTRODUCTION: MELODRAMA, LIMINALITY, AND POST-POLITICS

1 See Springer 2007 for an excellent discussion of post-feminist black female stereo-types.

2 Projansky argues that black women stand "next-to-but-just-outside-of postfemi-nism" (Projansky 2001, 193). This is true, if dominant political discourse is the reference point; I recover her insights regarding varieties of post-feminism in explaining its operation in black politics.

3 Tanya Ann Kennedy (2017, 5–7) also connects racial politics with post-feminism; however, she focuses on the emergence of the term "postfeminism," situating it broadly within the Reagan era. She recounts, more specifically, the use of the term "postfeminism" in a public controversy about a black newswoman, Jacqueline Trescott, who makes a choice to have a child as a single woman. This controversy included references to normative expectations about marriage and childbear-ing and the implications of single motherhood for black women in particular. Kennedy usefully underscores how the white TV character Murphy Brown was used to discuss this scenario on screen, thus "whitening" the real-life case and obfuscating the connection between race and post-feminism that emerged with this example of one of the earliest uses of the term in popular discourse.

4 President Barack Obama's My Brother's Keeper initiative and White House sum-mit on Advancing Equity for Women and Girls of Color: A Research Agenda for the Next Decade are both examples of programs that support race, gender, and class management. They focus, among other things, on private-sector support for undemocratic forms of self-help or uplift and fail to address black communities as political constituencies that are positioned to make demands on the state.

5 Like Courtney (2005, 295), while I find elements of Williams's study illuminating, her analysis problematically suggests that people are necessarily bound up with racially oriented thinking as it concerns the "Tom" and "anti-Tom" frames she assesses.

6 This phrasing is inspired by the notion "affective turn" developed by Patricia Clough.

7 Cynthia Burack (2004) and Jane Flax (2010), white feminist political theorists in political science, have used psychoanalytic frames to analyze race/gender in assessing black feminism and identity politics and the role of melancholia as a defining feature of US politics, respectively. My work advances the project of integrating psychoanalytic frames by presenting a black feminist approach to

psychoanalytic political theory that draws not only from feminist theory but also a broad range of work in postcolonial studies, black feminism, and black studies in general. In addition, while many political theorists address general audiences and texts as they relate to race or black politics, my work also incorporates work in the field of black politics within political science. It also complements existing work in political science on political psychology, which tends to focus on measures of black attitudes as they interface with quantitative measurements of political behavior.

CHAPTER 1. SPLITTING CONDI(LICIOUS)

1 As I will note, this seeming contradiction—that the storyline of closeness can generate competing interpretations and effects—is a function of the instability of the black woman as a sign (or symbol). The Condi-vs.-Condilicious melodrama storylines meet or have in common the notion of closeness, but with very different results.

2 James Clingman, "Blackonomics; Sad to Watch 'Condo' Condescend," *The Sacramento Observer*, October 22, 2003, sec. C., http://proquest.umi.com; Oscar W. King, III, "Condoleezza, Are You Fact or Fiction?," *Michigan Citizen*, February 19, 2005, sec B, http://proquest.umi.com; Gilbert Price, "Conservatives Playing Race Card on Richard Clarke and Condoleezza Rice," *Call and Post*, April 14, 2004, sec. A, http://proquest.umi.com; Sonya M. Toler, "Who Is Condoleezza Rice?," *New Pittsburgh Courier*, December 20, 2000, city edition, sec. A, http://proquest .umi.com.

3 Lizette Alvarez, "Butterfly McQueen Dies at 84; Played Scarlett O'Hara's Maid." *New York Times (1857–Current File)*, December 23, 1995, 28, http://proquest .umi.com.

4 The song "Fergalicious" invokes the hypersexualization of black womanhood embodied in Destiny's Child's 2001 mega-hit "Bootylicious," written and performed by black female lead singer Beyoncé Knowles. In a striking parallel to the evolution of blackface minstrelsy, Fergie, as a white female, enacts a personae based on black stereotype that is later performed or copied by a black female actress in the "Condilicious" video. For a discussion of minstrelsy, see Rogin (1996).

5 Feminist political theorist Linda Zerilli (1994 5, 142) explains that worries about gender norms are generated "in part" by women who challenge them. What intersectionality theory—or more specifically, a constitutive model of identity—suggests is that the norms in question and responses to their transgression will reflect the race, class, gender, and sexuality of these boundary-crossing or "disorderly and disordering" women.

6 This is true even in Rice's sexualized power dressing (in 2005, Rice appeared at Wiesbaden Army Airfield in a black *Matrix*-style topcoat and knee-length boots) on the international stage (Givhan 2005). It is interesting that Rice, who is aware that she is in the limelight, has been adamant about defying stereotypes about blacks, and is concomitantly conscious of her self-presentation, would choose this attire.

It could be that her performance of racialized gender identity at this moment (and, in general) can be read as her effort to exert agency that functions to defy and disrupt the Western racialized gender matrix (Butler 1990). Inhabiting racialized phallic power by affirming white political power and white masculinist modes of being (i.e., through clothing, public address, and the cultivation of cultural markers that are valued by white society as a means of legitimacy and efficacy) is ultimately ineffective. Challenging stereotypes can be beneficial in negotiating a racist and sexist terrain (Jones and Shorter-Gooden 2003), but Rice moves beyond negotiation to imitation. Rice, in her performance of racialized phallic power, remains caught in and scripted by the gaze of white masculinist authority.

CHAPTER 2. UNPACKING PRESIDENT BARACK OBAMA'S "IMPROBABLE STORY"

1 For a complete rendering of her typology, see Gillespie's "Meet the New Class: Theorizing Young Black Leadership in a 'Postracial' Era" (2010).

2 For scholars such as Aimee Carrillo Rowe (Rowe 2007) and Hsu (2006), miscegenation fantasies utilize an Africanist Presence as a primary vehicle for channeling and narratively resolving gender and race anxieties about change in ways that rearticulate white racial hierarchy.

3 See DuCille (1996), for a related discussion of the "browning" of Nicole Simpson.

4 For disparate views of the role of intersectionality in black male–focused programs and schools, see Butler (2013) and Lindsay (2018).

5 For an example of women who supported Obama's MBK initiative, see an open letter to the president titled "National Women Leadership Supporting My Brother's Keeper" (2014).

6 "Constructive critique" is the description used by Kimberlé Crenshaw to describe the approach.

CHAPTER 3. DIARY OF A MAD BLACK (WO)MAN

1 Indeed, given their derogatory nature, it is especially odd that black women enjoy and applaud *Diary* and other movies featuring Madea and other characters based on black female stereotypes. Although Madea is a "woman" it is significant that she is played in drag, given the ideological messages she supports regarding black women and the family. Might it be that black women who are in want of male attention and life partners are riveted by these performances because Perry is male and his character, Madea, promises a brass ring of wedded bliss?

2 Lee sees some of Perry's characters as providing access to redemption, forgiveness, and other black cultural resources. Such characters, however, arguably serve as an Africanist presence, functioning to redeem or transform white characters.

CHAPTER 4. THE REALITY OF THE WHITE MALE RAPIST

1 It should go without saying, but at times bears pointing out, that the United States is but one country in North America, and there is a separate South American

continent. Therefore, although it may seem a somewhat awkward locution, I specify "US-based American political development" in order to be precise and also to disrupt an arguably imperialist, First World hegemonic naming of the field.

2 According to Ritter (2008, 16), "Civic membership is conceived of . . . as a broader term than citizenship and allows us to consider the rights, status, and obligations of all those governed under U.S. political authority (Ritter 2006), including those who are not formally counted as citizens, such as immigrants, Native Americans prior to the twentieth century, or residents of the territories taken in the Spanish American war at the turn of the century."

3 Even though theorists have built on and challenged these seminal works and Pateman and Mills have themselves recognized in important ways the need to think about race and gender in tandem, there has been relatively little theorizing among political theorists or philosophers from a constitutive or intersectional view of identity. *Contract and Domination*, the book written by Pateman and Mills (2007) has essays by both authors and a conversational essay, but there is still little effort invested in thinking through and reshaping their work in light of the other's. For a critique of Pateman's social contract that focuses attention on the constructions of dominant forms of masculinity and femininity, as opposed to the rubric of contract as it relates to founding political narratives, see Wendy Brown (1995).

4 In 2008, for instance, a twelve-year-old girl, Dymond Milburn, was assaulted and almost kidnapped in front of her home in Galveston, Texas, under the false assumption that she was a prostitute. The plainclothes officers were ostensibly responding to a call concerning three white women soliciting a white male and a black male drug dealer approximately two blocks away. See *Emily Milburn v. Sergeant Gilbert Gomez et al.* (United States District Court for the Southern District of Texas, Galveston Division, 2010).

5 Some might also argue that the movie shows female cooperation and consciousness raising, in the relationships between Skeeter and the maids in general and Millie and white women in particular. As Kennedy (2017) argues, however, the movie, among other things, problematically suggests that the domestic Minnie, a character cast stereotypically as an angry black woman, can be tamed or reformed through a relationship with her white employer whom Minnie comes to view sympathetically and as suffering her own forms of trauma.

6 Importantly, it also provides a plot device that anchors the story in a way that highlights a split between past and present, situating racism as something kept alive by an older, dying generation. Skeeter's mother stands in for not only her generation, but also Skeeter's contemporaries in Mississippi, who fail to see the absurdity of race, and its basis not in biology, but in ideology. Skeeter's mother throughout the story is signified as someone beholden to tradition (in dress, gender expectations, and in racial attitudes). Skeeter's misalignment with the priorities, gender expectations, and racial attitudes of her peers situates her as the "new

woman," a contemporary woman with more progressive attitudes. Just as Skeeter's mother is sick and dying of cancer throughout the novel, racism is figured as something that is dying a seemingly slow but certain death.

7 Although my use of "haunting" is directly inspired by Rashkin (2008), it is important to underscore that haunting is a concept that has been explored across various fields in different registers of meaning. See, for instance, Jordan-Zachery (2019), for a discussion of haunting as it relates to black women's experiences with raced-gendered oppression in academe. See, also, Philip Bromberg's (2003) "One Need Not Be a House to Be Haunted," for a discussion of how dissociation of "not-me" self-states can "haunt" psychoanalytic treatment.

CHAPTER 5. METOO?

1 See Williams (2002) for another take on sadomasochism and sexual harassment.

REFERENCES

AAMC (Association of American Medical Colleges). 2016. *Diversity in Medical Education: Facts and Figures 2016*, accessed June 16, 2019, www.aamcdiversityfactsandfig ures2016.org/.

ABC News. 2018. "Cosby Supporters React to Verdict." Posted by *Good Morning America* on April 27, 2018. YouTube video, 4:20, www.youtube.com/watch?v =8TLjDJywc1M.

Ablogalypse Now. 2005. "All Hail Admiral Rice," January 28, http://paiz.typepad.com.

Abraham, Nicolas, and Maria Torok. 1994. *The Shell and the Kernel: Renewals of Psychoanalysis, Vol. I*. Translated and edited by Nicholas Rand. Chicago: University of Chicago.

Ahad, Badia Sahar. 2010. *Freud Upside Down: African American Literature and Psychoanalytic Culture*. Urbana: University of Illinois Press.

Ahmed, Sara. 2012. *On Being Included: Racism and Diversity in Institutional Life*. Durham, NC: Duke University Press.

Alcoff, Linda Martín, and Laura Gray-Rosendale. 2018. "Speaking 'as.'" In Linda Alcoff, *Rape and Resistance: Understanding the Complexities of Sexual Violation*, 176–202. Medford, MA: Polity Press.

Alexander-Floyd, Nikol G. 2003. "Theorizing Race and Gender in Black Studies: Reflections on Recent Examinations of Black Political Leadership." *International Journal of Africana Studies* 9, no. 1: 57–73.

———. 2004. "Interdisciplinarity, Black Politics, and the Million Man March: A Case Study." In *An Introduction to Interdisciplinary Studies*. Edited by Michael Herndon, 90–110. Dubuque, IA: Kendall/Hunt.

———. 2007. *Gender, Race, and Nationalism in Contemporary Black Politics*. New York: Palgrave Macmillan.

———. 2012a. "Disappearing Acts: Reclaiming Intersectionality in the Social Sciences in a Post-Black Feminist Era." *Feminist Formations* 24, no. 1: 1–25.

———. 2012b. "'But I Voted for Obama': Melodrama and Post–Civil Rights, Post-Feminist Ideology in *Grey's Anatomy*, *Crash*, and Barack Obama's 2008 Presidential Campaign." *National Political Science Review* 13 (2012): 23–39.

Alford, C. Fred. 1989. *Melanie Klein and Critical Social Theory: An Account of Politics, Art, and Reason Based on Her Psychoanalytic Theory*. New Haven, CT: Yale University Press.

———. 2000. "What Would It Matter If Everything Foucault Said about Prison Were Wrong? Discipline and Punish after Twenty Years." *Theory and Society* 29, no. 1: 125–46.

———. 2001. *Whistleblowers: Broken Lives and Organizational Power*. Cornell paperbacks ed. Ithaca, NY: Cornell University Press.

Allen, Stephanie. 2016. "Who's Your Mammy? Tyler Perry Created a Phenomenon." In *The Problematic Tyler Perry*. Edited by Brian Johnson, 79–91. New York: Peter Lang.

Ampersand. 2004. "Racist Cartoons of Condoleezza Rice?" *Alas! A Blog*, accessed November 20, http://amptoons.com.

Anker, Elisabeth. 2014. *Orgies of Feeling: Melodrama and the Politics of Freedom*. Durham, NC: Duke University Press.

Archer, Diane. 2020. "22 Studies Agree: 'Medicare for All' Saves Money." *The Hill*, February 24, www.thehill.com.

Arnold, Chris. 2020. "Forgiving Student Debt Would Boost Economy, Economists Say." *National Public Radio*, November 25, www.npr.org.

Baker, Al, and Steven Erlanger. 2011. "*I.M.F. Chief, Apprehended at Airport, Is Accused of Sexual Attack*." *New York Times*, May 14, www.nytimes.com.

Baker, Carrie. 2008. *The Women's Movement against Sexual Harassment*. Cambridge: Cambridge University Press.

Bartlett, Katharine T., and Rosanne Kennedy. 2018. *Feminist Legal Theory: Readings in Law and Gender*. New York: Routledge, Taylor & Francis.

Bay, Mia. 2009. *To Tell the Truth Freely: The Life of Ida B. Wells*. New York: Hill and Wang.

Beirich, Heidi. 2019. *The Year in Hate: Rage against Change*. Southern Poverty Law Center, February 20, www.splcenter.org.

Berger, Arthur Asa. 2012. *Media Analysis Techniques*. Los Angeles: Sage.

Berger, Michele, and Kathleen Guidroz, eds. 2009. *The Intersectional Approach: Transforming the Academy through Race, Class, and Gender*. Chapel Hill: University of North Carolina Press.

Bernard, Peter S., and James M. Wallace. 2002. *Turbulent Flow: Analysis, Measurement, and Prediction*. Hoboken, NJ: John Wiley & Sons.

BET-Staff. 2008. "Obama Delivers Some Tough Love in Texas." *Black Entertainment Television (BET)*, March 3, www.bet.com.

Bickel, Ofra. 1992. "*Frontline*: Clarence Thomas and Anita Hill: Public Hearing, Private Pain." VHS tape. Ofra Bikel Productions Corp. for *Frontline*.

Bird, Sharon R. 1996. "Welcome to the Men's Club." *Gender and Society* 10, no. 2: 120–32.

Bobo, Jacqueline. 1993. "Reading through the Text: The Black Woman as Audience." In *Black American Cinema*. Edited by Manthia Diawara, 272–87. London: Routledge.

Bogel, Donald. 1974. *Blacks, Coons, Mulattoes, Mammies, and Bucks: An Interpretive History of Blacks in American Film*. New York: Garland.

Bollas, Christopher. 2009. *The Evocative Object World*. New York: Routledge.

Bowley, Graham, and John Hurdle. 2018. "Bill Cosby Is Found Guilty of Sexual Assault." *New York Times*, April 26, www.nytimes.com.

Bowley, Graham, Richard Pérez-Peña, and Jon Hurdle. 2017. "Bill Cosby's Sexual Assault Case Ends in a Mistrial." *New York Times*, June 17, www.nytimes.com.

Bowman, Barbara. 2014. "Bill Cosby Raped Me. Why Did It Take 30 Years for People to Believe My Story?" *Washington Post*, November 13, www.washingtonpost.com.

"Box Office Mojo." 2019. *Box Office Mojo*, accessed August 7, www.boxofficemojo.com.

Brewer, Craig. 2005. *Hustle and Flow*, featuring Taraji P. Henson and Terrence Howard, Warner Bros., DVD, 117 mins.

Bromberg, Philip. 2003. "One Need Not Be a House to Be Haunted: On Enactment, Dissociation, and the Dread of 'Not-Me'—A Case Study." *Psychoanalytic Dialogues* 13, no. 5: 689–709.

Brooks, Peter. [1976] 1995. *The Melodramatic Imagination: Balzac, Henry James, Melodrama, and the Mode of Excess*. New Haven, CT: Yale University Press.

Brown, Nadia. 2014. *Sisters in the Statehouse: Black Women and Legislative Decision Making*. New York: Oxford University Press.

Brown, Ruth Nicole. 2013. *Hear Our Truths: The Creative Potential of Black Girlhood*. Urbana: University of Illinois Press.

Brown, Wendy. 1995. *States of Injury: Power and Freedom in Late Modernity*. Princeton, NJ: Princeton University Press.

———. 2015. *Undoing the Demos: Neoliberalism's Stealth Revolution*. New York: Zone Books.

Brüning, Kristina. 2018. "Olivia Pope: A Black Post-Feminist Subject? Analyzing Scandal's Intersecting Post-Feminist and Colorblind Discourses." *Feminist Media Studies*, DOI:10.1080/14680777.2018.1508049.

Bullock, Penn. 2016. "Transcript: Donald Trump's Taped Comments about Women." *New York Times*, October 8, www.nytimes.com.

Bumiller, Elisabeth. 2007. *Condoleezza Rice: An American Life*. New York: Random House.

Burack, Cynthia. 2004. *Healing Identities: Black Feminist Thought and the Politics of Groups*. Ithaca, NY: Cornell University Press.

Bush, Harold, Jr. 2007. "Grief Work: After a Child Dies." *Christian Century* 124, no. 5: 36–39.

Butler, Anne E. 2007. "Big Love." In *Dr. Rice in the House*. Edited by Amy Scholder, 83–92. New York: Seven Stories Press.

Butler, Judith. 1990. *Gender Trouble: Feminism and the Subversion of Identity*. New York: Routledge.

———. Butler, Judith. 1993. *Bodies that Matter: On the Discursive Limits of "Sex."* New York: Routledge.

Butler, Paul. 2013. "Black Male Exceptionalism?: The Problems and Potential of Black Male-Focused Interventions." *DuBois Review* 10: 485–511.

Carby, Hazel. 1987. *Reconstructing Womanhood: The Emergence of the Afro-American Woman Novelist*. New York: Oxford University Press.

Carissimo, Justin. 2019. "R. Kelly Charged with 11 New Counts of Sexual Assault and Abuse." *CBS News*, updated May 31, 2019, www.cbsnews.com.

Carroll, Matt, Sacha Pfeiffer, Michael Rezendes, and Walter Robinson. 2002a. "Spotlight Church Abuse Report: Church Allowed Abuse by Priests for Years, Part 1 of 2." *Boston Globe*, January 6, www.bostonglobe.com.

———. 2002b. "Spotlight Special Report: Geoghan Preferred Preying on Poorer Children, Part 2 of 2." *Boston Globe*, January 7, www.bostonglobe.com.

Celona, Larry. 2011. "Whiny IMF Head Finally Agrees to Medical Exam; Set for Arraignment Today." *New York Post*, May 16, https://nypost.com.

Chancer, Lynn S. 1992. *Sadomasochism in Everyday Life: The Dynamics of Power and Powerlessness*. New Brunswick, NJ: Rutgers University Press.

Charlton, Lauretta. 2014. "A Brief History of America Ignoring Bill Cosby Rape Allegations." *Complex*, November 19, www.complex.com.

Chaudhry, Lakshmi. 2007. "What Women See When They See Hillary." *The Nation*, July 2.

Clarke, Richard A. 2004. *Against All Enemies: Inside America's War on Terror*. New York: Free Press.

Clark-Lewis, Elizabeth. 1994. *Living In, Living Out: African American Domestics in Washington, D.C., 1910–1940*. Washington, DC: Smithsonian Institution Press.

Cleage, Pearl. 1993. *Deals with the Devil and Other Reasons to Riot*. New York: Ballantine Books.

Clinton, Hillary. [1996] 2016. "1996: Hillary Clinton 'Superpredators.'" Posted by C-Span, last modified February 25, 2016. YouTube video, 2:02. https://www.youtube.com/watch?v=jouCrA7ePno.

———. 2008. "Sen. Hillary Clinton (D-NY) Addresses the DNC." Posted by C-Span, August 27, 2008. YouTube video, 27:45, https://www.youtube.com/watch?v=MeFMZ7fpGHY.

Cohen, Cathy J. 1999. *The Boundaries of Blackness: AIDS and the Breakdown of Black Politics*. Chicago: University of Chicago Press.

Cohen, Philip. 2018. *Enduring Bonds: Inequality, Marriage, Parenting, and Everything Else That Makes Families Great and Terrible*. Oakland: University of California Press.

Cole, Johnnetta B. 1994. *Conversations: Straight Talk with America's Sister President*. New York: Anchor Books.

Collins, Patricia Hill. 1990. *Black Feminist Thought: Knowledge, Consciousness, and the Politics of Empowerment*. New York: Routledge. Reprint, 1991, New York: Unwin Hyman. Page references are to the Unwin Hyman edition.

———. 2005. *Black Sexual Politics: African Americans, Gender, and the New Racism*. New York: Routledge.

———. 2006. *From Black Power to Hip Hop: Racism, Nationalism, and Feminism*. Philadelphia: Temple University Press.

Collins, Patricia Hill, and Sirma Bilge. 2016. *Intersectionality*. Malden, MA: Polity Press.

Condit, Celeste. 1989. "The Rhetorical Limits of Polysemy." *Critical Studies in Mass Communication* 6: 103–22.

Connell, Raewyn. 2012. "Masculinities and Globalization." In *Feminist Frontiers*. Edited by Verta A. Taylor, Nancy Whittier, and Leila J. Rupp. Ninth ed., 87–98. New York: McGraw Hill.

Cooper, Brittney. 2014. "Clair Huxtable Is Dead: On Slaying the Cosbys and Making Space for Liv, Analise, and Mary Jane." *Crunk Feminist Collective*, October 23, www.crunkfeministcollective.com.

———. 2017. *Beyond Respectability: The Intellectual Thought of Race Women*. Urbana: University of Illinois Press.

"Coronavirus in the US: Latest Map and Case Count." 2020. *New York Times*, accessed April 7, www.nytimes.com.

Cosby, Bill. 2004. "Bill Cosby: Address at the NAACP on the 50th Anniversary of Brown v. Board of Education," delivered May 17, 2004. *American Rhetoric*, accessed March 8, 2020, www.americanrhetoric.com.

Cosby, Bill, and Alvin Poussaint. 2007. *Come on People: On the Path from Victims to Victors*. Nashville: Thomas Nelson.

Cosby, Camille. 2018. Official Statement from Camille O. Cosby. *Facebook*, May 3, www.facebook.com.

Courtney, Susan. 2005. *Hollywood Fantasies of Miscegenation: Spectacular Narratives of Gender and Race, 1903-1967*. Princeton, NJ: Princeton University Press.

Cramer, Renee Ann. 2016. *Pregnant with the Stars: Watching and Wanting the Celebrity Baby Bump*. Stanford, CA: Stanford University Press.

Crenshaw, Kimberlé. 1989. "Demarginalizing the Intersection of Race and Sex: A Black Feminist Critique of Antidiscrimination Doctrine, Feminist Theory and Antiracist Politics." *University of Chicago Legal Forum* (1989): 139–67.

———. 1991. "Mapping the Margins: Intersectionality, Identity Politics, and Violence against Women of Color." *Stanford Law Review* 43, no. 6: 1241–99.

———. 2014. "The Girls Obama Forgot." *New York Times*, July 29, www.nytimes.com.

Curtis, Mary. 2013. "Strom Thurmond's Black Daughter: A Symbol of America's Complicated Racial History." *Washington Post*, February 5, www.washington post.com.

Daniels, Lee, dir. 2013. *Lee Daniels' The Butler*, written by Danny Strong, featuring Forest Whitaker, Oprah Winfrey, and John Cusak, Weinstein Company/Anchor Bay, DVD, 132 mins.

Dargis, Manohla. 2010. "A Powerful Chorus Harmonizing 'Dark Phrases of Womanhood.'" *New York Times*, November 4, www.nytimes.com.

Davidson, Peter. 2015. *Turbulence: An Introduction for Scientists and Engineers*. Second ed. Oxford: Oxford University Press.

Davies, Carole Boyce. 2007. "Con-di-fi-ca-tion: Black Women Leadership and Power." *Feminist Africa* (March): 66–88.

———. 2014. "12 Years a Slave Fails to Represent Black Resistance to Enslavement." *The Guardian*, January 10, www.theguardian.com.

Davis, Adrienne D. 2004. "Slavery and the Roots of Sexual Harassment." In *Directions in Sexual Harassment Law*. Edited by Catharine A. MacKinnon and Reva B. Siegel, 457–78. New Haven, CT: Yale University Press.

Davis, Angela Y. 1981. "Rape, Racism, and the Myth of the Black Rapist." In *Women, Race, and Class*, 172–201. New York: Vintage.

———. 2000. "Reflections on the Black Woman's Role in the Community of Slaves." In *A Turbulent Voyage: Readings in African American Studies*. Edited by Floyd Hayes. Third ed., 83–96. San Diego, CA: Collegiate Press.

Davis, Ronald. 2008. "Achieving Racial Harmony for the Benefit of Patients and Communities: Contrition, Reconciliation, and Collaboration." *Journal of the American Medical Association* 300, no. 3: 323–25, doi:10.1001/jama.300.3.323.

Dawson, Michael. 1995. *Behind the Mule: Race and Class in African-American Politics.* Princeton, NJ: Princeton University Press.

Department of Finance Canada. 2020. "Government Introduces Canada Emergency Response Benefit to Help Workers and Businesses." *Canada Department of Finance* (News Release), March 25, www.canada.ca.

Dicker, Ron. 2018. "Tyler Perry is Killing Off His Madea Character Once and for All." *Huffington Post*, October 30, www.huffpost.com.

Dill, Bonnie Thornton, and Ruth Zambrana. 2009. *Emerging Intersections: Race, Class, and Gender in Theory, Policy, and Practice.* New Brunswick, NJ: Rutgers University Press.

Doggart, Sebastian, prod. and dir. 2008. *Courting Condi*, written by Sebastian Doggart, featuring Devin Ratray, Journeyman Pictures, DVD, 127 mins.

———. 2009. *American Faust: From Condi to Neo-Condi*, written by Sebastian Doggart. Journeyman Pictures, DVD, 86 mins.

Donovan, Doug, Natalie Sherman, and Catherine Rentz. 2017. "Crowds Travel from, through Baltimore to Women's March on D.C." *Baltimore Sun*, January 21, www.baltimoresun.com.

Dowd, Ann Reilly. 2005. "What Makes Condi Run." *AARP the Magazine*, September/October.

DuCille, Ann. 1996. *Skin Trade.* Cambridge, MA: Harvard University Press.

Dwyer, Jim, and Michael Wilson. 2011. "Strauss-Kahn Accuser's Call Alarmed Prosecutors." *New York Times*, July 1, www.nytimes.com.

Earle, Steve. 2004. "Condi, Condi." *The Revolution Starts Now.* Warner Records.

———. 2006. "Condi, Condi." *Steve Earle: Live at Montreaux 2005.* Eagle.

Ecke, Jonas. 2020. "Would Dying for the Economy Help Anybody?" *Counterpunch*, April 3, www.counterpunch.org.

Edmondson, Jacqueline. 2006. *Condoleezza Rice: A Biography.* Westport, CT: Greenwood.

Ehrenstein, David. 2007. "Obama the 'Magic Negro.'" *Los Angeles Times*, March 19, www.latimes.com.

Eisenstein, Zillah. 2007. *Sexual Decoys: Gender, Race, and War in Imperial Democracy.* New York: Zed Books.

Elber, Lynn. 2014. "Video: Janice Dickinson Says Bill Cosby Raped Her in 1982." *Los Angeles Daily News*, November 18; Updated August 28, 2017, www.dailynews.com.

Elders, Jocelyn, and David Chanoff. 1996. *Jocelyn Elders, M.D.: From Sharecropper's Daughter to Surgeon General of the United States of America.* New York: William Morrow & Co.

Eligon, John. 2011. "Judge Denies Bail to I.M.F. Chief in Sexual Assault Case." *New York Times*, May 16, www.nytimes.com.

Elsaesser, Thomas, and Malte Hagener. 2010. *Film Theory: An Introduction through the Senses.* New York: Routledge.

Eng, David, and David Kazanjian. 2003. "Introduction: Mourning Remains." In *Loss: The Politics of Mourning*. Edited by David Eng and David Kazanjian, 1–28. Berkeley: University of California Press.

Eng, Joyce. 2009. "Tyler Perry's Mother, Inspiration for Madea, Dies." *TV Guide*, accessed December 9, 2009, www.tvguide.com.

Entman, Robert M., and Andrew Rojecki. 2001. *The Black Image in the White Mind: Media and Race in America*. Chicago: University of Chicago Press.

Estrada, Sheryl. 2017. "TIME Magazine Excluding Tarana Burke from #MeToo Cover Speaks Volumes." *Diversity Inc.*, last modified December 11, www.diversityinc.com.

Fanon, Frantz. 2008. *Black Skin, White Masks*. Translated by Richard Philcox. New York: Grove Press.

Farley, Robert. 2019. "The Facts on White Nationalism." *FactCheck*, March 20, www.factcheck.org.

Felix, Antonia. 2002. *Condi: The Condoleezza Rice Story*. New York: Threshold Editions.

Felsenthal, Edward. 2017. "The Choice." *Time*, December 18, 32–33.

Fernandes, Leela. 1997. *Producing Workers: The Politics of Gender, Class, and Culture in the Calcutta Jute Mills*. Philadelphia: University of Pennsylvania Press.

Ferri, Beth A., and David J. Connor. 2006. *Reading Resistance: Discourses of Exclusion in Desegregation and Inclusion Debates*. New York: Peter Lang.

Fischer, Frank. 2003. *Reframing Public Policy: Discursive Politics and Deliberative Practices*. Oxford: Oxford University Press.

Flax, Jane. 2010. *Resonances of Slavery in Race/Gender Relations: Shadow at the Heart of American Politics*. New York: Palgrave Macmillan.

Fleming, Victor. 1939. *Gone with the Wind* (2009, 70th anniversary edition), featuring Clark Gable and Vivien Leigh, Warner Home Video, DVD, 233 mins.

Foden, Glenn. 2007. "Rice, Condoleezza Cartoons." *Cartoon Stock*, March 13, www.cartoonstock.com.

Fogel, Matthew. 2005. "'Grey's Anatomy' Goes Colorblind." *New York Times*, May 8 www.nytimes.com.

Forgey, Quint. 2018. "Trump: 'I'm a Nationalist.'" *Politico*, updated October 22, 2018, www.politico.com.

Franco, Michael. 2007. "Goodbye Guitar Town: An Interview with Steve Earle." *Pop Matters*, September 23, www.popmatters.com.

Frank, Justin A. 2011. *Obama on the Couch: Inside the Mind of the President*. New York: Free Press.

Franklin, Sekou. 2010. "Situational Deracialization, Harold Ford, and the 2006 Senate Race in Tennessee." In *Whose Black Politics? Cases in Post-Racial Black Leadership*. Edited by Andra Gillespie, 133–54. New York: Routledge.

Freud, Anna. 1937. *The Ego and the Mechanisms of Defense*. Translated by Cecil Baines. Third ed. London: Hogarth Press and the Institute of Psycho-Analysis.

Freud, Sigmund. [1914] 1958. "Remembering, Repeating, and Working Through: Further Recommendations on the Technique of Psycho-Analysis II." In *The Standard

Edition of the Complete Psychological Works of Sigmund Freud. Vol. XII (1911–1913): *The Case of Schreber, Papers on Technique and Other Works*, translated from the German under the General Editorship of James Strachey, in collaboration with Anna Freud, assisted by Alix Strachey and Alan Tyson, 145–56. London: Hogarth Press and the Institute of Psycho-Analysis.

———. 1989. *Introductory Lectures on Psycho-Analysis.* Translated and edited by James Strachey. New York: W. W. Norton & Company.

———. [1995] 2010. *The Interpretation of Dreams: The Complete and Definitive Text.* Translated and edited by James Strachey. New York: Basic Books.

Fuentes, Marisa J. 2016. *Dispossessed Lives: Enslaved Women, Violence, and the Archive.* Philadelphia: University of Pennsylvania Press.

Gane-McCalla, Casey. 2009. "Spike Lee Compares Tyler Perry to Amos and Andy." *News One*, May 28, https://newsone.com.

Gardner, Amy, Krissah Thompson, and Philip Rucker. 2010. "Beck, Palin Tell Thousands to 'Restore America.'" *Washington Post*, August 29, www.washingtonpost.com.

Gavanas, Anna. 2004. *Fatherhood Politics in the United States: Masculinity, Sexuality, Race, and Marriage.* Urbana: University of Illinois Press.

Gay, Roxane. 2014. "Bill Cosby and the Rape Accusers: Stop Looking Away and Start Believing." *The Guardian*, November 21, www.theguardian.com.

Gay, Verne. 2014. "Bill Cosby Booking on 'Late Show with David Letterman' Canceled." *Newsday*, updated November 14, www.newsday.com.

Gaztambide, Daniel José. 2019. *A People's History of Psychoanalysis: From Freud to Liberation Psychology.* Lanham, MD: Lexington Books.

Génz, Stéphanie, and Benjamin A. Brabon. 2009. *Postfeminism: Cultural Texts and Theories.* Edinburgh: Edinburgh University Press.

Gerson, Michael. 2008. "A Speech That Fell Short." *Washington Post*, March 19, www.washingtonpost.com.

Giddings, Paula. 1984. *When and Where I Enter: The Impact of Black Women on Race and Sex in America.* New York: W. Morrow.

Gill, R., and C. Scharff. 2011. *New Femininities: Postfeminism, Neoliberalism, and Subjectivity.* London: Palgrave Macmillan.

Gillespie, Andra. 2010. "Meet the New Class: Theorizing Young Black Leadership in a 'Postracial' Era." In *Whose Black Politics?: Cases in Post-Racial Black Leadership.* Edited by Andra Gillespie, 9–42. New York: Routledge.

———. 2019. *Race and the Obama Administration: Substance, Symbols, and Hope.* Manchester: Manchester University Press.

Gillman, Laura. 2010. *Unassimilable Feminisms: Reappraising Feminist, Womanist, and Mestiza Identity Politics.* New York: Palgrave Macmillan.

Gilroy, Paul. 2006. *Postcolonial Melancholia.* New York: Columbia University Press.

Givhan, Robin. 2005. "Condoleezza Rice's Commanding Clothes." *Washington Post*, February 25, www.washingtonpost.com.

Glymph, Thavolia. 2008. *Out of the House of Bondage: The Transformation of the Plantation Household.* New York: Cambridge University Press.

Goldberg, David Theo. 2009. *The Threat of Race: Reflections on Racial Neoliberalism*. Malden, MA: Wiley-Blackwell.

Gordon-Reed, Annette. 1998. *Thomas Jefferson and Sally Hemings: An American Controversy*. Charlottesville: University of Virginia Press.

Gramsci, Antonio. [1971] 2008. *Selections from the Prison Notebooks of Antonio Gramsci*. Edited and translated by Quintin Hoare and Geoffrey Nowell Smith. New York: International Publishers Co.

Grant, Darren, dir. 2005. *Tyler Perry's Diary of a Mad Black Woman*, written by Tyler Perry, featuring Kimberly Elise, Steve Harris, Tyler Perry, and Cisely Tyson, Lionsgate, DVD, 116 mins.

Gray, Herman. 1995. *Watching Race: Television and the Struggle for Blackness*. Minneapolis: University of Minnesota Press.

Green, Tamara. 2014. "Accuser to Bill Cosby: Take Up for Women, Try to Do Something Heroic." *Entertainment Tonight*, November 19, www.etonline.com.

Greer, Christina M. 2013. *Black Ethnics: Race, Immigration, and the Pursuit of the American Dream*. New York: Oxford University Press.

Grey's Anatomy. 2006. "Damage Case." Episode number 24. Directed by Tony Goldwyn Written by Shonda Rhimes and Mimi Schmir. Aired May 7 on NBC.

Grindstaff, L. A. 1994. "Double Exposure, Double Erasure: On the Frontline with Anita Hill." *Cultural Critique* 27 (Spring): 29–60.

Guy-Sheftall, Beverly. 1995. "Introduction: The Evolution of Feminist Consciousness among African American Women." In *Words of Fire: An Anthology of African American Feminist Thought*. Edited by Beverly Guy-Sheftall, 1–22. New York: New Press.

Guy-Sheftall, Beverly, and Johnetta Betsch Cole, eds. 2010. *Who Should Be First? Feminists Speak Out on the 2008 Presidential Campaign*. Albany: State University of New York Press.

Haggis, Paul. 2005. *Crash*, featuring Sandra Bullock, Don Cheadle, and Matt Dillon. Artisan/Lionsgate Home Video, DVD, 112 mins.

Hampton, Dream. 2019. *Surviving R. Kelly*. Season 1. Bunim-Murray Productions (BMP) and Kreativ. Released January 3. Aired on Lifetime Network.

Hancock, Ange-Marie. 2004. *The Politics of Disgust: The Public Identity of the Welfare Queen*. New York: New York University Press.

Hare, Nathan, and Julia Hare. 1984. *The Endangered Black Family: Coping with the Unisexualization and Coming Extinction of the Black Race*. San Francisco: Black Think Tank.

Harris, Duchess. 2018. *Black Feminist Politics from Kennedy to Trump*. New York: Palgrave Macmillan.

Harris, Fredrick C. 2012. *The Price of the Ticket: Barack Obama and the Rise and Decline of Black Politics*. New York: Oxford University Press.

Harris, Hamil. 2004. "Some Blacks Find Nugget of Truth in Cosby Speech." *Washington Post*, May 26, www.washingtonpost.com.

Harris, Kamala. 2019. *The Truths We Hold: An American Journey*. New York: Penguin.

Harris, Rose. 1999. "Signifying Race and Gender in Feminist Theory." Ph.D. diss. Rutgers University.

Harris-Perry, Melissa V. 2011. *Sister Citizen: Shame, Stereotypes, and Black Women in America*. New Haven, CT: Yale University Press.

Harvey, Steve. 2009. *Act Like a Lady, Think Like a Man: What Men Really Think about Love, Relationships, Intimacy, and Commitment*. Hardcover ed. New York: HarperCollins.

Harzewski, Stephanie. 2011. *Chick Lit and Postfeminism*. Charlottesville: University of Virginia Press.

Herbert, Bob. 2008. "With a Powerful Speech, Obama Offers a Challenge." *New York Times*, March 25, www.nytimes.com.

Higginbotham, Evelyn Brooks. 1994. *Righteous Discontent: The Women's Movement in the Black Baptist Church, 1880–1920*. Cambridge, MA: Harvard University Press.

Hine, Darlene Clark. 1989. "Rape and the Inner Lives of Black Women in the Middle West: Preliminary Thoughts on the Culture of Dissemblance." *Signs: Journal of Women in Culture and Society* 14, no. 4: 912–20.

Holmes, David G. 2007. "The Civil Rights Movement according to *Crash*: Complicating the Pedagogy of Integration." *College English* 69, no. 4: 314–20.

Holmes, Rachel. 2007a. *African Queen: The Real Life of the Hottentot Venus*. New York: Random House.

———. 2007b. "Identity over Politics." In *Dr. Rice in the House*. Edited by Amy Scholder, 65–73. New York: Seven Stories.

hooks, bell. [1984] 2015. *Feminist Theory: From Margin to Center*. New York: Routledge.

———. 2004. *We Real Cool: Black Men and Masculinity*. New York: Routledge.

Hsu, Hsuan L. 2006. "Racial Privacy, the L.A. Ensemble Film, and Paul Haggis's *Crash*." *Film Criticism* 31, no. 1/2: 132–56.

Hunter, Tera. 1997. *To Joy My Freedom: Southern Black Women's Lives and Labors after the Civil War*. Cambridge, MA: Harvard University Press.

Hurt, Charles. 2008. "Jesse Jackson Says He Wants to Cut Obama's 'Nuts Out.'" *New York Post*, July 9, https://nypost.com.

Inskeep, Steve. 2020. "Asian Americans Are Blamed by Some for COVID-19 Outbreak." *National Public Radio*, March 27, www.npr.org.

Irving, Toni. 2004. "Race, Rape and Third Wave Feminism: A Tale of Two Cities." *Black Renaissance* 6, no. 1: 45–60.

Ishikawa, Tanya. 2009. "Sebastian Doggart on American Faust." Posted on December 7, 2009, YouTube video, 8:20, www.youtube.com/watch?v=btL6ZdPQIAU.

Italiano, Laura. 2011. "DA Set to Drop Charges vs. DSK." *New York Post*, July 5, https://nypost.com.

Izrael, Jimi. 2010. *The Denzel Principle: Why Black Women Can't Find Good Black Men*. New York: St. Martin's Press.

Jewell, K. Sue. 1993. *From Mammy to Miss America and Beyond: Cultural Images and the Shaping of US Social Policy*. New York: Routledge.

Johnson, Cedric. 2011. "Preface: Obama's Katrina." *The Neoliberal Deluge: Hurricane Katrina, Late Capitalism, and the Remaking of New Orleans*. Edited by Cedric Johnson, vii–xvi. Minneapolis: University of Minnesota Press.

Johnson, Devon, Patricia Warren, and Amy Farrell, eds. 2015. *Deadly Injustice: Trayvon Martin, Race, and the Criminal Justice System*. New York: New York University Press.

Jones, Charisse, and Kumea Shorter-Gooden. 2003. *Shifting: The Double Lives of Black Women in America*. New York: HarperCollins.

Jones, Jacqueline. 2010. *Labor of Love, Labor of Sorrow: Black Women, Work, and the Family from Slavery to the Present*. New York: Basic Books.

Jones, Mack H. 1987. "The Political Thought of the New Black Conservatives: An Analysis, Explanation, and Interpretation." In *Readings in American Political Issues*. Edited by Franklin D. Jones and Michael O. Adams with Sanders Anderson Jr. and Tandy Tollerson, 23–49. Dubuque, IA: Kendall/Hunt.

———. 2014. *Knowledge, Power, and Black Politics: Collected Essays*. Albany: State University of New York Press.

Jones, Martha, and Hanna Rosen. 2020. "The Celia Project: A Research Collaboration on the History of Slavery and Sexual Violence," accessed March 16, 2020, https://sites.lsa.umich.edu/celiaproject.

Jordan-Zachery, Julia. 2009. *Black Women, Cultural Symbols, and Social Policy*. New York: Routledge.

———. 2014. "'I Ain't Your Darn Help': Black Women as the Help in Intersectionality Research." *National Political Science Review* 16: 19–30.

———. 2017. *Shadow Bodies: Black Women, Ideology, Representation, and Politics*. New Brunswick, NJ: Rutgers University Press.

———. 2019. "Licking Salt: A Black Woman's Tale of Betrayal, Adversity, and Survival." *Feminist Formations* 31, no. 1: 67–84, doi:10.1353/ff.2019.0009.

Joseph, Miranda. 2002. *Against the Romance of Community*. Minneapolis: University of Minnesota Press.

Katz, Michael B. 1989. *The Undeserving Poor: From the War on Poverty to the War on Welfare*. New York: Pantheon Books.

Keizer, Arlene R. 2010. "African American Literature and Psychoanalysis." In *A Companion to African American Literature*. Edited by Gene Andrew Jarrett, 410–20. Malden, MA: Wiley-Blackwell.

Kelleter, Frank, Barbara Krah, and Ruth Mayer, eds. 2007. "The Melodramatic Mode Revisited: An Introduction." *Melodrama!: The Mode of Excess from Early America to Hollywood*. Edited by Frank Kelleter, Barbara Krah, and Ruth Mayer, 7–17. Heidelberg: Universitatsverlag Winter.

Kellogg, Carolyn. 2011. "Kathryn Stockett and Janet Evanovich Become Kindle Million-Sellers." *LA Times*, August 16, https://latimesblogs.latimes.com.

Kelly, Gene. 2016. "Tyler Perry as Madea: Homophobia Gets a Pass When It's a Man in a Dress." In *The Problematic Tyler Perry*. Edited by Brian Johnson, 115–32. New York: Peter Lang.

Kempley, Rita. 2003. "Too, Too Divine." *Washington Post*, June 7, www.washington post.com.

Kenneally, Tim. 2011. "Lionsgate Re-Ups Tyler Perry with Multi-Year Deal." *The Wrap*, last modified March 31, 2011, www.thewrap.com.

Kennedy, Tanya Ann. 2017. *Historicizing Post-Discourses: Postfeminism and Postracialism in United States Culture*. Albany: State University of New York Press.

Kessler, Glenn. 2007. *The Confidante: Condoleezza Rice and the Creation of the Bush Legacy*. New York: St. Martin's Press.

Kim, Kyle, Christina Littlefield, and Melissa Etehad. 2018. "Bill Cosby: A 50-Year Chronicle of Accusations and Accomplishments." *Los Angeles Times*, September 25, www.latimes.com.

King, Martin Luther, Jr. [1968] 1986. "I See the Promised Land." In *A Testament of Hope: The Essential Writings and Speeches of Dr. Martin Luther King, Jr*. Edited by James M. Washington, 279–86. New York: HarperCollins.

Klein, Aaron. 2006. "'Black Spinster' Label Pinned on Condi Rice." *WorldNetDaily*, July 31, www.WorldNetDaily.com.

Klein, Melanie. [1946] 1975. "Notes on Some Schizoid Mechanisms." *Envy and Gratitude and Other Works, 1946–1963*, 1–24. New York: Free Press.

Kloer, Phil. 2006. "Many Relate to the Values of Madea's Family Reunion Star." *Atlanta Journal-Constitution*, February 23, www.accessatlanta.com.

Knouse, Jessica. 2016. "Playing with Gender, Queering Lines: Should We be Mad at Madea?" In *The Problematic Tyler Perry*, edited by Brian Johnson, 96–114. New York: Peter Lang.

Kramer, Stanley. 1967. *Guess Who's Coming to Dinner* (40th Anniversary Edition), featuring Sidney Poitier, Spencer Tracy, Katharine Hepburn, and Cecil Kellaway, Sony Pictures Home Entertainment, DVD, 107 mins.

Kreider, Rose M., and Renee Ellis. 2011. *Number, Timing, and Duration of Marriages and Divorces: 2009*. Washington, DC: US Census Bureau.

Krugman, Paul. 2020. "Covid-19 Brings Out All the Usual Zombies." *New York Times*, March 28, www.nytimes.com.

Kunjufu, Jawanzaa. 1985. *Countering the Conspiracy to Destroy Black Boys*. Chicago: African American Images.

———. 1986. *Countering the Conspiracy to Destroy Black Boys, Vol. II*. Chicago: African American Images.

———. 1990. *Countering the Conspiracy to Destroy Black Boys, Vol. III*. Chicago: African American Images.

Kurtzman, Daniel. 2004. "Is Condi Rice Secretly in Love with President Bush?" *About*, April 19, http://politicalhumor.about.com.

———. 2007. "Late-Night Jokes about Secretary of State Condoleezza Rice." *About*, accessed July 15, 2007, http://politicalhumor.about.com.

Laplanche, Jean, and Jean-Bertrand Pontalis. 1988. *The Language of Psycho-analysis*. London: Karnac Books.

"Latest News (Official Book Website for *The Help* by Kathryn Stockett)." 2019. *Penguin*, accessed August 20, 2019. www.penguin.com.

Lattuca, Lisa. 2001. *Creating Interdisciplinarity: Interdisciplinary Research and Teaching among College and University Faculty*. Nashville: Vanderbilt University Press.

Lee, Shayne. 2015. *Tyler Perry's America: Inside His Films*. Lanham, MD: Rowman & Littlefield.

Legette, Willie. 1999. "The Crisis of the Black Male: A New Ideology in Black Politics." In *Without Justice for All: The New Liberalism and Our Retreat from Racial Equality*. Edited by Adolph Reed Jr., 291–324. Boulder, CO: Westview Press.

"Letter of 250+ Concerned Black Men and Other Men of Color Calling for the Inclusion of Women and Girls in 'My Brother's Keeper.'" 2014. *African American Policy Forum*, May 30, http://aapf.org.

Lewis, Angela. 2013. *Conservatism in the Black Community: To the Right and Misunderstood*. New York: Routledge.

Lichfield, John. 2015. "Dominique Strauss-Kahn 'Had Brutal Anal Sex with Prostitute at Orgy,' Pimping Trial Hears." *Independent*, February 10, www.independent.co.uk.

Lindsay, Keisha. 2018. *In a Classroom of Their Own: The Intersection of Race and Feminist Politics in All-Black Male Schools*. Urbana: University of Illinois Press.

Lionsgate. 2011. "Press Release: Lionsgate Extends Partnership with Tyler Perry with New Multiyear Deal." *PRNewswire via COMTEX*, March 31, www.prnewswire.com.

Lipsitz, George. 1997. "The O. J. Simpson Trial: The Greatest Story Ever Sold: Marketing and the O. J. Simpson Trial." In *Birth of a Nation'Hood: Gaze, Script, and Spectacle in the O. J. Simpson Case*. Edited by Toni Morrison and Claudia Brodsky Lacour, 3–29. New York: Pantheon.

Littlefield, Marci Bounds. 2008. "The Media as a System of Racialization: Exploring Images of African American Women and the New Racism." *American Behavioral Scientist* 51, no. 5: 675–85.

Locke, Mamie. 1990. "From Three-Fifths to Zero: Implications of the Constitution for African-American Women, 1787–1870." *Women & Politics* 10, no. 2: 33–46.

Lott, Eric. 1995. *Love and Theft: Blackface Minstrelsy and the American Working Class*. New York: Oxford University Press.

Lowndes, Joseph E., Julie Novkov, and Dorian Todd Warren, eds. 2008. *Race and American Political Development*. New York: Routledge.

Lubiano, Wahneema. 1992. "Black Ladies, Welfare Queens, and State Minstrels: Ideological War by Narrative Means." In *Race-Ing Justice, En-Gendering Power: Essays on Anita Hill, Clarence Thomas, and the Construction of Social Reality*. Edited by Toni Morrison, 323–63. New York: Pantheon.

Lusane, Clarence. 2006. *Colin Powell and Condoleezza Rice: Foreign Policy, Race, and the New American Century*. Westport, CT: Praeger.

Mabry, Marcus. 2007. *Twice as Good: Condoleezza Rice and Her Path to Power*. New York: Modern Times.

Mack, Melanie. 2006. "'Crash' Breaks the Mountain at Academy Awards." *Los Angeles Sentinel*, Mar 9–15.

MacKinnon, Catharine. 1989. "Rape: On Coercion and Consent." In *Toward a Feminist Theory of the State*. Cambridge, MA: Harvard University Press.

Maguire, Sharon, dir. 2001. *Bridget Jones's Diary*, featuring Renée Zellweger, Colin Firth, and Hugh Grant, Miramax, DVD, 98 mins.

Manigault-Bryant, LeRhonda, Tamura Lomax, and Carol Duncan. 2014. "Introduction." In *Womanist and Black Feminist Responses to Tyler Perry's Productions*. Edited by LeRhonda Manigault-Bryant, Tamura Lomax, and Carol Duncan, 1–14. New York: Palgrave Macmillan.

Matthews, Dylan. 2014. "Why Hannibal Buress Won't Let People Forget That 13 Women Have Accused Bill Cosby of Rape." *Vox Media*, October 21, www.vox.com.

May, Vanessa H. 2011. *Unprotected Labor: Household Workers, Politics, and Middle-Class Reform in New York, 1870–1940*. Chapel Hill: University of North Carolina Press.

May, Vivian M. 2015. *Pursuing Intersectionality, Unsettling Dominant Imaginaries*. New York: Routledge.

McAdam, Doug. 1999. *Political Process and the Development of Black Insurgency, 1930–1970*. Second ed. Chicago: University of Chicago Press.

McClintock, Anne. 1995. *Imperial Leather: Race, Gender, and Sexuality in the Colonial Conquest*. New York: Routledge.

McCormick, Joseph, and Charles Jones. 1993. "The Conceptualization of Deracialization: Thinking through the Dilemma." In *Dilemmas of Black Politics: Issues of Leadership and Strategy*. Edited by Georgia Persons, 66–84. New York: HarperCollins College Publishers.

McKinley, James, and Robbie Brown. 2010. "Sex Scandal Threatens a Georgia Pastor's Empire." *New York Times*, September 25 ,www.nytimes.com.

McKittrick, Katherine. 2006. *Demonic Grounds: Black Women and the Cartographies of Struggle*. Minneapolis: University of Minnesota Press.

McLaurin, Melton. 1991. *Celia, A Slave*. Athens: University of Georgia Press.

McQueen, Steve, dir. 2013. *Twelve Years a Slave*, written by John Ridley, based on *Twelve Years a Slave* by Solomon Northrup, featuring Benedict Cumberbatch, Brad Pitt, and Chiwetel Ejiofor, 20th Century Fox, DVD, 134 mins.

McRobbie, Angela. 2007. "Postfeminism and Popular Culture: Bridget Jones and the New Gender Regime." In *Interrogating Postfeminism: Gender and the Politics of Popular Culture*. Edited by Yvonne Tasker and Diane Negra, 27–39. Durham, NC: Duke University Press.

Mehta, Akash. 2020. "Even in a Pandemic, Andrew Cuomo Is Not Your Friend." *Jacobin*, March 27, https://jacobinmag.com.

"'Me Too' Creator Tarana Burke: 'We Have to Make Movements Ourselves.'" 2017. *CBS News*, October 20, www.cbsnews.com.

Miller, Elaine. 1992. *Running Mate: Gender and Politics in the Editorial Cartoons*. New York: First Run/Icarus Films.

Mills, Charles W. 1997. *The Racial Contract*. Ithaca, NY: Cornell University Press.

Mitchell, Juliet. [1974] 2000. *Psychoanalysis and Feminism: A Radical Reassessment of Freudian Psychoanalysis*. New ed. of second revised ed. New York: Basic Books.

Mitchell, Stephen A., and Margaret J. Black. 1995. *Freud and Beyond: A History of Modern Psychoanalytic Thought*. New York: Basic Books.

Modleski, Tania. 1991. *Feminism without Women: Culture and Critique in a "Postfeminist" Age*. New York: Routledge.

Morris, Edward. 2004. "Steve Earle Launches Anti-War Album." *Country Music Times*, September 4, www.CMT.com.

Morris, Wesley. 2018. "Cliff Huxtable Was Bill Cosby's Sickest Joke." *New York Times*, April 26, www.nytimes.com.

Morrison, Toni, ed. 1992. *Race-Ing Justice, En-Gendering Power: Essays on Anita Hill, Clarence Thomas, and the Construction of Social Reality*. New York: Pantheon.

———. 1993. *Playing in the Dark: Whiteness and the Literary Imagination*. New York: Vintage.

———. 1997. "The Official Story: Dead Man Golfing." In *Birth of a Nation'hood: Gaze, Script, and Spectacle in the O. J. Simpson Case*. Edited by Toni Morrison and Claudia Brodsky Lacour, vii–xxviii. New York: Pantheon.

———. 2000. "Unspeakable Things Unspoken: The Afro-American Presence in American Literature." In *A Turbulent Voyage: Readings in African American Studies*. Third ed. Edited by Floyd Hayes III, 246–67. San Diego, CA: Collegiate Press.

Moynihan, Patrick. [1965] 1967. "The Negro Family: The Case for National Action." In *The Moynihan Report and the Politics of Controversy: A Trans-Action Social Science and Public Policy Report. Including the Full Text of the Negro Family: The Case for National Action by Daniel Patrick Moynihan*. Edited by Lee Rainwater and William Yancey, 41–124. Cambridge, MA: MIT Press.

———. 1996. *Miles to Go: A Personal History of Social Policy*. Cambridge, MA: Harvard University Press.

Mulraney, Frances, and Marlene Lenthang. 2020. "Conservative Commentator Glenn Beck, 56, Says He 'Would Rather Die' Than Continue Shutdown and That Over 50s Should Work to Keep the Economy Going Because 'the Country Is Dying.'" *Daily Mail*, March 25, www.dailymail.co.uk.

Murray, Melissa. 2017. "We Won't Let 'TIME' Erase Tarana Burke from the Movement She Started." *Black Entertainment Television (BET)*, December 7, www.bet.com.

Murray, Shailagh, and Dan Balz. 2008. "Obama Urges US: 'Move beyond Our Old Racial Wounds.'" *Washington Post*, March 19, www.washingtonpost.com.

Musser, Amber. 2016. "Queering Sugar: Kara Walker's Sugar Sphinx and the Intractability of Black Female Sexuality." *Signs: Journal of Women in Culture and Society* 42, no. 1: 153–74.

Narea, Nicole. 2020. "The Missing Piece in the Coronavirus Stimulus Bill: Relief for Immigrants." *Vox*, April 1, www.vox.com.

Nash, Jennifer. 2014. *The Black Body in Ecstasy: Reading Race, Reading Pornography*. Durham, NC: Duke University Press.

Nast, Heidi J. 2000. "Mapping the 'Unconscious': Racism and the Oedipal Family." *Annals of the Association of America Geographers* 90, no. 2: 215–55.

"National Women Leadership Supporting My Brother's Keeper." 2014. Open Letter, National Women Leadership Supporting My Brother's Keeper to President Barack Obama, Jun. 29, 2014, Washington, DC.

Nawaz, Amna. 2020. "Manhattan DA Cyrus Vance on Weinstein Verdict and Why His Office Didn't Prosecute in 2015." *PBS News Hour*, February 25, www.pbs.org.

Ndubuizu, Rosemary. 2014. "(Black) Papa Knows Best: Marion Barry and the Appeal to Black Authoritarian Discourse." *National Political Science Review* 16: 31–48.

Negra, Diane. 2009. *What a Girl Wants?: Fantasizing the Reclamation of Self in Post-feminism*. New York: Routledge.

New York Times. 2008. "Obama's Speech on Race Played Well, a Poll Finds." March 22, www.nytimes.com.

———. 2010. "The New York Times Bestsellers." *New York Times*, October 3, www.nytimes.com.

Nunley, Vorris. 2007. "SYMPOSIUM: *Crash*: Rhetorically Wrecking Discourses of Race, Tolerance, and Privilege." *College English* 69, no. 4: 335–46.

Obama, Barack. [1995] 2004. *Dreams of My Father: A Story of Race and Inheritance*. New York: Three Rivers Press.

———. 2006. *Audacity of Hope: Thoughts on Reclaiming the American Dream*. New York: Three Rivers Press.

———. 2008a. "The Great Need of the Hour." In *An American Story: The Speeches of Barack Obama*. Edited by David Olive, 238–44. Toronto: ECW Press.

———. 2008b. "A More Perfect Union (transcript)." *National Public Radio*, March 18, www.npr.org.

———. 2008c. "Obama's Father's Day Remarks (transcript)." *New York Times*, June 15, www.nytimes.com.

———. 2014. "Remarks by the President on 'My Brother's Keeper' Initiative." *Obama Whitehouse Archives*, February 27, https://obamawhitehouse.archives.gov.

———. 2015. *Obama in Kenya: President Barack Obama's Speech at Kasarani-Full*. Posted by *Daily Nation*, July 6, 2015, YouTube video, 44:59, www.youtube.com/watch?v=MNCN4B8xbuo.

Obama, Michelle. 2018. *Becoming*. New York: Crown.

Obama Foundation, The. 2019. "Town Hall with President Barack Obama and Steph Curry." Filmed in Oakland, California, February 19, 2019. YouTube video, 1:05:29,www.youtube.com/watch?v=c_zoh9mTefY&t=3524s.

Omi, Michael, and Howard Winant. 1986. *Racial Formation in the United States*. New York: Routledge.

Painter, Nell Irvin. 2002. *Southern History across the Color Line*. Chapel Hill: University of North Carolina Press.

Parker, Nate, dir. 2016. *The Birth of a Nation*, written by Nate Parker, featuring Nate Parker, Armie Hammer, and Penelope Ann Miller, Walt Disney Studio Home Entertainment, DVD, 120 mins.

Pateman, Carole. 1988. *The Sexual Contract.* Cambridge: Polity Press.

Pateman, Carole, and Charles Mills. 2007. *Contract and Domination.* Malden, MA: Polity Press.

Pérez-Peña, Richard. 2017. "Woman Linked to 1955 Emmett Till Murder Tells Historian Her Claims Were False." *New York Times,* January 27, www.nytimes.com.

Perry, Tyler. 2007. *Don't Make a Black Woman Take Off Her Earrings: Madea's Uninhibited Commentaries on Love and Life.* New York: Riverhead Books.

———. 2020. "Author Essay." *Penguin,* accessed January 3, 2020, www.penguinrandom house.com.

Pew Research Center. 2018. *Wide Gender Gap, Growing Educational Divide in Voters' Party Identification.* Washington, DC: Pew Research Center.

Philip, Marlene Nourbese. 1997. "Dis place—The Space Between." *Genealogy of Resistance and Other Essays,* 74–112. Toronto: Mercury Press.

Philpot, Tasha S. 2007. *Race, Republicans, and the Return of the Party of Lincoln.* Ann Arbor: University of Michigan Press.

———. 2018. *Conservative but not Republican: The Paradox of Party Identification and Ideology among African Americans.* New York: Cambridge University Press.

Pickens, Therí. 2012. "My Body Is Your Problem (Not Mine)." *Cultural Front,* August 3, www.culturalfront.com.

Pratt, Mary Louise. 1992. *Imperial Eyes: Studies in Travel Writing and Transculturation.* New York: Routledge.

Press, Alex. 2018. "It's Time to Acknowledge That Strikes Work." *Washington Post,* May 31, www.washingtonpost.com.

Prestage, Jewell. 1991. "In Quest of the African American Political Woman." *Annals of the American Academy of Political and Social Science* 515: 88–103.

Price, Melanye T. 2016. *The Race Whisperer: Barack Obama and the Political Uses of Race.* New York: New York University Press.

Projansky, Sarah. 2001. *Watching Rape: Film and Television in Postfeminist Culture.* New York: New York University Press.

Purnell, Derecka. 2019. "Why Does Obama Scold Black Boys?" *New York Times,* February 23, www.nytimes.com.

Puwar, Nirmal. 2004. *Space Invaders: Race, Gender, and Bodies Out of Place.* Oxford: Berg.

Quinn, Eithne. 2005. *Nuthin' but a 'G' Thang: The Culture and Commerce of Gangsta Rap.* New York: Columbia University Press.

Raley, R. Kelly, Megan Sweeney, and Danielle Wondra. 2015. "The Growing Racial and Ethnic Divide in US Marriage Patterns." *Future Child* 25, no. 2: 89–109, www.ncbi .nlm.nih.gov/pmc/articles/PMC4850739/.

Rashkin, Esther. 2008. *Unspeakable Secrets and the Psychoanalysis of Culture.* Albany: State University of New York Press.

Ray, Sangeeta. 2007. *Crash* or How White Men Save the Day, Again. *College English* 69, no. 4: 350–54.

Redden, Molly. 2019. "The Human Cost of Kamala Harris' War on Truancy." *Huffington Post,* March 27, www.huffpost.com.

Reed, Jr., Adolph L. 1996. "The Curse of Community." *Village Voice*, January 16.

———. 2008. "Obama No." *The Progressive*, April 28, https://progressive.org.

Reed, Touré F. 2008. *Not Alms but Opportunity: The Urban League and the Politics of Racial Uplift, 1910–1950*. Chapel Hill: University of North Carolina Press.

Reeves, Marcus. 2011. "Tyler Perry Tells Spike Lee to 'Go Straight to Hell.'" *Black Entertainment Television (BET)*, April 21, https://www.bet.com.

Regan, Helen. 2014. "Netflix Postpones a Bill Cosby Comedy Special as Fallout Mounts." *Time*, November 19, https://time.com.

Renold, Caroline, Alessandro Chechi, and Marc-André Renold. 2013. "Case: Sarah Baartman—France and South Africa," *Platform ArThemis*, Art-Law Centre, University of Geneva, http://unige.ch/art-adr.

Rein, Martin, and Donald A. Schön. 1993. "Reframing Policy Discourse." In *The Argumentative Turn in Policy Analysis and Planning*. Edited by Frank Fischer and John Forester, 145–66. Durham, NC: Duke University Press.

Reny, Tyler, and Matt Barreto. 2020. "Americans Who Are Biased against Asians Are More Likely to Fear the Coronavirus." *Washington Post*, April 1, www.washingtonpost.com.

Rice, Condoleezza. 2010. *Condoleezza Rice: A Memoir of My Extraordinary, Ordinary Family and Me*. New York: Delacorte Press.

Riggs, Marlon, prod. and dir. 1986. *Ethnic Notions*. California Newsreel, VHS tape, 54 mins.

Ritter, Gretchen. 2008. "Gender as a Category of Analysis in American Political Development." In *Political Women and American Democracy*. Edited by Christina Wolbrecht, Karen Beckwith, and Lisa Baldez, 12–30. New York: Cambridge University Press.

"R. Kelly Come & Get 'Em! Concert Seats Available Amid 'Cult' Rumors." 2017. *TMZ*, July 28, www.tmz.com.

Roach, Joseph. 1992. "Mardi Gras Indians and Others: Genealogies of American Performance." *Theatre Journal* 44, no. 4: 461–83.

Robnett, Belinda. 1997. *How Long? How Long?: African American Women in the Struggle for Civil Rights*. New York: Oxford University Press.

Rogin, Michael. 1996. *Blackface, White Noise: Jewish Immigrants in the Hollywood Melting Pot*. Berkeley: University of California Press.

Rohan, Tim. 2012. "Sandusky Gets 30 to 60 Years for Sexual Abuse." *New York Times*, October 9, www.nytimes.com.

Roig-Franzia, Manuel. 2018. "Bill Cosby Convicted on Three Counts of Sexual Assault." *Washington Post*, April 26, www.washingtonpost.com.

Rowe, Aimee Carrillo. 2007. "Feeling in the Dark: Empathy, Whiteness, and Miscege-Nation in *Monster's Ball*." *Hypatia* 22, no. 2: 122–42.

Russ, Hillary 2020. "Instacart, Amazon Workers Strike as Labor Unrest Grows during Coronavirus Crisis." *Reuters*, March 30, www.reuters.com.

Rustin, Bayard. 1965. "From Protest to Politics: The Future of the Civil Rights Movement." *Commentary* 39, no. 2 (February): 25–31.

Salam, Maya. 2019. "R. Kelly: Why So Many Ignored the Warning Signs." *New York Times*, January 11, www.nytimes.com.

Samuels, David. 2007. "Grand Illusions." *Atlantic Monthly*, June.

Sanday, Peggy Reeves. 2007. *Fraternity Gang Rape: Sex, Brotherhood, and Privilege on Campus*. New York: New York University Press.

Sandler, Joseph, and Anna Freud. 1985. *The Analysis of Defense: The Ego and the Mechanisms of Defense Revisited*. New York: International Universities Press.

Schoenemann, Deborah, with Spencer Moran. 2004. "Armani's Exchange . . . Condi's Slip . . . Forget the Alamo." *New York Magazine*, April 26, https://nymag.com.

Schram, Sanford F. 2015. *The Return of Ordinary Capitalism: Neoliberalism, Precarity, Occupy*. Oxford: Oxford University Press.

Schram, Sanford F., and Philip Neisser, eds. 1997. *Tales of the State: Narrative in Contemporary US Politics and Public Policy*. Lanham, MD: Rowman and Littlefield.

Schultz, Connie. 2009. "His Grandmother, My Father, Your Uncle . . ." In *The Speech: Race and Barack Obama's "A More Perfect Union."* Edited by T. Denean Sharpley-Whiting, 102–12. New York: Bloomsbury.

Scott, Darryl. 2018. "This Does a Disservice to Our Ancestors, Women, and History." *Facebook*, September 25, www.facebook.com.

Scott, Janny. 2011. *A Singular Woman: The Untold Story of Barack Obama's Mother*. New York: Riverhead Books.

Secret, Mosi. 2011. "Police Seek Evidence from I.M.F. Chief on Sex Attack." *New York Times*, May 15, www.nytimes.com.

Shapiro, Eliza. 2020. "New York City Public Schools to Close to Slow Spread of Coronavirus." *New York Times*, March 15, www.nytimes.com.

Sharpley-Whiting, T. Denean. 2009. "Introduction: Chloroform Morning Joe!" In *The Speech: Race and Barack Obama's "A More Perfect Union."* Edited by T. Denean Sharpley-Whiting, 1–15. New York: Bloomsbury.

Shear, Michael, and Maggie Haberman. 2017. "Trump Defends Initial Remarks on Charlottesville; Again Blames 'Both Sides.'" *New York Times*, August 15, www.nytimes.com.

Simien, Evelyn M. 2011. *Gender and Lynching: The Politics of Memory*. New York: Palgrave Macmillan.

———. 2016. *Historic Firsts: How Symbolic Empowerment Changes U.S. Politics*. New York: Oxford University Press.

Simmons, Aishah Shahidah, dir. 2006. *No!: The Rape Documentary*. 4.3 Digital. AfroLez Productions, LLC.

Simmons, Russell. 2013. "Harriet Tubman Sex Tape." Posted on August 15, 2013. YouTube video, 3:08, www.youtube.com/watch?v=78OvnOmZvTg&list=PLZsFXoOzx GAzH85gHvQe19FFQByYTSB9q.

Smith, Candis Watts. 2014. *Black Mosaic: The Politics of Black Pan-Ethnic Diversity*. New York: New York University Press.

Smith, Robert C. 1996. *We Have No Leaders: African Americans in the Post–Civil Rights Era*. Albany: State University of New York Press.

Smooth, Wendy. 2013. "Black Politics, as If Black Women Mattered." *National Political Science Review* 15: 79–82.

———. 2018. "Hyde-Smith and the Test of Women's Descriptive Representation." *Gender Watch 2018*, last modified December 6, www.genderwatch2018.org.

Snow, David, Rochford E. Burke Jr., Steven Worden, and Robert Benford. 1986. "Frame Alignment Processes, Micromobilization, and Movement Participation." *American Sociological Review* 51, no. 4: 464–81.

Solomon, John. 2012. *DSK: The Scandal That Brought Down Dominique Strauss-Kahn.* New York: Thomas Dunne.

Sonmez, Felicia, and Ashley Parker. 2019. "As Trump Stands by Charlottesville Remarks, Rise of White-Nationalist Violence Becomes an Issue in 2020 Presidential Race." *Washington Post*, April 28, www.washingtonpost.com.

Sparx, Rosa. 2007. "Condoleezza Rice Is a White Man." *Insultadarity*, accessed January 4, 2007, http://insultadarity.blogspot.com.

Spence, Lester K. 2016. *Knocking the Hustle: Against the Neoliberal Turn in Black Politics.* New York: Punctum Books.

Spillers, Hortense. 2003. *Black, White, and in Color: Essays on American Literature and Culture.* Chicago: University of Chicago Press.

———. 2012. "Destiny's Child: Obama and Election '08." *Boundary 2* 39, no. 2: 3–32.

Spillers, Hortense, Saidiya Hartman, Farah Jasmine Griffin, Shelly Eversley, and Jennifer L. Morgan. 2007. "'Whatcha Gonna Do?'—Revisiting 'Mama's Baby, Papa's Maybe: An American Grammar Book': A Conversation with Hortense Spillers, Saidiya Hartman, Farah Jasmine Griffin, Shelly Eversley, & Jennifer L. Morgan." *Women's Studies Quarterly* 35, no. 1/2: 299–309.

Spivak, Gayatri Chakravorty. 1988. "Can the Subaltern Speak?" In *Marxism and the Interpretation of Culture.* Edited by Cary Nelson and Lawrence Grossberg, 271–313. Urbana: University of Illinois Press.

Springer, Kimberly. 2005. *Living for the Revolution: Black Feminist Organizations, 1968–1980.* Durham, NC: Duke University Press.

———. 2007. "Divas, Evil Black Bitches, and Bitter Black Women: African American Women in Postfeminist and Post-Civil-Rights Popular Culture." In *Interrogating Post-Feminism: Gender and the Politics of Popular Culture.* Edited by Yvonne Tasker and Diane Negra, 249–76. Durham, NC: Duke University Press.

Stark, Evan. 2007. *Coercive Control: How Men Entrap Women in Personal Life.* New York: Oxford University Press.

Steenhuysen, Julie. 2008. "Physicians' Group Apologizes to Black Doctors." *Reuters*, July 10, www.reuters.com.

Steinberg, Stephen. 1989. *The Ethnic Myth: Race, Ethnicity, and Class in America.* Boston: Beacon.

Stephens, Dionne, and Layli Phillips. 2003. "Freaks, Gold Diggers, Divas, and Dykes: The Sociohistorical Development of Adolescent African-American Women's Sexual Scripts." *Sexuality and Culture* 7, no. 1: 3–49.

Stephens, Michelle Ann. 2014. *Skin Acts: Race, Psychoanalysis, and the Black Male Performer*. Durham, NC: Duke University Press.

Stewart, Bob, and Nancy Dillon. 2018 . "Cosby Called Pills He Gave to Accuser Andrea Constand 'Your Friends,' She Says in Graphic Retrial Testimony." *New York Daily News*, April 13, www.nydailynews.com.

Still, Ashlyn, Heather Long, and Kevin Uhrmacher. 2020. "Calculate How Much You'll Get from the $1,200 (or More) Coronavirus Checks." *Washington Post*, April 2, www.washingtonpost.com.

Stockett, Kathryn. 2009. *The Help*. Large print ed. Detroit: Gale, Cengage Learning.

Stone, Deborah. 1988. *Policy Paradox and Political Reason*. New York: HarperCollins.

Street, Paul. 2009. *Barack Obama and the Future of American Politics*. Boulder, CO: Paradigm.

———. 2010. *The Empire's New Clothes: Barack Obama in the Real World of Power*. New York: Routledge.

Swain, Carol M. 2002. *The New White Nationalism in America: Its Challenge to Integration*. Cambridge: Cambridge University Press.

Swarns, Rachel. 2016. "Trying to Separate Bill Cosby from Cliff Huxtable." *New York Times*, January 31, www.nytimes.com.

Tarantino, Quentin, dir. 2013. *Django Unchained*, featuring Jamie Foxx, Christopher Waltz, Leonardo DiCaprio, Kerry Washington, Samuel L. Jackson, Artisan/Lionsgate, DVD, 165 mins.

Tasker, Yvonne, and Diane Negra, ed. 2007. *Interrogating Postfeminism: Gender and the Politics of Popular Culture*. Durham, NC: Duke University Press.

Tate, Claudia. 1996. "Freud and His Negro: Psychoanalysis as Ally and Enemy of African Americans." *Journal for the Psychoanalysis of Culture and Society* 1, no. 1: 53–62.

———. 1998. *Psychoanalysis and Black Novels: Desire and the Protocols of Race*. New York: Oxford University Press.

Tatum, Beverly Daniel. 2003. *"Why Are All the Black Kids Sitting Together in the Cafeteria?" and Other Conversations about Race*. New York: Basic Books.

Taylor, Anthea. 2012. *Single Women in Popular Culture: The Limits of Postfeminism*. New York: Palgrave Macmillan.

Taylor, Keeanga-Yamahtta. 2019. "Succeeding While Black." *Boston Review*, March 13, https://bostonreview.net.

This Just In. 2007. "Condilicious." Posted on February 6, 2007. YouTube video, 2:04, www.youtube.com/watch?v=Cof2dHJ6A18.

Thomas, Dominic. 2009. "L'Effet Obama: Diversity and 'A More Perfect Republic.'" In *The Speech: Race and Barack Obama's "A More Perfect Union."* Edited by T. Denean Sharpley-Whiting, 119–31. New York: Bloomsbury.

Thompson, Clara. [1950] 1964. "Some Effects of the Derogatory Attitude toward Female Sexuality." In *Interpersonal Psychoanalysis: The Selected Papers of Clara Thompson*. Edited by M. R. Green, 248–56. New York: Basic Books.

Threadcraft, Shatema. 2016. *Intimate Justice: The Black Female Body and the Body Politic*. New York: Oxford University Press.

Tillet, Salamishah, and Scheherazade Tillet. 2019. "After the 'Surviving R. Kelly' Documentary, #MeToo Has Finally Returned to Black Girls." *New York Times*, January 10, www.nytimes.com.

Tomlinson, Yolande. 2014. "'A People That Would Take Care of Ourselves': Tyler Perry's Vision of Community and Gender Relations." In *Womanist and Black Feminist Responses to Tyler Perry's Productions*. Edited by LeRhonda Manigault-Bryant, Tamura Lomax, and Carol Duncan, 91–106. New York: Palgrave Macmillan.

Trubey, J. Scott. 2019. "Director, Actor, and Now Developer: Tyler Perry Opens Studio with Gala." *Atlanta Journal-Constitution*, October 4, www.ajc.com.

Tucker, Susan. 1988. *Telling Memories among Southern Women: Domestic Workers and Their Employers in the Segregated South*. Baton Rouge: Louisiana State University Press.

Tyler, Imogen. 2013. *Revolting Subjects: Social Abjection and Resistance in Neoliberal Britain*. New York: Zed Books.

"Tyler Perry to Spike Lee: 'Go Straight to Hell.'" 2011. *Huffington Post*, April 20, www.huffingtonpost.com.

"Tyler Perry's Traumatic Childhood." 2010. *Oprah.com*, October 20, www.oprah.com.

Urie, Rob. 2020. "Bailouts for the Rich, the Virus for the Rest of Us." *Strategic Culture Foundation*, March 28, https://www.strategic-culture.org.

Vaillant, George. 1992. *Ego Mechanisms of Defense: A Guide for Clinicians and Researchers*. Washington, DC: American Psychiatric Press.

Vande Berg, Leah R. 1996. "Liminality: Worf as Metonymic Signifier of Racial, Cultural, and National Differences." In *Enterprise Zones: Critical Positions on Star Trek*. Edited by Taylor Harrison, Sarah Projansky, Kent Ono, and Elyce Rae Helford, 51–68. Boulder, CO: Westview.

Vedantam, Shankar. 2018. "The Psychological Forces behind a Cultural Reckoning: Understanding #MeToo." *NPR*, February 5, www.npr.org.

Wallace, Michelle. 1990. "Variations on Negation and the Heresy of Black Feminist Creativity." In *Reading Black, Reading Feminist: A Critical Anthology*. Edited by Henry Louis Gates Jr., 52–67. New York: Meridian.

Walters, Ronald. 2003. *White Nationalism, Black Interests: Conservative Public Policy and the Black Community*. Detroit: Wayne State University Press.

Walton, Hanes. 1985. *Invisible Politics: Black Political Behavior*. Albany: State University of New York Press.

Walton, Hanes, and Robert Smith. 2001. *American Politics and the African American Quest for Universal Freedom*. New York: Longman.

Washington-Williams, Essie Mae, and William Stadiem. 2005. *Dear Senator: A Memoir by the Daughter of Strom Thurmond*. New York: HarperCollins.

Wells, Jeffrey. 2014. "Another Cosby Victim Comes Out." *Hollywood Elsewhere*, November 16, http://hollywood-elsewhere.com.

Whack, Errin H. 2018. "Bill Cosby Verdict Met with Conflicting Emotions by Some African-Americans." *AP News*, April 27, https://apnews.com.

Whitaker, Mark. 2014. *Cosby: His Life and Times*. Hardcover ed. New York: Simon and Schuster.

White, Deborah Gray. 1999a. *Ar'nt I a Woman?: Female Slaves in the Plantation South*. Revised ed. New York: W. W. Norton & Co.

———. 1999b. *Too Heavy a Load: African American Women in Defense of Themselves, 1894–1994*. New York: W. W. Norton & Co.

———.2017. *Lost in the USA: American Identity from the Promise Keepers to the Million Man March*. Urbana: University of Illinois Press.

White, E. Frances. 2001. *Dark Continent of Our Bodies: Black Feminism and the Politics of Respectability*. Philadelphia: Temple University Press.

"Why We Can't Wait: Women of Color Urge Inclusion in 'My Brother's Keeper.'" 2014. *African American Policy Forum*, June 17, http://aapf.org.

Williams, Christine. 2002. "Sexual Harassment and Sadomasochism." *Hypatia* 17, no. 2: 99–117.

Williams, Linda. 2001. *Playing the Race Card: Melodramas of Black and White from Uncle Tom to O. J. Simpson*. Princeton, NJ: Princeton University Press.

Williams, Patricia J. 1991. *The Alchemy of Race and Rights: Diary of a Law Professor*. Cambridge, MA: Harvard University Press.

Williams, Timothy. 2018. "Did the #MeToo Movement Sway the Cosby Jury?" *New York Times*, April 26, www.nytimes.com.

Willis, Deborah, ed. 2010. *Black Venus 2010: They Called Her "Hottentot."* Philadelphia: Temple University Press.

Wilson, William Julius. 1980. *The Declining Significance of Race: Blacks and Changing American Institutions*. Chicago: University of Chicago Press.

Wineinger, Catherine. 2019. "How Can a Black Woman Be a Republican? An Intersectional Analysis of Identity Claims in the 2014 Mia Love Campaign." *Politics, Groups, and Identities*, doi: 10.1080/21565503.2019.1629316.

Wright, Colin. 2013. "Sadomasochism and the Body of Law: Lacan's Reconceptualization of Perversion as Père-Version." *Theory & Event* 16, www.muse.jhu.edu/article/530499.

Wright, Elizabeth. 1992. "Introduction." In *Feminism and Psychoanalysis: A Critical Dictionary*. Edited by Elizabeth Wright, xiii–xix. Cambridge, MA: Blackwell.

Zacharek, Stephanie, Eliana Dockterman, and Haley Sweetland Edwards. 2017. "2017 Person of the Year: The Silence Breakers." *Time*, December 18, 34–70.

Zerilli, Linda M. G. 1994. *Signifying Woman: Culture and Chaos in Rousseau, Burke, and Mill*. Ithaca, NY: Cornell University Press.

Žižek, Slavoj. 1989. *The Sublime Object of Ideology*. New York: Verso.

INDEX

Page numbers in *italics* indicate figures and tables.

ABOUT THE AUTHOR

Nikol G. Alexander-Floyd is Associate Professor of Political Science at Rutgers University, New Brunswick. She is the author of *Gender, Race, and Nationalism in Contemporary Black Politics* and coeditor of *Black Women in Politics: Demanding Citizenship, Challenging Power, and Seeking Justice*, with Julia Jordan-Zachery.